MEDIEVALIA ET HUMANISTICA

MEDIEVALIA ET HUMANISTICA

STUDIES IN MEDIEVAL & RENAISSANCE CULTURE

NEW SERIES: NUMBER 13

EDITED BY
PAUL MAURICE CLOGAN

1985
ROWMAN & ALLANHELD
PUBLISHERS

ROWMAN & ALLANHELD

Published in the United States of America in 1985
by Rowman & Allanheld, Publishers
(A division of Littlefield, Adams & Company)
81 Adams Drive, Totowa, New Jersey 07512

The Library of Congress has cataloged this serial
publication as follows:

Medievalia et humanistica. fasc. 1- jan. 1943- ; new
ser. no. 1- 1970-
Totowa, N.J. [etc.] Rowman and Allanheld [etc.]

no. 26 cm.
Annual, 1943-
"Studies in medieval and renaissance culture."
Vols. for 1970–72 issued by the Medieval and Neo-Latin Society; 1973-
by the Medieval and Renaissance Society.
Key title: Medievalia et humanistica, ISSN 0076-6127.
1. Middle Ages—History—Periodicals. 2. Civilization, Medieval—Periodi-
cals. 3. Renaissance—Periodicals. I. Medieval and Neo-Latin Society. II.
Medieval and Renaissance Society.
D111.M5   940.105   47-36424
                        MARC-S
ISBN 0-8476-7209-3
Library of Congress   [8101]

85 86 87 / 10 9 8 7 6 5 4 3 2 1

Printed in the United States of America

Contents

vi   *Contents*

Editorial Note

Since 1970, this new series has sought to promote significant scholarship, criticism, and reviews in the several fields of medieval and Renaissance studies. It has published articles drawn from a wide variety of disciplines and has given attention to new directions in humanistic scholarship and to significant topics of general interest. This series has been particularly concerned with exchange between specializations, and scholars of diverse approaches have complemented each other's efforts on questions of common interest.

Medievalia et Humanistica is sponsored by the Modern Language Association of America, and publication in the series is open to contributions from all sources. The Editorial Board welcomes scholarly, critical, or interdisciplinary articles of significant interest on relevant material and urges contributors to communicate in a clear and concise style the larger implications, in addition to the material of their research, with documentation held to a minimum. Texts, maps, illustrations, diagrams, and musical examples will be published when they are essential to the argument of the article. In preparing and submitting manuscripts for consideration, potential contributors are advised to follow carefully the instructions given on page xiii. Articles in English may be submitted to any of the editors. Books for review and inquiries concerning *Fasciculi* I–XVII in the original series should be addressed to the Editor, *Medievalia et Humanistica*, P.O. Box 13348, North Texas Station, Denton, Texas 76203.

Inquiries concerning subscriptions should be addressed to the publisher.

Preface

The present volume, the thirteenth in the new series, is a collection of original articles in the area of history and literature. The first two articles were originally presented in 1982 at the B. K. Smith Lectures in History at the University of St. Thomas, entitled Women in the Middle Ages and Renaissance. Professors Sheehan and Herlihy draw on the experiences of women from Chaucer's fictional Wife of Bath to the real-life St. Catherine of Siena to engage in some scholarly speculations about the lives of women from the fourth century to the early 1400s. According to Sheehan and Herlihy, women in those days were not as inconsequential or as invisible as traditional history—mostly written by and about men—would have us believe. This volume also presents nine articles in the areas of medieval and Renaissance studies and a review article that evaluates significant new publications. Each article makes a contribution to its own specialized field and is presented in such a way that its significance may be appreciated by nonspecialists. Together, these articles should provide the scholar and serious student with new insights into current research.

I am grateful to the Editorial Board and in particular to the staff of Rowman & Allanheld for their patience and help.

P.M.C.

MEDIEVALIA ET HUMANISTICA

New Series

Paul Maurice Clogan, EDITOR
North Texas State University

EDITORIAL BOARD

Articles for Future Volumes Are Invited

Articles may be submitted to any of the editors, but it would be advisable to submit to the nearest or most appropriate editor for consideration. A prospective author is encouraged to contact his editor at the earliest opportunity to receive any necessary advice and a copy of the style sheet. The length of the article depends upon the material, but brief articles or notes are normally not considered. The entire manuscript should be typed, double-spaced, on standard 8½″ X 11″ bond paper with ample margins and documentation should be held to a minimum. Endnotes, prepared according to *A Manual of Style*, thirteenth edition (University of Chicago Press), should be double-spaced and numbered consecutively and appear at the end of the article. All quotations and references should be carefully verified before submission. The completed article should be in finished form, appropriate for printing. Only the original manuscript (not photocopy or carbon) should be submitted, accompanied by a stamped, self-addressed manuscript envelope.

The addresses of the American editors can be determined by their academic affiliations. The addresses of the editors outside the United States are:

Mr. Peter Dronke, Clare Hall, Cambridge CB3 9DA, England (Medieval Latin Poetry and Thought)

Professor J. R. Hale, Department of Italian, University College London, Gower Street, London WC1E 6BT, England (Renaissance History)

Professor Ian D. McFarlane, Wadham College, Oxford OX1 3NA, England (Renaissance French and Neo-Latin Literature)

Professor Jean-Claude Margolin, 75 Bld Richard-Lenoir, 75011 Paris, France (Humanism, Renaissance Philosophy and Neo-Latin)

Did Women Have a Renaissance?: A Reconsideration

DAVID HERLIHY

Interest in the history of women now forces historians to reexamine the large epochs into which they have traditionally divided the past. Conventional divisions, such as medieval or modern, which have long seemed valid and valuable in the light of masculine doings, seem quite different when measured by the experiences of women.

Of all conventional periods, the one that has proved most vulnerable to feminist reassessment has been the Renaissance. In the old and familiar view, the Renaissance of the fifteenth and sixteenth centuries, beginning in Italy and then spreading to all Europe, transformed European culture through the revived appreciation of classical learning. Supposedly, too, it was an age of individualism. It liberated men, or some men, from the social and intellectual trammels of medieval society. It liberated men, but what did it do for women? In a seminal article published in 1977 and entitled "Did Women Have a Renaissance?" Joan Kelly-Gadol gave a forthright answer: this supposedly progressive period did nothing for women.[1] And most feminist historians have agreed with her. By many social indicators—access to property, power or knowledge—the position of women deteriorated across the long centuries of the Middle Ages. Women in fact fared better in barbarian Europe of the sixth or seventh centuries than they did in the cultured Europe of the fifteenth and sixteenth. In her recent study of early medieval women, Suzanne Wemple affirmed that as early as the Carolingian empire in the ninth century, "women of the aristocracy faced a decline in the number of social options open to them."[2] The Renaissance with all its overtones of progress and improvement is thus judged meaningless when applied to women and their history.

In this essay, I will reexamine this now widely shared assumption: that women lost status and visibility from the beginning to the end of the Middle Ages. To encapsulate the history of approximately one-half the members of an entire civilization, over more than a millenium of human history, is clearly a formidable task. To apply a fair test to the thesis, we need some sort of

This paper was presented as a Smith Lecture at the University of St. Thomas, Houston, in March 1982.

1

Medievalia et Humanistica, New Series, Number 13 (Paul Maurice Clogan, ed.). Rowman & Allanheld, Totowa, NJ. 1985.

yardstick that will allow us to compare how women fared in the various periods of medieval history. There is one documentary genre that might permit such comparisons: the lives of women saints, whom these Christian centuries produced in abundant numbers.

WOMEN AND SANCTITY

Hagiographical records are, to be sure, notoriously difficult to use.[3] Few of the early hagiographers, fewer still of the earliest, had a personal knowledge of their holy subjects. Lacking direct observations, the authors had ready recourse to legend. When even legends could not serve, they stitched together clichés and commonplaces. Many saints' lives are little more than compilations of edifying *topoi*. On the other hand, these sources offer some singular advantages to the social historian. They are, to begin with, numerous—even for periods, such as the early Middle Ages, not well served by source survivals. While the particulars of the narratives are rarely to be trusted, the lives undoubtedly reflect common social situations, common attitudes and assumptions. Finally—and this is the crucial consideration—they pay attention to women. In the lives of saints, women make more than token appearances. Most medieval writers, in depicting a woman, adhered to the advice given by the ghost of Hamlet's father: they ignored her; they left her to heaven. Hagiographers did so too, but also charted her ascent.

We shall try to use these lives, antedating 1500, to illuminate the fluctuating fortunes of women. To be sure, our test applies to only one sector of social life, religious experiences. But it is a fair assumption that visibility among the blessed paralleled visibility in the secular world as well. Even the pursuit of sainthood required resources. The dumb priest, according to an Irish saying, never got a parish; the repressed and ignored woman, however holy, never won a cult.

To permit comparisons, our census of medieval saints must include men as well as women. The counting of saints has in fact become a popular exercise among medieval historians, but these efforts differ quite a bit from each other according to the sources used and the time and space surveyed.[4] Our basic source will be the standard bibliography of medieval hagiographical writings, the *Bibliotheca Hagiographica Latina*, the two volumes and supplement published by the Bollandist society.[5] In making our census, we count as members of the court of heaven only individually named saints. Groups are ignored. Otherwise, the 11,000 virgins martyred with St. Ursula would throw our sex ratios hopelessly awry. We enter the name of the saint by date of death assigned by the Bollandists, and we make no effort to screen out mythical from historical figures. We shall not usurp St. Peter's functions. When the death can be dated only by century—as for example, the seventh century—we enter the death in the middle year of the period, 650 (see Table 1).

The total number of named saints for the period of Church history, dead

Table 1

Saints by Periods

Period	Men	Women	Total	Sex Ratio (men to women)	Density Women	Density Men
1–313	767	158	925	4.85	.51	2.45
313–475	327	51	378	6.41	.32	2.01
476–750	755	111	866	6.80	.41	2.76
751–850	102	13	115	7.85	.13	1.03
851–999	112	21	133	5.33	.14	.75
1000–1150	217	18	235	12.06	.12	1.44
1151–1347	255	69	324	3.69	.35	1.30
1348–1500	63	24	87	2.64	.16	.41
Not given	156	57	213	2.74		
Total	2754	522	3276	5.28	.35	1.84

Source: *Bibliotheca Hagiographica Latina.*

before 1500 and entered into the *Bibliotheca*, is 3276. Of these 522 are women. The sex ratio among the blessed is thus about five males for every female.

To illustrate changes in the distribution of saints across the Middle Ages, we can further divide this lengthy span into eight shorter periods, commonly used in ecclesiastical history.[6] We can then calculate a kind of density index —number of saints divided by number of years in the period. The results of this exercise are also presented in Table 1. Although the index shows wide fluctuations, the overall trend is nonetheless clear. Saints become markedly fewer as the Middle Ages progress. Saints of both sexes are numerous during the age of persecutions, ending in 313, when the Edict of Milan brought peace to the Church. They are numerous too under the Christian Roman empire, lasting in the West to 476. But perhaps most unexpected is their continued, or rather enhanced, importance in the barbarian Europe of the early Middle Ages, which we date from the fall of the Roman empire in the West in 476, to the establishment of the Carolingian dynasty by Pepin the Short in 751. This epoch yields more saints per year than any other age of the ancient or medieval Church.

After 751 and the establishment of the Carolingian empire, the relative number of saints falls continuously, to reach its lowest levels in the closing century of the Middle Ages. For several reasons the ranks of recognized saints grow thin as we approach modern times. It was fairly easy to establish a cult during the early Middle Ages. A reputation for sanctity during life and a few opportune miracles performed at the candidate's tomb after death usually sufficed to inscribe a new name on the liturgical books of a local church.[7] Then, too, the tumultuous times of the early Middle Ages favored the cultivation of heroic virtues. The local churches were contending with a deeply ingrained paganism; they were eager to identify and celebrate champions, of whatever sex.

But the uncontrolled proliferation of cult figures created problems too, and from the eleventh century, the universal Church sought to impose strict controls over local cults. From about 1200, the papacy reserved to itself the right to canonize saints, and the procedures it gradually laid out took on all the aspects of a trial, replete with judges, lawyers, experts, and witnesses.[8] To promote the cause of a servant of God now required a lengthy and expensive process. Typically, only big religious orders, or prominent lay families, had the resources needed to initiate and carry through these proceedings. It is understandable, therefore, that the total number of saints drops precipitously over the late Middle Ages.

But even as the totals were falling, the relative proportions of male and female saints were shifting too. Women saints are numerous among the martyrs of the early Church. More surprising is the continued importance of female saints even after the persecutions ceased. They are especially common in the period of barbarian Europe, between 476 and 751. Indeed, the density of women saints then surpasses that of any other of our eight periods, saving only the age of persecutions. The social and religious prominence of early medieval women is confirmed.

After 751, as the Carolingian empire grew and then disintegrated, the relative number of female saints registers a marked decline. Women saints are at their fewest right in the middle of the Middle Ages, from about 1000 to 1150. During that span of 150 years, male saints outnumber female by 12 to 1.[9] Powerful movements were then transforming Western society: the Gregorian reform of the Latin Church, which sought to extirpate clerical marriage and win for the clergy freedom from lay control; the rise of effectively governed feudal principalities; the beginnings of commercial revival and the rebirth of towns; the expansion of Europe, through crusades and colonization. And yet the visibility of women was fading, according to our index. Here, again, the experiences of men and of women in the past seemed not to be congruent.

The thesis, that the status of women deteriorated across the Middle Ages, is thus partially sustained. But not entirely: after 1151, the relative proportion of women saints begins again to expand. Over the years 1348 to 1500, although the number of saints is small, still the sex ratio drops to the lowest levels so far attained.[10] In other words, the trend marked out by women's involvement with holiness is not linear. Rather, the relative distribution of female saints lies like a slack rope across the medieval centuries, high at the beginning and at the end, but drooping low in the middle ranges of this millenial span.

It can further be argued that women, while becoming relatively more frequent among late-medieval saints, were also moving upward in the heavenly hierarchy. What male saints of the fourteenth century, for example, rival Catherine of Siena or Bridget of Sweden in spiritual, or even political, influence?

To explain these shifts in the relative number of female saints, we must look more closely at their personalities and careers. Here we shall develop a crude typology of sainthood. We can distinguish those who owed their elevation, at least in part, to high status or connections with great and powerful families, from those who earned their reputations through personal charisma, through going the way of prophecy and mysticism.

In our census of saints it is easy to identify women associated with great families and to trace the frequency of their appearances across the centuries. It is less easy to sort out the charismatic figures. To measure their appearances we must use proxy types, that is, identifiable categories of women saints likely to include many charismatics. Martyrs can serve this purpose, as martyrs were venerated for their personal courage and commitment, not for high office or even high achievement. But martyrs are rare after the age of persecution. In the late Middle Ages many female mystics were associated with the new mendicant orders, the Franciscans or Dominicans. That association was often loose. For example, St. Christina of Stommeln, a thirteenth-century visionary from the Rhineland, spent most of her career as a beguine, a religious woman following no recognized rule, before she entered the Dominican Order and, incidentally, found a biographer.[11] St. Catherine of Siena, perhaps the greatest mystic of the fourteenth century, was a member of the sisters of penitence of St. Dominic.[12] But she was not cloistered and remained free to travel widely, to Florence, Pisa, Avignon and Rome, where she, the daughter of a cloth dyer, instructed and exhorted the mighty of the world. Her extraordinary career would have been inconceivable had she been tied to a cloistered community. At times the association of these holy women with the established orders was entirely fictional. The mendicants posthumously coopted them into their ranks, even though they had never during their lives been formally associated.[13]

Table 2 shows the distributions over time of these principal types of female saints: martyrs, queens, abbesses and mendicants.

Our basic distinction, between status (family connections) and charisma (personal magnetism) evokes this further comment. These two routes to sainthood were not easily combined, whether by men or by women. High office or a high place in society carried weighty responsibilities, which tended to dampen or suppress mystical exuberance. A prelate or prince who received,

Table 2

A Typology of Medieval Female Saints

Period	Martyrs	Abbesses	Queens	Mendicants
1–313	136	0	0	0
313–475	17	1	1	0
476–750	12	36	6	0
751–850	1	2	1	0
851–99	11	3	2	0
1000–1150	0	1	3	0
1151–1347	3	10	2	23
1348–1500	0	1	1	4
Not given	31	0	0	0

Source: *Bibliotheca Hagiographica Latina.*

or thought he was receiving, direct instructions from heaven could easily rock Church or society. On the other hand, freedom from administrative or social responsibilities conveyed evident benefits on the charismatic or mystic; such duties were likely to demand time and divert psychic energies. St. Francis of Assisi never received Holy Orders; the responsibilities of the priesthood might well have repressed his mystical vision. Catherine of Siena, although she attracted a "joyous brigade" of followers, both men and women, never assumed official responsibilities within the Dominican Order. Office represses the spirit; freedom from office gives it life.

Status and charisma thus offered medieval women two alternate routes to social influence, social visibility, among the saints and in secular life, too. Concerning status, this further observation can be made. Much more than the males, medieval women were crucially dependent upon the family to gain access to power and property with which to influence society.[14] Either they inherited office directly as queens or princesses, or, as regents for their frequently absent husbands or sons, they gained it through close relationship with powerful families. Finally, through their rights of inheritance over family property, they acquired the wealth that allowed them to found or endow religious communities and, as abbesses, to take a prominent role in their management. On the other hand, women fared rather poorly under social systems where families had no exalted functions—in republican regimes, for example, where offices were elective and not linked to family membership. It would be possible to write the political history of medieval city-states, for example, Florence or Venice, and scarcely mention women.

A further, important conclusion follows from this argument. If women depended upon the family for status, wealth, office, and power, so their position within the family and their public role in society were intimately connected. If the first weakened, so also would the second.

Female saints who gained recognition by status and those who did so by charisma do not show the same distributions across the Middle Ages. In the earliest period, the age of persecutions, women were numerous among the martyrs. It would be easy to attribute their prominence to the persecutions themselves; opportunities for the exercise of heroic virtue abounded. But more profoundly, the importance of women among the martyrs reflects the highly mystical, charismatic flavor of religious life in the early Christian communities. The martyrs, of course, appear to us through clouds of legend, and it is hard to gain a sense of their personalities and character. In regard to female martyrs, the capital text is surely the passion of the two women of Carthage, Perpetua and Felicity, martyred in 202 or 203. In a big segment of their Life (chapters 3 to 10), Perpetua relates in the first person the story of her trial and passion, and concludes with an apocalyptic vision of heaven.[15] The Life overflows with allusions to her emotions and inner experiences. Perpetua is a young matron, aged 22, with a baby at her breast; she fears for her baby's fate, yet still invites martyrdom. In one of her visions she is turned into a man: "I am stripped and I am made male."[16] This, not so much out of modesty; she wishes more powerfully to wrestle with the devil. In her last agony, she asks for a hairpin. She wants to set her hair, lest she appear sad and unkempt at this moment of supreme satisfaction and ecstatic joy. Felicity, her slave girl, is pregnant when arrested and delivers her baby in prison. The husbands of the women are nowhere identified. Scholars have discerned in the Life strong influences of the Montanist heresy, an eschatological movement originating in Asia Minor, which counted among its early leaders two women prophets, Priscilla and Maximilla.[17] In the Montanist vision, all Christians, even the humble and the unlearned, even women and slaves, could prophesy under the promptings of the Holy Spirit. Charismatic women fitted, and helped form, the religious style of the age.

The peace of the Church in 313, the stabilization of ecclesiastical structure and discipline, and perhaps too the decline of urban communities and an urban culture in the western provinces of the empire, stilled the voice of feminine prophets and mystics within the Latin Church. These changes did not reduce the number of female saints, only changed their character. The great female saints of the early Middle Ages—St. Radegund of Gaul, St. Brigid of Ireland, St. Lioba of England and Germany—were abbesses, queens, wonderworkers, but none of them was truly a mystic.[18] In the early medieval world, office rather than charisma distinguished the female saints. Out of 54 sainted abbesses, 37, nearly 70 percent, lived before 751; so also did nearly one-half the queens. Thereafter, holy queens retained importance chiefly in central Europe—in Germany, Hungary, and Poland.[19]

Our count of women saints confirms their prominence in the early Middle Ages, but also marks a deterioration in their status from the Carolingian age on. Women saints, as we have mentioned, marshal their fewest number in the middle of the Middle Ages, from about 1000 to 1150.

Why did holy queens and abbesses fade from the ranks of the blessed in the central Middle Ages? One reason often given for their deteriorating status is the changes wrought by the Gregorian Reform, in particular the removal of women from centers of authority within the Church.[20] The frequency of clerical marriages in the pre-reform Church gave to women, if not ecclesiastical office, then at least proximity to it. In a Lombard charter dated 724, the wife of a priest is even called *presbitera*, "priestess."[21] Marozia, the lady senator of Rome, ruler of the city from 928 to 932, was the concubine of one pope and the mother of another.[22] Her career would have been inconceivable in the absence of clerical marriage or concubinage. The reformers were intent on placing distance between the now-celibate clergy and women. One casualty of their policies was the double monastery, including both nuns and monks, common in the early Middle Ages and especially in England.[23] Usually, the feminine component had dominated these co-residential institutions. But this close association of the sexes was anathema to the reformers.

The reform, in sum, unquestionably restricted the functions of women within the Church and so also their access to sainthood—or at least one style of sainthood. Still, it would seem an exaggeration to attribute the declining number of women saints solely to the Gregorian movement. In fact the number of women saints was falling well before the Gregorian epoch. Women, it would appear, fell victim to a more profound and powerful social movement. I would argue that the declining number of holy queens and abbesses reflects their deteriorating position within the elite family of medieval Europe, their weakening grasp over its resources. In the second part of this essay, I will examine the changing status of women within elite households, across the medieval centuries.

WOMEN AND THE FAMILY

How can we evaluate the position of medieval women within the family? We shall utilize three indicators: the place and role of women within the kinship systems of the Middle Ages; the function of women in passing on property down the generations; and the contributions of women in the production and management of wealth. All these topics are large and complicated, and all have attracted much study in recent years.[24] The following remarks will summarize what seems to be the thrust of current research.

In describing the kinship system of the early Middle Ages, we can take as a convenient point of departure a treatise written about 1063 by the Italian reformer and saint Peter Damian.[25] It is entitled "On the Degrees of Kinship"; Damian wrote it at the request of the Florentines. They were confused— many persons in the early Middle Ages must have been—about the methods of calculating degrees of kinship and why it all mattered. They sought enlightenment from jurists at Ravenna, and Damian was in essence replying to what he thought to be their erroneous opinions.

Jurists and theologians of the period had in fact several models of kinship from which to choose. In the ancient world, Roman law had measured the degrees of kinship by counting backward from Ego to the common ancestor, and then forward again to the targeted relative.[26] The Romans had defined the degrees, within which marriages were prohibited, as a narrow four. In the early Middle Ages, a new method of reckoning degrees of kinship emerged, called Germanic and later accepted as canonical. This method struck forth in a direct path from Ego to the targeted relative and counted the lines of descent that had to be crossed or touched to reach the target. And a council at Rome, held in the year 721, defined the degrees within which marriage was prohibited as seven.[27] The new boundaries and the new methods of calculating kinship expanded the kin group to enormous, truly unrealistic dimensions. How many people in early medieval society could trace their ascendants back seven generations, as the system required? Realistically then, Pope Gregory II in 726, and several councils after him, affirmed that a vague sense of kinship, a suspicion of relationship, was sufficient to define a kinship group and to prohibit marriage within its bounds.[28]

To set the stage for his disquisition on kinship, Damian first sought to justify why blood relationship should matter at all in determining eligibility for marriage. Here, he makes much use of earlier writers—St. Augustine, Isidore of Seville, Burchard of Worms—but he still describes ideas and a system very much alive in the eleventh century.

All human beings, he reminds his readers, are descendants of the same first parents, Adam and Eve, and all are therefore members of the same descent group, a *genus cognationis*. Human beings, unlike animals, have only a single pair of first parents; this should remind all human beings that they are in fact brothers or sisters, members of the same clan. But in fact, over time, the lines of descent—*progenies*, in Peter's technical terminology— grow apart. As the distance among them increases, so their mutual love cools and dies. This distancing of the strands stemming from a common source, this extinction of love, threatens social peace. The descent groups could easily turn to war, against their now-estranged neighbors. Here, marriage and affinity perform their essential services to society. "When blood relationship," he writes, "along with the terms that designate it, expire, the law of marriage takes up the function, and reestablishes the rights of ancient love among new men."[29] Marriage is thus much more than the casual union of two persons.

Rather, it ties together two clans; it restores affection between two hitherto alienated lines of descent. It reintegrates human solidarity, which time and divergence of family lines relentlessly pull asunder. On marriage and its integrating, reconciling powers, social harmony crucially depends.

Now, if members of the same clan were allowed to marry, this would obviously defeat the sublime purposes of exogenous marriage. Members of the same group are already morally obligated to love one another, by reason of their common blood. They have no further need of cohesion; they have much need to seek through exogenous marriages the reestablishment of "ancient love," as Damian says, "among new men."

Damian expresses a further, and for our purposes, a crucial principle. The right to inherit from a person is conclusive proof of kinship relation with him or her, but the same right to inherit totally excludes the right to marry. He explains: "One right excludes the other, so that the woman from whom one could inherit cannot be taken as a legitimate spouse, even as the women whom one can legally marry can have no title of inheritance [over her husband's property]."[30]

The kin group which Damian describes thus possesssed the following characteristics: it was Ego-focused, in sense that all lines stretch out, and are measured from, the place which Ego holds among the lines of descent. This means that the descent group, or *genus*, in Damian's language, was redefined every new generation, as its focus settled upon a new person, a new Ego. It did not accumulate members over time. Its limits were precisely defined, however they be measured, whether over four or seven degrees. It was obviously cognatic or bilineal, as the strands of relationship ran indifferently through men and women. It assumed that women too, as authentic kins, enjoyed rights of inheritance over the property the kin group carried with it over time.

Damian's model fits well with the little that we know of kinship organization in the early Middle Ages. Given the imperfection of genealogical memory, it would then have been very difficult to distinguish patrilineal from matrilineal relationships stretching far backward into time. Pope Gregory II thought that proof of kinship ties required only a vague sense of relationship; how could he have demanded more?

Then too, the sexual practices of the early medieval elites were singularly loose, even promiscuous, both for men and for women.[31] Polygyny or sexual promiscuity in any form has the result of obscuring the line of descent through males—patrilineal linkages, in sum—and of emphasizing the importance of descent through females. Here, we cite only two of many possible examples. King Hugh of Italy (926-947) allegedly ignored his queen and consorted with three concubines, who were popularly nicknamed after pagan goddesses, Venus, Juno, and Semele. He sired children on all of them. Or did he? "As the king was not the only man who enjoyed their favours," our source, Liutprand of Cremona, relates, "the children of all three are of uncertain parentage."[32] (He wrote *parentage*, but he meant *paternity*.) As late as the eleventh century, Emperor Henry IV for long refused to accept a legal wife, but kept two or three concubines simultaneously. If he discerned among his courtiers an attractive wife or daughter, he attempted promptly to seduce her; if his suit failed, he sometimes resorted to violent abduction. Women who came to court with petitions he also seduced. When he tired of them, he discarded them and gave them in marriage to his servants. Once, he persuaded a courtier to undertake the seduction of his queen, in order to disgrace her. His plot failed, but clearly he believed that success was in the realm of possibility. He tolerated the rape of his own sister.[33] The account we have of the mores of his court and courtiers, from Bruno of Saxony, is admittedly biased. But if their behavior in any way resembled what Bruno describes, it would have been hard to trace with confidence patrilineal relationships at Henry's court. In this social environment, women, and relationships to women, were the surest indicators of close kin.

The importance of women, in indicating to Ego who his certain relatives were, further affected, it would appear; our second indicator; the role of women in passing property down the generations, through inheritance customs and marriage settlements.[34] As Damian asserts, women as full-fledged members of the *genus* must have a right to inherit. To be sure, the various legal traditions of the early Middle Ages defined that right in particular ways. But even in the worst case—such as the provisions of the famous Salic law—women were postponed in regard to brothers, not totally excluded, from the inheritance of real property; and all the traditions gave them a right to inherit movables. By the eighth century, when our oldest charters survive, women commonly appear as holders of inherited land.[35]

Marriage settlements, the second great channel through which the old directed wealth to the young, also favored women. In A.D. 98 Tacitus, in his famous description of the Germans, observed that among these barbarians, the groom brought the dowry to the bride, not the bridge to the groom, as was the Roman practice.[36] This system of reverse dowry or of bridewealth became, as far as we can judge, the universal practice in early medieval Europe, even in areas, such as the Mediterranean lands, where Roman traditions remained strong.[37] It is interesting to note that the marriage goods Tacitus described—oxen, a horse and bridle, a shield and spear—were clearly intended, as he himself remarked, for male use, though given to the bride. The descent group used an affine, the daughter-in-law, as a kind of trustee, offering assurance that these resources would flow to the certain benefit of the clan, even its male descendants. The system survived intact into the early Middle Ages. "The dowry," reads a charter from St. Gall in 758, "which my father gave to my mother, and I have given to my wife."[38]

In sum, from even this brief consideration of early medieval inheritance and marriage settlements, there emerges a special relationship between women and property.[39] Their control over wealth equipped them to be founders of monasteries and benefactors of religion, and famed throughout their communities.

Women in early medieval society had a special role not only in the conveyance of wealth down the generations, but also in its production and management—our third indicator of their status. At humble social levels, still according to Tacitus, women performed the principal agricultural labors, while the free adult male was either away at war or at home in indolence.[40] Women seem to have exerted a virtual monopoly over the processes of cloth production. The large estates of the period typically contained a *gyneceum*, a workshop which, as its name suggests, was staffed by women engaged in making cloth. Even the dyeing of cloth seems to have been a specifically feminine skill.[41] The Life of the ninth-century German saint, Liutberg, depicts a servant in an aristocratic household, as *"multorum muliebrium operum artifex"* (skilled in many feminine labors). Among them was the *"ars texturae"* (the art of weaving); she also kept a vat in her room filled with burning coals, in order to dye cloth with diverse colors.[42] St. Severus of Ravenna, according to his ninth-century life (he lived in the fifth), was so humble that he labored with his wife and daughter, "with whom he did women's works . . . he was accustomed to weave wool after the manner of women."[43]

Among the arts considered appropriate, at least for elite women, were reading and writing. The eighth-century nuns Herlindis and Renildis were trained in "reading, singing, chanting psalms . . . also writing and painting." They copied and decorated the four gospels, a psalter, and "many other texts."[44] They were "perfect workers" "in skills of every kind, which are usually done by women"; among the skills mentioned are weaving, sewing, and embroidery.[45] Even lay noblewomen seem often to have been literate. The lady Gisila read her psalter so often that it angered her husband, Count Eppo, who threw the book into the fire.[46] The association of women with special skills, *muliebria opera*, which men did not understand—with dyeing, brewing, milking cows and churning butter, and of course with cooking— may have suggested that they were proficient in occult arts as well, with magic and witchcraft. Witchcraft too was, after all, a *muliebre opus*.

Aristocratic women also played a prominent role in administration, in marshaling and managing resources. A curious passage out of Irish historiography tells of the three orders of the saints of Ireland. The oldest order flourished in Ireland soon after the time of St. Patrick and consisted of 350 bishops, renowned for their chastity and sanctity. "They did not," says the passage, "spurn the company of women, or their administration."[47] What service did women perform for these chaste bishops? Perhaps continental sources can offer some illumination. Under the Carolingians, the stewards, the managers of the royal estates, presented their accounts to the queen, at least during the absences of her husband, which were likely to be frequent and prolonged. The queen also guarded the royal treasure, and seems to have had chief responsibility for distributing the yearly gifts to the knights at court, the equivalent of their salaries.[48] Women, in sum, maintained a stable, continuous administration of household and estates. Their services freed elite males for their preferred activities, high politics and war.

Women in the early Middle Ages thus played a major role in the display of kin connections; they were also stations in the flow of wealth down the generations; they were supervisors, managers, producers. Their services won them high visibility in society and a strong voice in the disposition of resources. Did not their celestial prominence, which our count of saints reveals, have a terrestial base? Status on earth helped assure to some women status in heaven.

From about the year 1000, a new type of kinship system made its appearance in Western Europe, specifically among the elite classes.[49] This was the patrilineal lineage. It did not so much replace, as it was superimposed upon, the earlier *genus*. But it differed from the older descent group in certain crucial ways. It was ancestor-focused, not Ego-focused, in the sense that it traced its line of descent back to a particular ancestor. Like all ancestor-focused descent groups, it was likely to grow larger with each generation. Members were never lost, as with Ego-focused groups, which were redefined every generation. Its solidarity with the past came early to be proclaimed through adoption of a family name, a coat of arms, mottoes, and sometimes even a mythology. And it was patrilineal or agnatic. Daughters, and their children, were excluded from the lineage. To be sure, cognate relationships were not ignored. They remained an essential consideration in negotiating marriages, in calculating degrees of kinship, and determining the eligibility for marriage of possible partners. But in most areas of social life, they took on only secondary importance. The elite family became a solidarity of males, linked one to the others by agnate bondings.

No longer a central signpost indicating kin, women further lost their functions as principal conduits in the flow of wealth down the generations. The patrilineal family now managed its resources primarily for the benefit of sons. Daughters lost their traditional claim to an equal share with their brothers in their parents' property. The terms of marriage also turned against them. The true dowry returned in much of Europe, and even where other types of marriage settlements prevailed, the bride, and her family, lost the strong negotiating position they had held in former times. The bride, or her family, was forced to assume the principal share of the "burdens of matrimony," the costs involved in creating a new household.[50]

Many changes—cultural, social, economic—contributed to this transformation. On the cultural level, a prerequisite to this definition of the elite family in patrilineal terms was the success, always limited but still substantial, of the Church's long campaign against extramarital sexual liaisons. As long as the European elites, women as well as men, strayed from strict monogamy, so any effort to define the family as a fellowship of agnates would be frustrated. Already in the ninth century, the Church seems to have enjoyed some success in setting stricter controls over sexual behavior.[51] The Gregorian reform of the eleventh century, and the centralized Church emerging out of it, imposed tighter ethical standards and a much closer scrutiny on the European elites. Lapses may have been frequent, but monogamy became established as the unquestioned rule of western marriage.

The Church's now-effective insistence on monogamous marriage was a precondition for this realignment of the elite family, but does not alone explain why realignment occurred. Simultaneously, the mode of life that these families adopted, or perhaps better, their strategies for survival, were also changing. Elite families always looked in two directions for economic support, to their landed properties and to the profits of war. But opportunities for pillage were diminishing in the post-Carolingian epoch, save along the frontiers or in the distant East. At the same time, their own growth in numbers threatened their other economic base, their landed patrimonies. The elites in response tried to preserve the integrity of their holdings, upon which their status now principally depended. Above all, they sought to prevent their division among numerous heirs. The defense of the patrimony required, in other words, that the claims of younger sons and of all daughters to shares in the inheritance be limited. Younger sons were typically required to delay marriage or to eschew it altogether. It is understandable that they filled the armies of adventurers, who from the eleventh century poured into frontier areas, including the Holy Land, where they hoped to make or repair their fortunes. Daughters did not have even this option. To some girls, their fathers and brothers provided the dowries they now needed to contract respectable marriages. Other daughters with paltry dowries had to marry well beneath their station or enter the religious life, with or without an authentic vocation.

Nor did the economic and urban revival of the eleventh century improve the social position of women. The relationship of women to production was especially complicated, and seems to have differed considerably across different trades and across geographic regions.[52] Women retained prominence in some skills, such as brewing or spinning. They early acquired importance in silk manufacture—a new and growing industry in the late Middle Ages. On the whole, however, the following principle seems to have prevailed. Where the work involved high levels of family participation, the contribution of women remained substantial. Where guilds dominated the productive processes, women played a diminished role. Although there were exceptions, guilds tended to exclude women. In the medieval economy as well as in politics, the family chiefly promoted the active engagement of women; but that support tended to weaken in an urban context.

Women, for example, dominated the processes of cloth manufacture in the early Middle Ages, including such skilled arts as dyeing and finishing cloth. Males took over these activities in the cloth towns. The diminished role of women in the production of wealth reduced the economic contribution they could make to their households, whether of origin or of marriage. Their families of origin were prone to look upon them as burdens and were eager to settle their future, to give them to a husband or to the religious life, usually at young ages, and under unfavorable terms.[53]

So also, at the highest echelons of society, among princes and barons, the growing role in government of trained clerks and professional officials, of staffs and bureaus, impinged upon and narrowed the traditional place of elite women in administration. In lage part, though never entirely, they lost to male officials the administrative functions that had been a chief support of their status in the early medieval household.[54]

By most social indicators, women, especially elite women, were losing status, power, and visibility as the Middle Ages progressed. By many indicators, but not by all. Women possessed, as we have argued, an alternate route to social influence and visibility: through personal charisma. Indeed, the exclusion of women from office seems often to have invited them and freed them to nurture their interior powers. Catherine of Siena here offers a superb example of the late-medieval, charismatic woman. Of humble origins, she held no high office, whether in Church or state. In one of her impassioned dialogues with God, she protested that her sex prevented her from fulfilling the commissions He had laid upon her. "My sex, you know," she reminded Him in familiar language, "is here an obstacle for many reasons, whether because men disparage it or because of modesty, for it is not good that a woman consort with men."[55] But God rejects her reasoning in an extraordinary passage: "Isn't it I who have created the human race, and divided it into male and female? I dispense where I want the grace of my spirit. In my eyes there is neither male nor female nor rich nor poor. All are equal, for I can work my will through all equally."[56] Joan of Arc would be another example of this common, late-medieval type. She too held no office and enjoyed no status. Her voices alone gave her unique authority and led her to extraordinary accomplishment.

Women dominated what might be called the charismatic sectors of late-medieval society. They figured prominently among the late-medieval mystics: Margery Kempe, Julian of Norwich, Catherine of Siena, Catherine of Genoa, and many others.[57] Their cultivation of the interior spirit led many of them beyond the bounds of orthodoxy. They were numerous, for example, in the heresy of the Free Spirit, which taught that office, structures, rules meant nothing; all that mattered was God's spirit within, which conveyed full and perfect freedom.[58] Even witches might be considered part of this charismatic sector; witchcraft, like mystical movements in orthodoxy, like heresy, swelled in strength in the late Middle Ages. The structure of late-medieval society may have restricted the access of women to property and office, but it could not silence or repress them.

Did women then have a Renaissance? Did they enjoy higher social status and more favorable social treatment at the end of the Middle Ages than at the beginning? The negative response, which feminist historiography has given to these questions, carries much conviction. Women did indeed lose over the course of the Middle Ages many functions, which had distinguished them and supported them in the early centuries. They came to play a reduced role in the identification of Ego's closest kin. They were no longer the important stations in the flow of property down the generations, the trustees who assured that the property devolved upon the surest members of the clan. Their importance in economic production at the lower social levels, and in administration and management at the highest, also diminished. To judge from office and authority, women were pushed to marginal positions in the structure of medieval society. Although these changes seem indisputable, yet the response they support, that women did not have a Renaissance, is not entirely satisfactory. It ignores entirely the alternate route to personal fulfillment and social leadership, that through charisma. It cannot make sense of a Catherine of Siena or a Joan of Arc. And these are figures whom no interpretation of the experiences of medieval women can leave isolated, accidental, uncomprehended.

In the traditional interpretation, the Renaissance represented a triumph of individualism over the collective restraints of traditional, medieval society. Catherine of Siena, Joan of Arc, and many other charismatic women of the epoch were individualists in the full meaning of the word, trusting in their interior voices, critical of the male-dominated establishment and the manner it was leading society. Charismatic women appear with extraordinary frequency in the late-medieval world. In at least one sector of social and cultural life, women had a Renaissance.

NOTES

1. Joan Kelly-Gadol, "Did Women Have a Renaissance?" *Becoming Visible: Women in European History*, ed. Renate Bridenthal and Claudia Koonz (Boston, 1977). The theme is expressed in several of the studies presented in *Women in Medieval Society*, ed. Susan Mosher Stuard (Philadelphia, 1976). Kelly-Gadol and others were in part reacting against a famous section (Book five, Chapter six) in Jacob Burckhardt's classic work, *The Civilization of the Renaissance in Italy* (New York, 1929). In one of the weakest parts of this great book, Burckhardt quite unrealistically lauds the freedom and equality of the lady in Renaissance Italy.

2. Suzanne Fonay Wemple, *Women in Frankish Society: Marriage and the Cloister, 500-900* (Philadelphia, 1981), p. 194.

3. For the early cult of saints and its relation to the veneration of heroes in pagan antiquity, see the stimulating essay by Peter Brown, "The Cult of Saints: Its Rise and Function in Latin Christianity" (Haskell Lectures, n.s. 2; Chicago, 1981). For introductions to the study of women and sainthood, see the collected essays *Women of Spirit: Female Leadership in the Jewish and Christian Traditions*, ed. Rosemary Radford Ruether and Eleanor McLaughlin (New York, 1979); and *Religion and Sexism: Images of Woman in the Jewish and Christian Traditions*, ed. Rosemary Radford Ruether (New York, 1974). More specialized is Ortrud Reber, *Die Gestaltung des Kultes weiblicher Heiliger im Spätmittelalter: Die Verehrung der Heiligen Elisabeth, Klara, Hedwig, und Birgitta* (Hersbruck, 1963). Biographies of women in early medieval sources, including saints' lives, are reviewed in Marie-Louise Portmann, *Die Darstellung der Frau in der Geschichtsscreibung des früheren Mittelalters* (Basler Beiträge zur Geschichtswissenschaft 69; Basel, 1958).

4. Recent examples of a quantitative approach to the study of saints are the following: Jane Tibbetts Schulenburg, "Sexism and the Celestial Gynaeceum, 500-1200," *Journal of Medieval History* 3 (1978):117-33, which examines women saints in the *Bibliotheca sanctorum* in 12 vols. (Rome, 1961-69); Michael Goodrich, "A Profile of Thirteenth Century Sainthood," *Comparative Studies in Society and History* 18 (1976): 429-37; Donald Weinstein and R. M. Bell, "Saints and Society: Italian Saints of the Late Middle Age and Renaissance," *Memorie Domenicane*, n.s. 4 (1973):180-94; Alexander Murray, *Reason and Society in the Middle Ages* (Oxford, 1978), pp. 338-49. In their 1973 study, Weinstein and Bell classified 485 saints by sixty-five variables for the period 1100 to 1425; their basic source was Alban Butler, *Lives of the Saints*, 2nd ed., ed. Herbert Thurston, S. J., 4 vols. (New York, 1963). See also, by the same authors, *Saints and Society: The Two Worlds of Western Christendom, 1000-1700* (Chicago, 1982), which examines 864 saints. Murray made use of the *Oxford Dictionary of Saints*, ed. D. H. Farmer (Oxford, 1979), to study saints who died between 900 and 1500. Many statistical tables are given in the large study by Andre Vauchez, *La sainteté en Occident aux derniers siècles du Moyen Age d'après les procès de canonisation et les documents hagiographiques* (Rome, 1981).

5. *Bibliotheca Hagiographica Latina antiquae et mediae aetatis*, ed. Socii Bollandiani, 2 vols., Subsidia Hagiographica, 6 (Brussels, 1898-1903); *Supplementi*, Subsidia Hagiographica, 12 (Brussels, 1913).

6. Many of the dates are approximations, but embrace recognizable periods of medieval history: the late Roman empire, to its fall in the west in 476; barbarian Europe, to the election of the first Carolingian king, Pepin, in 751; the Carolingian empire, to the middle ninth century (850); the disintegration of the empire and renewed invasions, to 1000; European recovery and reorganization, to 1151; the height of medieval civilization in the "long" thirteenth century, to the outbreak of the bubonic plague in 1348; the crisis and transformation of medieval society, to 1500.

7. For a recent, full survey of the development of the cult of saints in the

early Middle Ages, see the first part of Vauchez, *Sainteté*, which is entitled "La discipline du culte des saints dès origines au XIIIe siècle" (pp. 13–68).

8. Ibid., pp. 39–67, with abundant bibliography.

9. For similar conclusions, see Weinstein and Bell, *Saints*, p. 220.

10. Vauchez, *Sainteté*, p. 243, goes so far as to speak of a "feminisation" of sainthood, most visible among the urban saints of late-medieval Italy. Weinstein and Bell, *Saints*, p. 221, also note this pronounced trend.

11. Christina fled her native village to escape an unwanted marriage and lived by begging in Cologne. See *Acta Sanctorum* (henceforth *ASS*), *Junii IV*, p. 431: "Cum autem esset duodecim annorum cum eam parentes ipsius matrimonio tradere vollent, Christi ancilla hoc renuens et parentibus ignorantibus fugiens, perrexit Coloniam, ubi pauperibus sociata, et fame atque siti cruciata, petiit alimoniam."

12. Blessed Raymond of Capua, *Vita di S. Caterina da Siena* (*n. 1347–m. 1380*), transl. P. Giuseppe Tinagli, O. P., Classici Cristiani, 47–49 (Siena, 1934). An English translation is *The Life of St. Catherine of Siena*, transl. George Lands (London, 1965).

13. St. Zita of Lucca (d. 1272) is an example of a saint coopted by the mendicants. See Vauchez, *Sainteté*, p. 246.

14. Joann McNamara and Suzanne Wemple, "The Power of Women through the Family in Medieval Europe: 500–1100," *Feminist Studies* 2 (1973): 126–41; reprinted in *Clio's Consciousness Raised: New Perspectives on the History of Women*, ed. Mary Hartman and Lois Banner (New York, 1974), pp. 103–18. The authors make the point that weak central government and the strength of great local families enhanced the status of women in the "first feudal age" (to ca. 1050). On the prominence of women in one dynastic line, see M. C. Facinger, "A Study of Medieval Queenship: Capetian France, 987–1237," *Studies in Medieval and Renaissance History* (1968):3–48.

15. "Passio Perpetuae et Felicitatis," in *The Acts of the Christian Martyrs*, ed. and transl. Herbert Musurillo (Oxford, 1972), pp. 106–31.

16. Ibid., p. 118: "et expoliata sum et facta sum masculus."

17. W. Le Saint, "Montanism," *New Catholic Encyclopedia*, vol. 9 (1967), pp. 1078–79.

18. On Lioba, see Rudolf, monk of Fulda, "Life of Saint Leoba," in *The Anglo-Saxon Missionaries in Germany*, ed. and transl. C. H. Talbot (New York, 1954), pp. 205–26. On Radegund, see Baudonivia, "De vita s. Radegundis Liber II," in *Passiones vitaeque sanctorum aevi Merovingici* (Monumenta Germaniae Historica [henceforth, MGH], ed. B. Krusch and W. Levison, Scriptores rerum Merovingicarum, vol. 2; Leipzig, 1920), pp. 377–95. One of several versions of the life of St. Brigid, and probably the oldest, is in *Vitae sanctorum Hiberniae ex codice olim salmanticensi nunc bruxellensi*, ed. W. W. Heist, Subsidia Hagiographica 28 (Brussels, 1966), pp. 1–37.

19. For example, Elizabeth of Thuringia (d. 1231) or Margaret of Hungary (d. 1271). See Vauchez, *Sainteté*, pp. 427–48.

20. The effects of the reform movements on female religious is treated

extensively in Philibert Schmitz, *Histoire de l'ordre de saint Benoit* (7 vols.; Paris, 1942–56). The entire seventh volume is given over to *les moniales*. On the relation of the reform to numbers of female saints, see also Jane Schulenburg in the article cited in note 4.

21. *Codice diplomatico longobardo,* ed. Luigi Schiaparelli, Fonti per la Storia d'Italia, 62–64 (Rome, 1929) I, 122, no. 34, October 724: "Romualdo prete cum coniuge mea presbitera nomine Ratperga . . ."

22. The career of Marozia and of other members of the House of Theophylact is primarily based on the account of Liutprand of Cremona, *Antapodosis* II, 48, in *Works,* transl. F. A. Wright (London, 1930), I, pp. 92–93.

23. Schmitz, *L'ordre de saint Benoit,* vol. 7, pp. 45–52. Schmitz believes that all English convents were double houses in the early Middle Ages. See also Mary Bateson, *Origin and Early History of Double Monasteries* (Royal Historical Society, Transactions, n.s. 13; London, 1899); Lina Eckenstein, *Women under Monastacism: Chapters on Saint-lore and Convent Life between A.D. 500 and A.D. 1500* (Cambridge, 1896); Ferdinand Hilpisch, *Die Doppelkloster: Entstehung und Organisation* (Munster, 1928); M. de Fantette, *Les religieuses à l'âge classique du droit canon: Recherches sur les structures juridiques des branches féminines des ordres* (Paris, 1967).

24. *Famille et parenté dans l'Occident médiéval; Actes du colloque de Paris (1974),* ed. G. Duby and J. LeGoff, Collection du l'Ecole française de Rome, 22 (Rome, 1977). On the character of the early medieval family, see the review article by Robert Fossier, "Les structures de la famille en occident au moyen-âge," XVe Congrès International des Sciences Historiques, *Rapports* II (Bucharest, 1980), pp. 115–32. See also Karl Schmid, "Heirat, Familienfolge, Geschlechter- bewusstsein," *Il matrimonio nella società altomedievale: Settimane di Studio del Centro Italiano sull' Alto Medioevo* (Spoleto, 1977), pp. 103–37; Georges Duby, "Structures de parenté et noblesse dans la France du nord au 11e et 12e siècles" (1967), reprinted in his *Hommes et structures du Moyen Age* (Paris, 1973), pp. 267–85. An English translation by Cynthia Postan appears in Georges Duby, *The Chivalrous Society* (London, 1977), pp. 134–48. Finally, see David Herlihy and Christiane Klapisch-Zuber, *Les Toscans et leurs familles: Une étude du catasto florentin de 1427* (Paris, 1978), pp. 525–51.

25. "De parentelae gradibus, ad Ioannem episcopum caesenatensem et d. d. archidiaconum ravennatem," *Patrologia Latina,* ed. J. P. Migne (Paris, 1853), 145, cols. 191–208. For Damian's sources, see the study by J. J. Ryan, *Saint Peter Damian and His Canonical Sources* (Toronto, 1956).

26. On degrees of kinship, see most recently Constance B. Bouchard, "Consanguinity and Noble Marriages in the Tenth and Eleventh Centuries," *Speculum* 56 (1981):268–87, with a chart on p. 270. For measurement of consanguinity from Roman times, the basic study is A. Esmein, *Le mariage en droit canonique,* 2nd ed., ed. R. Genestal (Paris, 1929), I, pp. 371–93.

20	*Medievalia et Humanistica*

27. For the council of Rome in 721, see J. D. Mansi, *Sacrorum conciliorum nova et amplissima collectio* (Venice, 1758–98), 12, pp 262–67.
28. "Dicimus, quod oportuerat quidem, quandiu se agnoscunt affinitate propinquos, ad hujus copulae non accedere societatem," letter of Gregory II, *Monumenta Germaniae Historica, Epistolarium*, vol. 3, p. 275, dated 726.
29. "De gradibus," col. 193.
30. Ibid., col. 194: "Quod quibus est jus haereditatis, est et affinitas generis."
31. On polygyny among the Merovingians, see most recently Wemple, *Women in Frankish Society*, pp. 51–70.
32. Liutprand of Cremona, *Antapodosis*, vol. 5, p. 32, transl. Wright, p. 199.
33. *Brunos Buch von Sachsenkrieg*, ed. Hans-Eberhard Lohman (Leipzig, 1937), p. 195. "Binas vel ternas simul concubinas habebat, nec his contentus, cuiuscumque filiam vel uxorem iuvenem et formosam audierat, si seduci non poterat, sibi violenter adduci praecipiebat."
34. The inheritance customs in the barbarian laws are reviewed in McNamara and Wemple, "The Power of Women," cited in note 14 above, although the authors tend to confuse postponement with exclusion from the inheritance. Katherine F. Drew, "The Law of the Family in the Germanic Barbarian Kingdoms: A Synthesis," *Studies in Medieval Culture* (Houston: Rice University, 1977).
35. Many examples appear in the *Codice diplomatico longobardo*, ed. Schiaparelli, no. 18, 27 November 714: a married couple donates "omnem facultatem nostram quam possidemus vel quam ex parentum successionibus seu ex regio." On women as property owners, see my study "Land, Family and Women in Continental Europe, 701–1200," *Traditio* 18 (1962):89–120.
36. *Taciti De origine et situ Germanorum*, ed. G. Forni, with commentary by F. Galli (Rome, 1964), cap. 18. p. 114. "Dotem non uxor marito, sed uxori maritus offert."
37. Diane Owen Hughes, "From Brideprice to Dowry in Mediterranean Europe," *Journal of Family History* 3 (1978):262–96.
38. *Ukrundenbuch der Abtei Sanct Gallen*, ed. H. Wartmann (Zurich, 1863–82), vol. I, no. 26 (year 758).
39. On women in barbarian law see Wemple, *Women in Frankish Society*, pp. 27–50; G. Merschberger, *Die Rechtsstellung der germanischen Frau* (Leipzig, 1937).
40. *De origine et situ Germanorum*, cap. 15, p. 107. "delegata domus et penatium et agrorum cura feminis senibusque et infirmissimo cuique ex familia"; ibid., cap. 25, p. 132, "cetera domus officia uxor ac liberi exsequuntur."
41. On the dyeing of cloth as woman's work among the Irish, see Charles Plummer, *Vitae sanctorum Hiberniae* (Oxford, 1910), p. ci.
42. *Vita Liutbirgae virginis: Das Leben der Liutbirg*, ed. O. Menzel (MGH, Deutsches Mittelalter, 3; Leipzig, 1939), p. 13, "propter diversorum tincturam colorum."
43. *ASS* I Februarii, Vita auctore Luidolpho prebytero, p. 88. "cum quibus

[Vincentia uxore et Innocentia filia] opera muliebria, victum quaeritans, operabatur. Nam lanam . . . more feminarum, texere solebat."

44. *ASS* III Martii, p. 384: "erant beatissimae Virgines erudiendae . . . id est, in legendo, modulatione cantus, psallendo, necnon quod nostris temporibus valde mirum est etiam scribendo atque pingendo." Ibid., p. 386: "Quatuor Evangelistarum scripta . . . honorifico opere conscripserunt. Nihilominus Psalmorum libellum, . . . aliasque quamplures Scripturas."

45. Ibid., p. 384: "Simili modo, in universi operis arte, quod manibus foeminarum diversis modis et varia compositione fieri solet, honestissime fuerant instructae, videlicet nendo et texendo, creando ac suendo, in auro quoque ac margaretis in serico componendis, miris in modis extiterant perfectae opifices."

46. *ASS* I Aprilis, p. 666. "Comes Eppo . . . librum unde illa sola solebat Psalmos decurrere, ad culinam detulit atque in ignem projecit."

47. The passage appears in several collections of saints' lives. See *Vitae*, ed. Heist, pp. 81-83.

48. The queen fulfilled this function in the Carolingian palace, as described by Hincmar of Rheims, "De ordine palatii" (written in 882, but utilizing earlier materials), *Capitularia regum francorum*, ed. A. Boretius (MGH, Legum Sectio II; Hanover, 1883), pp. 517-30.

49. As well as the literature cited in note 20 above, see Georges Duby, *Medieval Marriage: Two Models from Twelfth-Century France*, transl. Elborg Forster, p. 10, on the gradual spreading among all levels of aristocratic society of a lineage-oriented family structure.

50. On the changing terms of marriage, see my own study, "The Medieval Marriage Market," *Medieval and Renaissance Studies* 6 (1976):3-27, reprinted in *The Social History of Italy and Western Europe, 700-1500* (London: Variorum Reprints, 1978), no. 14.

51. See the comments of Wemple in "The Ascent of Monogamy", *Women in Frankish Society*, pp 75-96.

52. For a positive assessment of women in the work force, see Eileen Power, *Medieval Women*, ed. M. M. Postan (London, New York, Melbourne, 1975), especially pp. 53-75, "The Working Woman in Town and Country."

53. The role of women within urban industries was also a function of the nature of the industry. Women seem to have been of scant importance in the manufactures of woolens, but played a significant role in the silk industry, perhaps because they were more dextrous than males in embroidery.

54. They retained some importance as administrators. The fifteenth century French poetess Christine de Pisane made the point that the daughters of barons must be taught how to read, as they will often have to administer the family's estates in the absence of the husband. See D. Herlihy, "Women in Medieval Society" (Houston: Smith Lecture, 1972), p. 12.

55. Raimondo da Campua, *Vita*, libro II, cap. 1 (ed. Tinagli), p. 169.

56. Ibid.

57. *The Book of Margery Kempe*, ed. W. Butler Bowdon (London, 1936; repr. New York, 1944); Julian of Norwich, *Revelations of Divine Love*,

transl. James Walsh (New York, 1962); *Catherine of Siena as Seen in Her Letters*, transl. Vida D. Scudder (London, 1926); Catherine of Genoa, *Treatise on Purgatory and the Dialogue*, transl. Charlotte Balfour and Helen Doublas Irvine (London, 1946).

58. Robert Lerner, *The Heresy of the Free Spirit in the Later Middle Ages* (Berkeley, Los Angeles, and London, 1972).

The Wife of Bath and Her Four Sisters: Reflections on a Woman's Life in the Age of Chaucer

MICHAEL M. SHEEHAN, C.S.B.

During the past decade many study sessions, numerous papers and collections of essays, and several monographs have been devoted to women's history in general or, more specifically, to the history of women in medieval Europe.[1] Much of this work is worthy of high praise. It is, however, not unfair to say that part of this literature suffers from a tendency to generalize: sometimes one wonders whether the notions advanced are applicable to any woman who actually lived.[2] To what extent can one write the history of "women" without further explication? In the description of attitudes, it is perhaps feasible to proceed in such general terms,[3] yet in several other areas of research, this approach is not entirely successful. There has been a tendency to forget that the study of the history of women in medieval Europe is by and large a new field of activity, one still at the stage of data collection and preliminary analysis. Much encouragement should be given to those who adopt a prosopographical approach, who seek to describe and reflect on the lives of individual women, and to those who concentrate their research on groups whose homogeneity permits the possibilities and realities of the lives of the women in question to be presented without danger of serious distortion.[4]

The second suggested approach, the analysis of homogeneous groups, will be employed in what follows, using the oldest tool of the social historian, the examination of law and its applications. In doing so, however, it is important not to fall into that error of vagueness criticized above. The intention is to identify and examine the lives of five women who will stand for groups within the three estates into which medieval authors long considered their society to be divided—those who pray, those who defend and govern, and those who work with their hands—and a fourth class, the merchants, whose importance was finally coming to be recognized. Chaucer can be of assistance in this enterprise: models are to be found in *The Canterbury Tales*, and to

This paper was presented as a Smith Lecture at the University of St. Thomas, Houston, in March 1982. An earlier form was read at the Caltech Invitational Conference, "Family and Property in Traditional Europe," 1981.

Medievalia et Humanistica, New Series, Number 13 (Paul Maurice Clogan, ed.). Rowman & Allanheld, Totowa, NJ. 1985.

the period of their composition—the last quarter of the fourteenth century —the following description applies.

First was the group whose law was the Common Law of England, the class that was landed and free. It extended through a wide spectrum of wealth and power, from the aristocracy, typified by Dorigen of the "Franklin's Tale", to a woman—the wife of the Yeoman, perhaps—whose husband possessed a little land and was free of the control of the manorial lord. But the Knight, whose Emily was the Dorigen of another age, was typical of that class. His wife—let us call her "Eleanor Knight"—can serve as model of the group.

Second were those women whose families provided the free burgesses, the citizens of the towns, a group that was growing in power in the period that is being examined.[5] Here, too, was a considerable spectrum of wealth and influence extending from the great merchant families down to those of the minor crafts; but all were citizens of the towns, and their lives were regulated by the customs of those towns. The Wife of Bath was one of them and, being involved in the cloth trade, enjoyed a position within the upper levels of urban society. Here it is not a question of those virtues that were especially her own and that would have propelled her to the head of any group, but of the advantages of the craft of which she was a member. She can serve as the model of the free townswoman.

Third were the women of the largest group in English society of the age, those whose rights and duties were stated in manorial custom. Two individuals can be isolated who would be typical of different classes among the peasantry. First was the wife of the Ploughman; let us call her "Joan."[6] If a little imagination is used, it is possible to say something of her. Since it was April, the heavy farm work of spring was finished, so the Ploughman could go on pilgrimage. There was still much to be done on the manor, and Joan was attending to it. She was married to a man who could afford to leave his land for a few days while he journeyed to Canterbury, who owned or had the use of a horse—not a very good one, but still a mount—and who was stoutly, if plainly, dressed. The Ploughman and his Joan can be seen as typical of the unfree peasants of some substance, tenants of a half or a whole virgate or even more, members of the group who constituted a third to a half of the village community.[7] Other members of this class had a more difficult lot. They extend from the quarter-virgator through the cottar, who held a few acres, to those nameless members of society who found a place in the village as servants or migrant workers. Within this group can be placed the Poor Widow of the "Nun's Priest's' Tale," the woman who owned Chauntecleer. The opening lines of the tale make her spring into life:

> A povre wydwe, somdeel stape in age
> Was whilom dwellyng in a narwe cotage,
> Biside a grove, stondynge in a dale.

By housbondrie of swich as God hire sente
She foond hirself and eek hir doghtren two.
Thre large sowes hadde she, and namo,
Three keen, and eek a sheep that highte Malle.

A yeerd she hadde, enclosed al aboute
With stikkes, and a drye dych withoute,
In which she hadde a cok, hight Chauntecleer.[8]

Joan Ploughman lived a much easier life than did a cottar like the Poor Widow; she could be expected to live longer, and more of her children would survive.[9] Even so, in terms of their positions within their respective families, they were possessed of similar rights and bound by similar obligations: their lives were circumscribed within the custom of the manor. The Poor Widow, whom Chaucer has presented so well, can serve as the type of the peasant woman.

Fourth were the women of a similar, lowly estate, but who lived in the towns. The lives of the men and women of this group are the most difficult to describe. In London they were called "foreigns."[10] They might be English or even have been born in London itself, but they did not possess the freedom of the city, and the very word used to identify them spoke of their alienation. No class of documents describes their role in society; we meet them when their activity threatened the business enterprises of the burgesses, in pleas of debt, and when they were involved in crime. It is estimated that in London they outnumbered adult members of the citizen class by three to one.[11] This group provided the porters, the hawkers, the innkeepers, the servants, and the working men and women of many of the crafts, yet they remain the most elusive of all. The nameless women in the background of the "Cook's Tale" or of that world in which the Miller and the Pardoner were so much at home were members of this class. It will be difficult to say much of these women with certainty; perhaps the main accomplishment of this essay will have been to insist on their existence. One of them—"Rose Foreign" is a suitable name for her—can stand for her class.

The fifth group and the last to be identified, was never numerous in medieval England. They were the women who chose to change their state and become religious.[12] Women of any class could find a place within religious life; indeed, the four types who have been identified thus far might have been received as choir nuns or as lay sisters in the greater nunneries, or as sisters attached to hospitals and other charitable institutions. Choir nuns were usually drawn from the upper classes, and women of the noble and knightly families as well as those of well-to-do burgesses were the principal sources of vocations. The Prioress might well have been a relative of Eleanor Knight, although the reference to her affectations may have had a snobbish overtone, implying that the Prioress was born into a family rather lower on the scale within the free classes.

The Prioress, Eleanor Knight, the Wife of Bath, the Poor Widow, and that unnamed woman of the towns whom we have called Rose Foreign will be the types to which the description that follows will refer. They have been isolated and identified because different sets of custom and law described, at least in part, the frame in which their lives developed. Before going further, however, it is important to recall that another kind of law was of general application to all these women. For three centuries before the period under discussion, there had been a revival of speculation on man and woman and their respective roles, speculation that considered all levels of society. This was the work of theologians, philosophers, and lawyers. In time, some of their ideas came to be accepted as social norms or rules of moral guidance and, in greater or lesser degree, became enforceable regulations in the form of religious or canon law. Many of its rules were of universal application, so they touched the lives of the Poor Widow and Rose Foreign as well as the lives of their more wealthy sisters.[13] These sets of regulations were a force within medieval society pressing toward generaral and consistent usage, a usage that transcended differences of class.

One final distinction must be made. It makes little sense in an essay to refer to the rights and responsibilities of a woman without noticing where she is located along the path of life. Recall that in the "Prologue" to *The Canterbury Tales* there are radically different expectations of the Knight and the Squire:

> A Knyght ther was, and that a worthy man, . . .
> And everemoore he hadde a sovereyn prys:
> And though that he were worthy, he was wys,
> And of his port as meeke as is a mayde.[14]

In contrast to this wise, responsible, grave and rather dull man is the Squire:

> A lovyere and a lusty bacheler,
> With lokkes crulle as they were leyd in presse. . . .
> Embrouded was he, as it were a meede
> Al ful of fresshe floures, whyte and reede,
> Syngynge he was, or floytynge, al the day;
> He was as fressh as is the month of May.[15]

Yet, from the point of view of this presentation, the Knight and the Squire are the same person seen at different moments of a single life.

Having made all the necessary distinctions, we will examine the women of England—somewhat more than a million individuals[16] living in an area one-fifth the size of the state of Texas—in terms of the regulations that applied to them about the year 1380. They are distinguished as four typical women within two traditional and one recently recognized lay groups: *bellatores*, *laboratores* and *mercatores*, and one typical of the status open to them all, that of *oratores*. Their rights and duties at each stage of life will be examined.

*   *   *

Birth

At birth all girl babies were allowed to live. The history of infanticide, especially female infanticide, is long, and there is evidence of it in various parts of Europe in the early Middle Ages.[17] Steady pressure to protect the life of the newborn was exerted by the leaders of society so that, well before the period that is the object of the present study, infanticide was forbidden and punishable in the courts. The research of Richard Helmholtz and Barbara Hanawalt during the past decade provides strong evidence that, in fourteenth-century England, the life of the newborn child was successfully protected by society.[18]

Childhood

Infant daughters of the free, landowning, and bourgeois classes could inherit and be recipients of landed property immediately after birth.[19] Rights, in fact, were vested even in the unborn child. Thus, in the case of uncertain inheritance, decisions as to the devolution of property were delayed until an expected child was born.[20] Money or chattels that came to little girls of these classes was considered to be the property of their fathers. Such, at least, was the law, although family attitudes on this matter are unclear and the practice revealed in testaments suggests that some, at least, intended that small children be the owners of legacies left to them.[21] If the father of little Eleanor Knight had died and she were his heiress, she and her estate would have been in the wardship of her feudal lord. If she were not the heiress, it is likely that her mother or other members of her family would assume the role, seeing to her nurture, administering her property and, eventually, arranging her marriage. Guardianship of the Wife of Bath during her childhood would probably be in the hands of the person chosen by her father or, in some towns, was exercised by the borough administration.[22] In the rare instance when property came to a Poor Widow or a Rose Foreign during her childhood, it was probably in the control of her father or the head of the family who raised her.

We know little of the early care and socialization of infant daughters. In the landholding and bourgeois classes they were often put out to wet nurse; there is some evidence in Coroners' rolls that this was done among the peasants, as well.[23] At all levels of society it was expected that the little ones would have adequate care to protect them from danger. Episcopal statutes were especially exercised to prevent neglect.[24] The little girls of the upper classes were probably trained by their mothers and servants with emphasis on

obedience to their fathers. Some evidence suggests that from about ages four
to seven the little peasant girls accompanied their mothers to work.[25]

Girlhood

At about seven, children were considered to come to moral responsibility.
This did not touch their right to control property but meant, among other
things, that they might be involved in the first step toward their adult vocation.
Thus, little girls of the class of Eleanor Knight or the Wife of Bath, whose
engagements were often made early (even before birth, on occasion), might
take part in a betrothal ritual.[26] The Prioress, who would be drawn from
those classes, may have entered a convent at this age, perhaps as a young
student, perhaps as a postulant. And in this period of life between responsibility and majority, the lives of the four types of women would begin to
diverge, and the fifth possibility become open to them. Eleanor Knight may
have been attached to the suite of a great lady in a household other than her
own where, in addition to training in deportment, she may have had some
opportunity for the study of letters.[27] Young women of the Wife of Bath's
group might enter apprenticeship in one of the crafts, such as the Silkworkers,
in which women played a major role, or she may have become involved in her
father's business in ways that were suitable for her.[28] The probability that she
would take a place in the business world ensured that she would at least learn
some mensuration; many city women were literate.[29]

   In these years the future Prioress learned the round of convent life,
including the recitation of the office in Latin, although probably by rote;
her reading would be in the vernacular.[30] Young peasant girls like the Poor
Widow's daughters found their places in the endless tasks of household and
field; many became servants. It is clear from recent work by Judith Bennett
that, on some manors at least, peasant girls maintained control of the money
they had received so that, when it became time for their marriage, they themselves were able to pay the marriage fine (*merchet*) to the lord of the manor,
rather than have it paid by their fathers or their future husbands.[31] Girls born
into the foreign class of the towns, of whom Rose is the type, probably began
to work as soon as they were able to be of use. Where their parents had
established themselves as workers attached to but not possessing the rights of
the craft guilds, they may have found a place by their side. A similar situation
probably obtained where parents were innkeepers or offered food-services as
hawkers. No doubt many were beggars and were already being drawn into
prostitution.[32]

Majority

At age twelve, young women began to enter their majority. It is necessary to
emphasize that this was but a beginning because, for them as for the young

women of our own age, majority came in stages: valid marriage became a possibility with the completion of the twelfth year, but the age at which disposition of property was permitted was considerably later.[33] At any rate, the time had come to think of a state in life. Marriage was the lot of most medieval women, but medieval society provided several honorable alternatives. One was religious life, considered to be a suitable vocation for women of Eleanor Knight's class or for that of the Wife of Bath. Their families would be expected to provide a dowry, although it would usually be considerably less than that for marriage. At this stage of life the young woman who had entered a convent in her childhood was permitted to take her final vows. The possibility of becoming a nun was also open to a woman at later stages of her life.[34] The fact that convents were often used as niches for women who had little or no desire for religious life was a contant threat to the monastic ideal and a cause of scandal as well: visitation records and the literature of the time leave no doubt in this regard.[35] The lay sisters (*conversae*) attached to the greater convents and those women who served in hospitals and other charitable institutions have not yet been studied. It is probable that some of them at least were recruited from the lower strata of society, that a Poor Widow or a Rose Foreign may have found a place among them.

Another possibility for the woman entering her majority was the single life in the world. The spinster in medieval England has proved to be a very elusive person but her name, at least, gives a clue to her place there. Spinsters probably existed in significant numbers among the sisters of the Wife of Bath and the Poor Widow, though they have left little trace. Testaments survive that are clear evidence of the activity of these women and, as well as other documents, have made it possible for scholars to begin the study of this group within English society.[36]

Marriage

The woman who became a wife and the married period of her life have thus far been the principal areas of research in the social history of her sex. Her betrothal and wedding, her rights during marriage, and the property distribution when her marriage ended have proved to be of special interest. At the social level of Eleanor Knight, the marriage of a woman at the minimum age of twelve was probably not uncommon, although a first union in the mid- or late teens would be more usual.[37] It will be remembered that the Wife of Bath insisted on her first marital adventure at twelve. She has sometimes been taken, at least in this matter, as a paradigm of the women of her class, but recent work suggests that first marriage usually occurred about five years later.[38] The possibility of a peasant woman finding a spouse was related to her succession to her parents' property at their death or retirement or the availability of land to the man she married. In either case the opportunity must often have been slow in presenting itself. In the conditions that obtained after the Black Death, however, land was more available. Thus the age of first marriage seems to have fallen, especially for peasant women like the Poor Widow, whose families held but little land.[39]

As to Rose Foreign, little more than surmise is possible. The completion of her twelfth year would be a requirement for a valid union, of course. For the upper levels of her class at least, the possibilities were similar to those of the Wife of Bath. Her marriage was probably less related to possessions than was the case with the women of the other groups and, therefore, may have occurred when she was quite young; but in her case, as that of the others, the question must be examined with more circumspection than has often been the case in the past. The older stereotypes of very early marriage in each of the four groups under examination must be set aside until much research has been completed; there are indications that first marriage toward the end of the second decade of a woman's life will prove to be the more common pattern.

Of similar difficulty is the question of the different individuals and groups who were expected to be involved in the choice of a woman's spouse. It can be taken as axiomatic that the higher a woman's position within the class structure, the more her marriage was a choice involving a wide circle of advisers. Thus the betrothal and marriage of Eleanor Knight would be a more complex arrangement than that of the Poor Widow or Rose Foreign. Depending on the class of the bride, in most cases her parents and wider family, neighborhood and parish, feudal and manorial lords might be expected to intervene. The twelfth and thirteenth centuries had seen a careful examination of the ways in which marriage was constituted. It resulted in a decision that is an example, as mentioned above, of a regulation that touched women of every class: the final say in establishing the marriage bond lay with the bridal pair. At the level of canonical theory it was insisted that, unless the couple consented to their union, that union did not occur. This regulation was implemented and enforced, often with serious consequences that touched dynasties and fortunes as well as the lot of the individuals concerned. Furthermore, the ancient usage whereby marriage could be a private act, that is, made by an exchange of consent by the couple without announcement and without witness, was still accepted. In fact, that kind of marriage, with all its possibility of mutual or self-deception, was to remain in force in England until the Marriage Act of 1753.[40] The motive for the "free choice" of spouse was not necessarily romantic; many other intentions might be at play.[41] But the stereotype of the young woman forced to marry against her will does not stand. The way in which fourteenth-century English society resolved the claims of individual freedom and the wider interests of those with some claim on the persons or property of the couple is a problem that has exercised several scholars for more than a decade.[42] It still has many uncertain elements, but it must be understood that, if any of the four women under discussion were to be married, she would have to consent to that union for it to occur.[43]

If the preparations for the marriages of Eleanor Knight and the Wife of Bath followed the path that society preferred, there would have been agreement between their parents or guardians and the future husbands and their families regarding the property that each would bring to the new menage and the settlement that would be made on the wife, were she widowed, and on the children born to the union. The women would be expected to bring a dowry (*maritagium*) to contribute to the household. In Eleanor's case this would likely involve some land and chattels as well. If she had no brother, her dowry might have been considerable indeed: potentially as much as her family inheritance. The Wife of Bath, too, may have brought tenements in the borough in which her family lived and other land as well, but chattels and money probably played a larger role in her case. Again, if there were no brother, to marry her might be to succeed to her father's estate and business. At the level of the peasantry a similar situation obtained, though the property involved would usually be much less. If a peasant woman had siblings, she probably brought some chattels—farm animals, linen, grain—to her marriage, and merchet would have been paid to the lord for her or by her. Once again, if she were an heiress, she would bring to her husband the parcel of land held by her parents. The Poor Widow's main contribution may have been her strong back and the ability to bear and nurture children.[44] As for Rose Foreign, once again records fail us. Presumably, if hers were a family that had found a place on the fringe of one of the trades, she would be expected to bring some dowry to her spouse; those of the poorest class would contribute what they could, presumably money and chattels that they had acquired themselves.

All four women came under the guardianship of their husbands when they married. The land that Eleanor Knight brought as *maritagium* and any land that came to her from family or other sources during her marriage passed into the control of her spouse.[45] He was not to alienate it although, as court records make abundantly clear, he frequently did so. In that case, if she survived him, Eleanor had an effective means of recovery at common law. If she died before a child were born, her land reverted to her family. If, as seems to have been Eleanor's case, a child survived its mother, her land was held by her husband during his lifetime, then passed to their offspring—in this case, the Squire. If the woman died giving birth to her child and the baby died too, as long as there was adequate proof that the infant was born alive—its cry was heard between four walls—then, by the courtesy of England, the husband held the property for his lifetime. On his death, it reverted to his wife's family. Any mobile property that Eleanor brought to the marriage, or that came to her later, by common law belonged to her husband. If she died before him, an attempt to dispose of these goods by testament was effective only inasmuch as he approved of it.[46]

The brutal simplicity of the property rights of married couples before common law was somewhat refined in the boroughs and on many manors. Thus, quite aside from the moral and perhaps physical authority that the Wife of Bath exercised over her husband, her position by right with regard to him was stronger than was Eleanor Knight's in regard to her spouse. Although her husband would usually speak for her in court, she and women of her class were sometimes in business for themselves and were considered legally capable of controlling funds required for their business and of answering for that business in borough court.[47] Furthermore, she could acquire landed property jointly with her husband in some boroughs and, again depending on local custom, could bequeath chattels and even land.[48] Patterns of peasant life, revealed by the anthropologist, in which the wife plays a major role in family support, often working closely with her husband, obtained among fourteenth-century peasantry; there were similar consequences. In many manors, villein tenements of husband and wife coalesced into a common possession. Furthermore, like her more wealthy sister in the borough, the Poor Widow during the time of her marriage may well have been in business for herself. She would most likely have been a brewer and would have been responsible for purchases, payments, and the fines to which ale-wives were so often subject.[49] The testamentary right of the villein was much debated in the fourteenth century. It can be demonstrated, however, that on some manors they did exercise that right and that some married women were included among the testators.[50] The testament of a Poor Widow would distribute small bequests and would likely be principally concerned with a gift in alms and her funeral.

When difficulties developed in a marriage, all four women had access to a remedy. It was the role of episcopal courts to protect the marriage rights of spouses and the bond that united them. Where the bond did not exist or proved to be intolerable, it was for the courts to provide an equitable separation. It is usually taken as axiomatic that the more wealthy were better suited to benefit from the remedies made available by the ecclesiastical courts. A first impression formed by a reading of papal registers and even those of the bishop's official is that Eleanor Knight and the Wife of Bath had a distinct advantage over the Poor Widow and Rose Foreign in these matters. It is clear that the marriage of Eleanor or of women of the higher aristocracy, was more likely to be considered in terms of its political consequences.[51] Yet it must be remembered that the jurisdiction in question functioned at the local level and that, by the time of interest to the present discussion, it was possessed of an efficient *ex officio* procedure. This meant that the hearing of cases touching marriage was not dependent on one of the parties being in a position to launch the case; hearings were often begun by the court itself when need was seen.[52] There is good evidence that assistance was available to men and women of the lowest levels of society.

Throughout their married years women would, in the ordinary course, be in charge of the day-to-day direction of their households and often, in the absence of their husbands, would see to its wider needs as well.[53] In these same middle years of life the women who followed the vocation of the Prioress would have settled into the monastic routine. Some of them would have begun to take on responsibilities as an obedientiary, in charge of a monastic department such as housekeeping, the cellar, or the sacristy or, as the Prioress herself, have accepted the charge of a nunnery.[54] Although Chaucer spoke rather lightly of her, it should not be forgotten that he gave the Prioress the most numerous suite in the pilgrimage. As a superior of religious women she exercised one of the most responsible roles open to women during the Middle Ages. Not only the direction of a major economic enterprise, but also the spiritual care of her sisters and their dependents were in her hands.

Widowhood

With the deaths of their husbands, the women representing the four lay groups suddenly sprang into full legal personality as expressed in the class to which they belonged. For those who had been married in their teens this was birth into a new kind of civil existence; for those who had married after a period of full adulthood, it was a rebirth.[55] Eleanor Knight would normally receive one-third of the landed property that her husband held during their marriage; it was hers for life, and she could use it as she saw fit so long as she did not alienate it. In addition, all the property she had brought to the marriage, and any that had accrued to her by inheritance or gift since that time, came under her control. She would be required to surrender the principal house of her husband's estate to the heir within forty days. It was customary that she would also receive a third part—or half, if there were no children —of her husband's chattels. By the period that is of interest here, the customary division of chattels was weakening in southern England to the detriment of the widow's right but, if the evidence of testaments can be trusted, wives were well provided for from the chattels of the household.[56] The Wife of Bath and her class usually enjoyed at least as generous a share of landed property and, since in some boroughs husbands were allowed to bequeath land to their wives, they might receive much more.[57] The wife's share of chattels remained the custom in the boroughs well past the period that is being described. In many manors, the Poor Widow benefited from the system of community property as her more wealthy sisters did not. She continued to hold the property that she had shared with her late husband and did not have to pay an entry fine. Thus she excluded the heir until she died or chose to relinquish the estate.[58]

Thus the widow faced the future not only with the wisdom that experience had given her, but often with a considerable fortune as well. She was free to remain single or to marry; in the latter case the choice of spouse was her own although, as was to be expected, she was often subject to much pressure in this regard. From many points of view, not least from that of wealth, the widow was an attractive candidate for marriage, and many of them entered into a second union soon after the deaths of their husbands.[59] On the other hand, it is clear that there were many widows at all levels of fourteenth-century society. Women like Eleanor Knight or a less matrimonially inclined Wife of Bath sometimes took vows and entered a convent. Others made a formal commitment to a life of continence and prayer while remaining in the world, even in charge of their own households. The study of this form of widowed life has only begun; it is impossible to state the numbers whose chose this path, though it is unlikely that they were numerous.[60] Peasant women were usually allowed to maintain their property and remain un-married as long as they were able to acquit their obligations to their lord. Often the best solution to the problems of a Poor Widow was to remarry, although it is clear that many did not do so.[61]

As those who remained in the world grew older and their powers failed, they or their families sometimes arranged that they enter convents or hospitals as pensioners. In a similar circumstance the Poor Widow might choose to surrender her little property with the understanding that it would be trans-ferred to an heir, or even to a stranger, who would be responsible for her support and care during the years that remained. Manorial court rolls illustrate this method of provision for old age and illustrate as well that these courts saw to the honoring of the agreement between the generations.[62] Religious like the Prioress could expect to be cared for by their communities until the end.[63]

Death and Burial

The description of the lives of these five typical women can be brought to a close with the final expression of affection and preoccupation with matters of the next world in their wills. According to the general law of the Church, religious were forbidden to own property and under ordinary circumstances were not to make wills.[64] In the somewhat relaxed state of monastic life in the later Middle Ages, however, these rules often proved difficult to maintain. Nuns accumulated chattels and sometimes sought to control their future use by will.[65] When one thinks of the Prioress, it is to wonder who next wore her brooch with the device "Amor vincit omnia"?[66] If Eleanor Knight died during her husband's lifetime she had no right to make a will, since she owned no chattels and landed property was not disposable by legacy. Moral guides urged that she make a will for charitable purposes and for the good of her soul, and Church courts would have given probate and would oversee its execution. They did not seek to exact that right from her husband.[67] If Eleanor were a widow, she had full control over all her chattels and could dispose of them as she wished. As was mentioned above, the Wife of Bath had a somewhat better chance of having a right to make a will during her husband's lifetime. As a widow she could sometimes bequeath both chattels and real estate.[68] By the last years of the fourteenth century, on many manors, the Poor Widow would be allowed to dispose of her chattels by will.[69] Of the last will of Rose Foreign little can be said with certainty. The more general freedom of bequest that obtained in borough custom suggests that, if she did make a will, it probably received probate and was implemented.

Adults had the right to choose their place of burial, and many of them stated it in their wills.[70] Widows usually chose to be buried with their husbands, but some, like Margaret Paston, preferred to return to the family that gave them birth.[71] An Eleanor Knight might be buried in the church of an abbey with which her husband's family was associated. The Prioress would rest in the choir of her convent church. For most of the women of England, burial was in their parish: the Wife of Bath would likely seek a place within the church; the Poor Widow and Rose Foreign would find rest in the churchyard. Women of all groups, like their male counterparts, sought to arrange by their wills that surviving relatives and friends reach into the next life to assist them by their prayers. The date of death of the Prioress would be entered in the beadroll of her house so that each year her anniversary would be remembered in the liturgy and, possibly, by the distribution of a pittance in her memory to her sisters. If confraternity provided suffrages for the dead were established between her convent and other houses, she would be remembered more widely. In addition to the masses and other prayers offered for Eleanor Knight and the Wife of Bath soon after their deaths, it is possible that they would establish a chantry or be included in one founded by their husbands or other family. There they would be remembered for years to come, perhaps until chantries were suppressed in the sixteenth century.[72] The Wife of Bath would also benefit from the suffrages offered on her behalf by her guild. Unless she had risen to a position where she belonged to some craft or parish guild, Rose Foreign was probably quickly forgotten after her death; there would soon be little sign of her passing in the busy town churchyard. The Poor Widow, buried in the cemetery that surrounded her parish church, the cemetery through which her friends passed every week, might not be forgotten so soon. Although it is unlikely that she would be remembered in an anniversary mass beyond the first year or two, the physical proximity of her place of burial would help to preserve her memory for a generation. The poorest women, as the richest, would be remembered in a general way on the feast of All Souls.

NOTES

1. For retrospective bibliography see Carolly Erickson and Kathleen Casey, "Women in the Middle Ages: A Working Bibliography," *Mediaeval Studies*

37 (1975):340-59; and Joan Kelly-Gadol, *Bibliography in the History of European Women* (Bronxville, N.Y., 1976). For current work, see *International Medieval Bibliography* (Leeds, 1967-   ), since July-December, 1976, "General Index," s.v. "women." On possible tensions between the study of the history of the family and the history of women, see Barbara J. Harris, "Recent Work on the History of the Family: A Review Article," *Feminist Studies* 3 (1976):159.

2. See the reflections of Ria Lemaire on the limitations of the conference "La femme dans la société des Xe-XIIIe siècles," held at Poitiers, September, 1976: "En marge du colloque . . . ," *Cahiers de civilisation médiévale* 20 (1977):261-63. For this and several other references my thanks to Sharon Ady.

3. E.g., Bede Jarrett, *Social Theories of the Middle Ages 1200-1500* (1926; reprint New York, 1966); "Women," pp. 69-93; and, more recently, G. H. Tavard, *Woman in Christian Tradition* (Notre Dame, Indiana, 1973); Vern L. Bullough and Bonnie Bullough, *The Subordinate Sex, a History of Attitudes towards Women* (Urbana, 1973); several essays in *Religion and Sexism: Images of Woman in the Jewish and Christian Traditions*, ed. R. R. Ruether (New York, 1974); Carolly Erickson, *The Medieval Vision* (London, New York, 1975), "The View of Women," pp. 181-212; M.-T. d'Alverny, "Comment les théologiens et les philosophes voient la femme," *Cahiers de civilisation médiévale* 20 (1977): 105-29; and M. C. Horowitz, "The Image of God in Man—Is Woman Included?," *Harvard Theological Review* 72 (1979):175-206.

4. Much progress has been made in obtaining data on the lives of individual women, including those of the lowest classes; see David Herlihy and Christiane Klapisch-Zuber, *Les Toscans et leurs familles* (Paris, 1978); for the English peasantry, see the work of J. A. Raftis in Toronto and R. H. Hilton in Birmingham and their students.

5. Although the population of London and a few other urban centers increased during the late fourteenth century, many English towns experienced serious decline: May McKisack, *The Fourteenth Century 1307-1399*, The Oxford History of England 5 (Oxford, 1959), pp. 380-81.

6. The Ploughman is seen here as the type of the substantial peasant, possessed of plough and team as well as land, rather than as the *famulus*, specializing in ploughing and attached to the demesne. Demesne farming was much reduced in the late fourteenth century, so there was little or no need for the ploughman in the older sense of *bovarius*: M. M. Postan, "The Famulus," *Economic History Review*, Supplement 2 (Cambridge, 1954), p. 12; and R. H. Hilton, *The English Peasantry in the Middle Ages* (Oxford, 1975), pp. 21-23.

7. In the changing conditions of the period, the economic position of this group was improving: see E. B. DeWindt, *Land and People in Holywell-cum-Needingworth* (Toronto, 1972), pp. 115-27, for the East Midlands; and Zvi Razi, *Life, Marriage and Death in a Medieval Parish* (Cambridge, New York, 1980), pp. 147-49 for Worcestershire; cf. M. M. Postan, "Medieval Agrarian Society in Its Prime; England," *Cambridge Economic*

History of Europe, Vol. 1, 2nd ed. (Cambridge, 1960), pp. 630–32. On Chaucer's view of the Ploughman as the ideal laborer, see Jill Mann, *Chaucer and Medieval Estate Satire: The Literature of Social Classes and the General Prologue to the "Canterbury Tales"* (Cambridge, 1973), pp. 67–70.

8. Geoffrey Chaucer, *The Canterbury Tales*, ed. F. N. Robinson, *The Works of Geoffrey Chaucer*, 2nd ed. (Boston, 1957), p. 199, ll. 2821–23, 2828–31, 2847–49.

9. Razi, *Life, Marriage and Death*, pp. 140–49.

10. See *Middle English Dictionary*, ed. Hans Kurath and Sherman M. Kuhn, Vol. E–F (Ann Arbor, 1952), p. 735 a–b, s.v. 'forein:1'. I am indebted to Professor R. H. Robbins for this reference and for valued assistance and advice touching many parts of this essay.

11. Elspeth M. Viale, "Craftsmen and the Economy of London in the Fourteenth Century," in *Studies in London History Presented to Philip Edmund Jones*, ed. A. E. J. Hollaender and W. Kellaway (London, 1969), pp. 136, 140–42, 163–64.

12. Eileen Power, *Medieval English Nunneries c. 1275 to 1535* (Cambridge, 1922), pp. 1–41; David Knowles, *The Religious Orders in England*, Vol. 2, *The End of the Middle Ages* (Cambridge, 1955), pp. 260–61.

13. René Metz, "Le statut de la femme en droit canonique médiéval," in *La femme*, Société Jean Bodin pour l'Histoire Comparative des Institutions 12, ii (1962):59–113; M. M. Sheehan, "The Influence of Canon Law on the Property Rights of Married Women in England," *Mediaeval Studies* 25 (1963):109–24.

14. Chaucer, *Canterbury Tales*, ed. Robinson, pp. 17–18, ll. 43, 67–69.

15. Ibid., p. 18, ll. 80–81, 89–92.

16. In a volume that, in spite of much criticism, has remained the benchmark of demographic study: *British Medieval Population* (Albuquerque, 1948), J. C. Russell estimated the population of England in 1377 at 2,232,373 (p. 146). In a review in *Revue Belge de philologie et d'histoire* 28 (1950):600–606, J. Stengers argued that numbers were considerably higher. Russell maintained that the population fell during the last quarter of the century (pp. 260–63), a position restated in *Late Ancient and Medieval Population*, Transactions of the American Philosophical Society, N.S. 48, pt. 3 (Philadelphia, 1958), pp. 118–19. For recent work on population trends 1350–1400, see Razi, *Life, Marriage and Death*, pp. 114–16. The numbers of men and women for this period were about equal: see Russell, p. 148, and S. L. Thrupp, "Plague Effects in Medieval Europe," *Comparative Studies in Society and History* 8 (1965–66):475.

17. Emily Coleman, "Medieval Marriage Characteristics: a Neglected Factor in the History of Medieval Serfdom," *The Journal of Interdisciplinary History* 2 (Autumn 1971):205–19, and "L'infanticide dans le haut moyen-âge?" *Annales: économies, sociétés, civilisations* 29 (1974):315–35. See Russell, *Late Ancient and Medieval Population*, passim.

18. R. R. Helmholz, "Infanticide in the Province of Canterbury during the Fifteenth Century," *History of Childhood Quarterly* 2 (1975):379–90;

B. A. Hanawalt, "Childrearing among the Lower Classes of Late Medieval England," *Journal of Interdisciplinary History* 8 (Summer 1977):1-22. The possibility that female infanticide is the explanation of the high sex ratios revealed in early fourteenth-century England and in London (1259-1330) is suggested by Russell, *British Medieval Population*, pp. 148-49, and by H. A. Miskimin, "The Legacies of London: 1250-1330" in *The Medieval City*, ed. H. A. Miskimin, David Herlihy, and A. L. Udovitch (New Haven and London, 1977), pp. 220-21, though the latter points out that underreporting is a plausible hypothesis. See Thrupp, "Plague Effects in Medieval Europe," pp. 474-83.

19. "Infant" is used to mean a very young child and not in the common-law sense of a minor. On the rights of the minor, see F. Joüon des Longrais, in "Le statut de la femme en Angleterre dans le droit commun médiéval," *La femme*, Société Jean Bodin pour l'Histoire Comparative des Institutions 12, ii (1962):148-63.

20. Testaments of the period provide for the child with which a wife is pregnant, or make bequests that are to be withdrawn if the pregnancy results in the birth of an heir.

21. Grandchildren are sometimes legatees; they would often be very young.

22. See *Borough Customs*, ed. Mary Bateson, Selden Society 21 (London, 1906), pp. 145-57.

23. Hanawalt, "Childrearing," p. 14.

24. See *Councils and Synods with Other Documents Relating to the English Church II A.D. 1305-1313*, Vol. 2, ed. F. M. Powicke and C. R. Cheney (Oxford, 1964), p. 1411: "General Index," s.v. "Children: safety measures for."

25. Hanawalt, "Childrearing," p. 18.

26. "A woman hath seven ages for severall purposes appointed to her by law: as seven years for the lord to have aid pur file marier," according to Coke on the first age of woman, as cited by Frederick Pollock and F. W. Maitland, *The History of English Law*, 2nd ed. (1898; rpt. Cambridge, 1978), 2:439, n. 3.

27. "Although the evidence of literacy among women is less conclusive . . . it appears that the typical upper-class education for women included reading knowledge of the vernacular, whether French or English, or possibly both, but little or no knowledge of Latin or of writing": J. H. Moran, "Educational Development and Social Change in York Diocese from the Fourteenth Century to 1548," (Ph.D. dissertation, Brandeis University, 1975), p. 235, n. 18. See her *Education and Learning in the City of York 1300-1560*, Borthwick Papers 55 (York, 1979), passim; and F. R. H. Du Boulay, *An Age of Ambition* (London, 1970), pp. 118-19.

28. See Marian K. Dale, "The London Silk-women of the Fifteenth Century," *Economic History Review* 4 (1933):324-35; S. L. Thrupp, *The Merchant Class of Medieval London* (1948; rpt. Ann Arbor, 1962), pp. 169-70; Viale, "Craftsmen and the Economy of London in the Fourteenth Century" (see n. 11, above), pp. 150-51; and Maryanne Kowaleski,

"Local Markets and Merchants in late Fourteenth-Century Exeter," (Ph.D. dissertation, University of Toronto, 1982), pp. 194-209, 220-25.

29. See Thrupp, *The Merchant Class*, pp. 170-71.

30. Power, *Medieval English Nunneries*, pp. 237-89, esp. pp. 245-50.

31. "Medieval Peasant Marriage: An Examination of Marriage License Fines in the *Liber Gersumarum*," in *Pathways to Medieval Peasants*, ed. J. A. Raftis (Toronto, 1981), pp. 193-246.

32. Viale, "Craftsmen and the Economy of London in the Fourteenth Century," pp. 141-43. See J. A. Brundage, "Prostitution in the Medieval Canon Law," *Signs, Journal of Women in Culture and Society* 1, no. 4 (Summer 1976):825-45.

33. On the different ages of majority, see Pollock and Maitland, *The History of English Law*, vol. 2, pp. 436-39, and M. M. Sheehan, *The Will in Medieval England* (Toronto, 1963), pp. 239-41. On proof of age, see Russell, *British Medieval Population*, pp. 92-117, and Sue S. Walker, "Proof of Age of Feudal Heirs in Medieval England," *Mediaeval Studies* 35 (1973):306-23.

34. Power, *Medieval English Nunneries*, pp. 38-41.

35. Ibid., pp. 25-38, 436-74, et passim; Sr. Mary of the Incarnation Byrne, *The Tradition of the Nun in Medieval England* (Washington, 1932), pp. 165-74; Mann, *Chaucer and Medieval Estate Satire*, pp. 128-37.

36. Annette Koren, "Provincial Women and Their Economic Status in Late Medieval England," a paper read at the Berkshire Conference of Women Historians, Vassar College, 1981. See the discussion of Cecilia Penifader, a spinster of Brigstock, Northants. (ca. 1316-ca. 1344), and her wide social network in Judith Bennett, "Gender, Family and Community: A Comparative Study of the English Peasantry, 1287-1349" (Ph.D. dissertation, Toronto University, 1981), pp. 108-13, 136, n. 63; and the earlier remarks of Eileen Power, "The Position of Women," in *The Legacy of the Middle Ages*, ed. G. C. Crump and E. F. Jacob (Oxford, 1926), pp. 411-15.

37. See Russell, *British Medieval Population*, p. 158.

38. See Thrupp, *The Merchant Class*, p. 196.

39. Razi found that, in the post-plague period, sons usually obtained land in the lifetime of their fathers and were able to marry earlier than had been the case before that time. They married at about twenty. The small sample that was available indicated marriage of women between twelve and nineteen. See Eleanor Searle, "Seigneurial Control of Women's Marriage: The Antecedents and Function of Merchet in England," *Past and Present* 82 (February 1979):3-43; and Chris Middleton, "Peasants, Patriarchy and the Feudal Mode of Production in England: A Marxist Appraisal. Part 2: Feudal Lords and the Subordination of Peasant Women," *Sociological Review* n.s. 29, no. 1 (1981):137-54.

40. See Christopher Lasch, "The Suppression of Clandestine Marriage in England: The Marriage Act of 1753," *Salmagundi* 26 (Spring 1974): 90-109. The possibility of a secret but valid union must be kept in mind

in the discussion of the marriage of all classes and in any analysis of the literature of the time; see K. P. Wentersdorf, "The Clandestine Marriages of the Fair Maid of Kent," *Journal of Medieval History* 5 (1979):203-31, and "Some Observations on the Concept of Clandestine Marriage in *Troilus and Criseyde*," *Chaucer Review* 15 (1980):101-26.

41. Cf. Jean Leclercq, *Monks on Marriage, a Twelfth-Century View* (New York, 1982), pp. 1-9, where the importance of the element of love in marriage is presented.

42. See Sue S. Walker, "Free Consent and Marriage of Feudal Wards in Medieval England," *Journal of Medieval History* 8 (1982):123-34. My thanks to Professor Michael Altschul for this reference and for other assistance in this essay.

43. See J. T. Noonan, Jr., "Power to Choose," *Viator* 4 (1973):419-34; and M. M. Sheehan, "Choice of Marriage Partner in the Middle Ages: Development and Mode of Application of a Theory of Marriage," *Studies in Medieval and Renaissance History* 1 (Vancouver, 1978):8-11.

44. B. A. Hanawalt, "Women's Contribution to the Home Economy in Late Medieval Europe," a paper read at the Berkshire Conference of Women Historians, Vassar College, 1981.

45. Joüon des Longrais, "Le statut de la femme," pp. 163-83; Pollock and Maitland, *The History of English Law*, 2:403-28.

46. William Holdsworth, *A History of English Law*, Vol. 3, 5th ed. (London, 1966), pp. 542-43. For a recent re-examination of the question, see Charles Donahue, Jr., "Lyndwood's Gloss propriarum uxorum: Marital Property and ius commune in Fifteenth-Century England," in *Europäisches Rechtsdenken in Geschichte und Gegenwart*, Festschrift für Helmut Coing zum 70. Geburtstag, ed. Norbert Horn (Munich, 1982), 1:19-37.

47. Thrupp, *The Merchant Class*, pp. 169-74, and Kowaleski, "Local Markets and Merchants in late Fourteenth-Century Exeter" (see n. 28, above), pp. 194-209, 220-25. See Bateson, *Borough Customs*, Selden Society 18:227-28.

48. Bateson, *Borough Customs*, Selden Society 21:106-11.

49. See J. A. Raftis, "Social Structures of Five East Midland Villages," *Economic History Review* 2 Ser. 18:1 (1965):91-92; DeWindt, *Land and People*, p. 235 and n. 157; Hilton, *The English Peasantry*, pp. 103-6; and especially Bennett, "Gender, Family and Community" (see n. 36, above), pp. 141-91, 262-74, and 320-29.

50. Holdsworth, *A History of English Law*, 3:542, and n. 23; see n. 69, below.

51. "Ubi non est consensus utriusque non est coniugium . . . nisi forte aliquando urgentissima interveniente necessitate pro bono pacis couniunctio talis toleretur." This text, c. 19 of the Council of Westminster (1175) was included in the *Extravagantes* of Gregory IX (4.2.2). See *Councils and Synods with Other Documents Relating to the English Church I A.D. 871-1204*, ed. D. Whitelock, M. Brett, and C. N. L. Brooke (Oxford, 1981), 2:991, 967 n. 3; and the discussion in M. M. Sheehan, "Marriage

Theory and Practice in the Conciliar Legislation and Diocesan Statutes of Medieval England," *Mediaeval Studies* 40 (1978):411. Dynastic and political aspects of marriage are well presented by H. A. Kelly in *The Matrimonial Trials of Henry VIII* (Stamford, California, 1975).

52. Slightly less than half of the marriage cases before the official of the bishop of Ely 1374-82 were *ex officio*. Several of them began because, at the reading of the banns of matrimony, objection was made to a proposed union. Learning of this, the court proceeded *ex officio* to investigate the case: M. M. Sheehan, "The Formation and Stability of Marriage in Fourteenth-Century England: Evidence of an Ely Register," *Mediaeval Studies* 33 (1971):256-62. On this matter generally, see R. H. Helmholz, *Marriage Litigation in Medieval England* (Cambridge, 1974), and *Select Cases from the Ecclesiastical Courts of the Province of Canterbury c. 1200-1301*, ed. Norma Adams and Charles Donahue, Jr., Selden Society 95 (London, 1981), "Introduction," pp. 81-84.

53. See Eileen Power, *Medieval People*, 10th ed. (New York, 1963), Ch. 5, "The Menagier's Wife," pp. 96-119; *Medieval Women* (Cambridge, 1975), pp. 9-34; and Hanawalt, "Women's Contribution" (see n. 44, above). A remarkable sense of women's administrative activity may be gained from the correspondence of Agnes Paston (1440-79) and Margaret Paston (1441-1484): *Paston Letters and Papers of the Fifteenth Century*, ed. Norman Davis, 2 vols. (Oxford, 1971-6), nos. 13-34, 434-36, and 124-230, 707-36.

54. Power, *Medieval English Nunneries*, pp. 42-95, 131-60.

55. Joüon des Longrais, "Statut de la femme," pp. 183-235; Pollock and Maitland, *The History of English Law*, 1:482-85.

56. See William Holdsworth, *A History of English Law*, pp. 554-56; M. M. Sheehan, "The Family in Late Medieval England, Extended or Nuclear? Evidence from Testaments," a paper read at the Fifth British Legal History Conference, University of Bristol, 1981.

57. Bateson, *Borough Customs*, 21:cviii-cxv.

58. On the customary rights of the peasant widow and the acquittal of the obligations of her holding, see George Homans, *English Villagers of the Thirteenth Century* (1941; rpt. New York, 1975), pp. 184-88; J. A. Raftis, *Tenure and Mobility* (Toronto, 1964), pp. 36-42; Edward Britton, *The Community of the Vill* (Toronto, 1977), pp. 20-22; and Hilton, *The English Peasantry*, pp. 98-100.

59. On the removal of the required interval of at least a year and a day between death of a husband and the remarriage of his widow, see Sheehan, "The Influence of Canon Law," p. 112.

60. A preliminary study of these women was presented by Sharon Ady in "Vows of Chastity and the Medieval English Widow" at the Sixteenth International Conference of Medieval Studies, University of Western Michigan, Kalamazoo, 1981. See J. R. Shinners, Jr., "Religion in Fourteenth-Century England: Clerical Standards and Popular Practice in the Diocese of Norwich" (Ph.D. dissertation, Toronto University, 1982), pp. 334-35.

61. See B. A. Hanawalt, "Widowhood in Medieval English Villages," a paper read at the Sixteenth International Conference of Medieval Studies, University of Western Michigan, Kalamazoo, 1981. Razi notes that peasant widows seem to have found it more difficult to marry in Worcestershire after the plague (*Life, Marriage and Death*, p. 138).
62. See Homans, *English Villagers*, pp. 144–46; Raftis, *Tenure and Mobility*, pp. 42–46; S. R. Burstein, "Care of the Aged in England from Medieval Times to the End of the 16th Century," *Bulletin of the History of Medicine* 22 (1948):738–43; and Elaine Clark, "The Quest for Economic Security in Medieval England," a paper read at the Medieval Conference: "Aging and the Aged in Medieval Europe" Part 1, Toronto, February 1983.
63. Powers, *Medieval English Nunneries*, p. 57.
64. The religious superior posed a special problem in this regard; see Sheehan, *The Will in Medieval England*, pp. 250–53.
65. Powers, *Medieval English Nunneries*, pp. 315–40; see Knowles, "The Wage-System and the Common Life," *The Religious Orders of England*, Vol. 2, pp. 240–47. For Bishop William of Wykeham's injunctions against the making of wills by nuns (1387), see Powers, op. cit., p. 337 and n. 6.
66. Chaucer, *The Canterbury Tales*, ed. Robinson, p. 18, ll. 158–62.
67. Sheehan, "The Influence of Canon Law," pp. 119–71; *The Will in Medieval England*, pp. 234–41. See n. 46, above.
68. See n. 48, above.
69. In the diocese of Rochester (1347–48), the testaments of 127 men, 33 married women, 20 widows, and 5 women (who were probably spinsters) were probated in groups. Many of these were the testaments of the very poor; see *Registrum Hamonis Hethe*, ed. C. Johnson, Canterbury and York Society 49 (Oxford, 1948), 2:923–26, 1000, et passim.
70. See Antoine Bernard, *La sépulture en droit canonique du* Décret *de Gratien au Concile de Trente* (Paris, 1933), pp. 85–104.
71. "First, I betake my sowle to God . . . and my body to be beried in the ele of the cherch of Mauteby byfore the ymage of Our Lady there, jn which ele reste the bodies of divers of myn aunceteres, whos sowles God assoile" (4 February 1482): *Paston Letters and Papers*, no. 230, 1:383.
72. See K. L. Wood-Legh, *Perpetual Chantries in Britain* (Cambridge, 1965), pp. 8–29, et passim; and Rosalind Hill, " 'A Chaunterie for Soules': Chantries in the Reign of Richard II," in *The Reign of Richard II: Essays in Honour of May McKisack*, ed. F. R. H. Du Boulay and Caroline M. Barron (London, 1971), pp. 243–55.

Why Did Jesus Use Parables?
The Medieval Discussion

STEPHEN L. WAILES

In the fourth chapter of the Gospel according to Mark, verses 11-12, Jesus explains the use of his parables in preaching. This explanation is repeated, though modified, in the later synoptic Gospels, and has come to be known as the Markan parable theory because of the compositional priority of that version. It is a problematic theory because it attributes to Jesus an interest in depriving the general public of his message, which was to be understood by only a chosen few (the disciples). We are told that Jesus used parables so that he would *not* be understood by those who might otherwise experience a change of heart, turn to God, and receive forgiveness of their sins.[1]

This passage is a crux of biblical scholarship, fraught with philological and theological difficulties. It is beyond the scope of this essay to discuss or even to summarize these—an ample literature already exists for that purpose.[2] We will try to view those verses from the Gospel of Mark and their parallels in which Jesus explains his use of parables, the characteristic form of his teaching, as students and teachers of Christian truth in the Middle Ages viewed them, and to show how they were interpreted by these readers. Whatever one's convictions regarding the exact meaning of the transmitted New Testament passages, and whether or not one agrees that the Markan parable theory is "perverse," "intolerable," and "lebensfremd,"[3] it is clear that the Latin Bible of the Middle Ages attributed a teaching to Christ that divided men into two groups on the basis of their amenability to truth, and that seemed to express Christ's indifference to those masses whose ignorance would preclude their salvation. In all synoptic Gospels the parable theory is framed by the parable of "The Sower" and Jesus' allegorical explanation of it to the disciples, which seemed to be a demonstration of the theory itself—Christ's teaching will be grasped only by the initiated. This context lent further weight to the critical verses in Mark and their parallels.

The parable theory was an important and difficult object of study. After a close examination of interpretations advanced from the Patristic period to the fourteenth century, we will consider certain implications of these ideas in several areas of medieval culture: exegesis, Church history, spirituality, philosophy, and literature. Though it might seem presumptuous to broach so

Medievalia et Humanistica, New Series, Number 13 (Paul Maurice Clogan, ed.). Rowman & Allanheld, Totowa, NJ. 1985.

many special domains in a few paragraphs, no activity engaged men in the Middle Ages more broadly and directly than understanding the Bible. It may therefore be justifiable to suggest connections of the Biblical parable theory, as explained and re-explained for nearly 1200 years, to issues in other areas of medieval civilization.

Medieval readers, accepting the divine inspiration and the truth of the Gospels, understood that when these appeared to disagree or to conflict with dogma, the exegete's task was to show the essential unity beneath any superficial disparity and to find the orthodox sense of seemingly doubtful passages. Augustine's long analysis of the relationship between the four Gospels, *De concensu Evangelistarum libri quattuor*,[4] had shown that Matthew was the earliest and most complete of the synoptic authors, being an eyewitness to Jesus' life. With respect to material treated in common, Mark depended on Matthew and tended to abbreviate the accounts that he repeated (*Marcus eum subsecutus tamquam pedisequus et breuiator eius uidetur*). Modern scholarship has rejected Augustine's judgment on this point, but its authority during the Middle Ages may be seen in the fact that around 1150 Zacharias Chrysopolitanus quotes extensively from *De concensu Evangelistarum* in the preface to his widely read commentary on the gospel harmony *In unum ex quattuor*, including the terms *pedisequus* and *breuiator* to characterize Mark in his relation to Matthew.[5] Thus the great majority of medieval authorities were concerned in the first place with the theory of parabolic teaching in Matthew 13:10–17 and 34, rather than with the account in the fourth chapter of Mark, just as far more commentaries were written on Matthew than on Mark or Luke. It is not the case, however, that Mark's version was simply disregarded in preference for Matthew, because Mark's has two features that commended it to the exegetes: it is more concise, lacking the theme of possession and want (verse 12 in Matthew), the explicit citation of Isaiah (verses 14–15), and commendation of the disciples' power of perception (verses 16–17); more important, the conjunction joining the ideas of parabolic teaching to the ignorance of the crowd is *ut* followed by *nequando* in Mark (*in parabolis . . . ut videntes videant et non videant . . . nequando convertantur*), whereas the syntax of Matthew was less plain, with *quia* followed by the prophecy quoted freely from Isaiah and *nequando* within this prophecy. Precisely because Mark was believed to be the follower and redactor of Matthew, his shorter and simpler account could serve as a guide to understanding the supposed eyewitness. The very brief version of Luke 8:10 played a tertiary role.

In the following pages we will analyze interpretations of the parable theory from the Fathers to Nicholas of Lyra and Ludolph of Saxony. Our sources are by no means exhaustive; for the period after 1250 their number reflects the relative paucity of edited material, yet they are sufficient to make clear the problems and the attempted solutions.[6] We will find that the exegetes generally represent the Judeo-Hellenic tradition of the parable "in der [sie] ein schwieriges, mitunter rätselhaftes, jedenfalls deutungsbedürftiges, nur besonderer Einsicht verständliches Wort ist" (Pesch, p. 240), as they explain the exclusion from understanding of those "outside." A different conception, transmitted by the Ciceronian school of rhetoric, is also present in many authorities: they recognize the parable as an effective teaching device. We will show the creative harmonization of these traditions by Albert the Great, then conclude with observations on the relevance of this question for other areas of medieval studies.

Although Luke provides virtually no scenic setting for Jesus' words in verse 10, Matthew and Mark agree that a very large crowd came to him at the lakeside and that he stepped into a boat and spoke in parables to the people on the shore. Hilary of Poitiers finds that this spatial separation agrees with figurative discourse, for the boat symbolizes the Church, and outside the Church there is no comprehension of the word. Like the sand on which it stands, the crowd separated from Jesus is sterile and useless (I, p. 296). This is the most severe of the judgments on the crowd, repeated in one of the major works of Carolingian exegesis, the commentary on Matthew by Paschasius Radbertus (col. 483C), and followed by Bruno of Segni ("illis autem non est datum. Quare? Quia non credunt; quia spiritualia non quaerunt," col. 187B). Jerome interprets the scenic information more temperately, suggesting that the crowd is at least removed from the sea of the world though it is not with the Lord, and this position is adopted by many authorities.[7] Aquinas combines Hilary's idea of the boat as *Ecclesia* with the crowd as catechumens (p. 425). Although most authorities discuss the text in Matthew, the influence of Mark's account seems likely from Jerome onward and is explicit in Aquinas, for Mark says that Jesus *taught* the crowd on the shore (*docere*, twice in verses 1–2), where Matthew uses *loquor* instead (verses 3, 13: cf. Aquinas, "per navem Ecclesia . . . significatur: ubi sedet per fidem et docet eos qui stant in littore," ibid.). We will return to this detail of Mark's account below, for it has considerable bearing on Jesus' resort to parables.

The Gospels leave unclear the location of the disciples when Jesus entered the boat and spoke from the water. Matthew notes that they approached him before asking why he spoke in parables ("et accendentes discipuli," v. 10); but Mark says they joined him when he was alone, having evidently withdrawn from the crowd ("et cum esset singularis," ibid.). Explaining Matthew's account, Jerome reasons that the disciples entered the boat with Jesus and so were able to approach him with their question, an idea repeated through the Middle Ages and that determined Ludolph of Saxony's first words on this subject in his fourteenth-century harmony ("prae turba ad eum congregata *ascendens* cum discipulis *in naviculam*," p. 277).[8] This question is important because it contributes to the identification of two groups, one with Jesus and one apart from him. Had the disciples not been understood to enter the boat with him, they would have been associated with the crowd on the shore, for not until verse 36 does Matthew mention a change of scene. At that point Jesus sends away the crowd and enters a house; the disciples come to him, thus establishing a private discussion such as the one introduced in the tenth verse of Mark.

The question asked by the disciples that elicits the parable theory is different in each gospel. Mark and Luke report it in indirect speech; it concerns, respectively, parables in general or "The Sower" ("interrogaverunt eum . . . . . . parabolas," "interrogabant . . . quae esset haec parabola"). Matthew offers a direct quotation of the disciples' words ("quare in parabolis loqueris eis"), which is, in content, easily the most appropriate query for the transmitted response. Matthew then introduces the passage regarding the failure of sight and hearing with the conjunction "quia," where both Mark and Luke have "ut" (vv. 13, 12, and 10 respectively), so that Jesus explains his custom of speaking in parables as the consequence of defects in others rather than the cause. This might have been construed positively, as an expression of Jesus' concern for the masses who were handicapped in their spiritual understanding, but in fact it was taken negatively: because the crowd was not adept, it was not worthy of plain speech. The passage from Isaiah was crucial for this interpretation because it was plainly a condemnation of the Jews, which, in its new context, seemed to condemn them yet again—for the rejection of Christ. John Chrysostom taught that the failure of the Jewish crowd's senses was caused by its wickedness ("ex eorum nequitia caecitas . . . quia vero sese pervertebant, in parabolis demum loquitur," *PG* 58:472); similarly, Rabanus ("Incrassatum est cor Judaeorum crassitudine malitiae, et abundantia peccatorum," col. 942D), Haimo of Auxerre ("propter superbiam caeci et surdi facti sunt," col. 166C), and others.[9]

Although it would have been possible to construe Matthew's account as showing the failure of sinful spirits to grasp *any* mode of discourse, parabolic or direct, the earliest authorities were apparently much swayed by the agreement between Mark and Luke on this question. Both evangelists set forth the use of parables for "outsiders" or "others" as deliberate obfuscation, hence punishment: "Illis autem qui foris sunt in parabolis omnia fiunt / ut videntes videant et non videant" (Mark 4:11); "Ceteris autem in parabolis / ut videntes non videant" (Luke 8:10). Given the conjunction *ut*, Jerome had no choice but to take parabolic speech as *ipso facto* obscure speech, the just portion of the willfully perverse (on verses 14–15, I, p. 268). Thus he arrived at one of the modern readings of the parable theory: "The synoptic witness to parable purpose . . . uniformly suggests . . . that Jesus' purpose in relating parables was to make obscure his message so that those who were enlightened might recognize truth while those not so gifted might remain in darkness."[10] Origen had thought the parable a kind of riddle and tried to show that Jesus never spoke to his disciples in the parable as such, but rather in some other figure of speech bearing the same name (!), or in the rhetorically distinct similitude.[11] Later authorities, accepting the parable as a technique of non-communication, associated Jesus' parable theory with his command in Matthew 7:6 ("Nolite dare sanctum canibus / neque mittatis margaritas vestras ante porcos"), as, for example, did Bonaventure: "*Ceteris autem in parabolis*, scilicet supple: datum est nosse, quod potius est ignorare . . . Et hoc facit iusto suo iudicio, quo non vult communicare sancta immundis . . . 'Nolite sanctum dare canibus' " (p. 193).[12]

To understand the Bible as saying that Christ sought to withhold his teaching from certain men through rhetorical obscurities strikes modern readers as perverse and intolerable. This idea was difficult for medieval readers as well, but they were obliged to explain it. The Arian author of the *Opus imperfectum*, which was attributed in the Middle Ages to Chrysostom, simply rejected the witness of Mark and Luke and the notion that Christ had not wished to speak plainly ("ut . . . non videant"). He identified the problem quite specifically as the unwillingness of the hearers to hear, but left no direct impress on tradition.[13] In a gospel commentary attributed to Jerome, the author reasons that Jesus obscured his message so that the people would have to turn for truth to the disciples, whom they despised (col. 603A), but this opinion was not influential. A far more popular approach was to analyze the fault that caused Christ justly to veil his meaning in parabolic speech. Bede, studying the phrase "qui foris sunt" in Mark's account, discovers a failure in the crowd when it condones its separation from the Lord: "Illis autem qui foris sunt *neque appropinquant pedibus domini ut accipiant de doctrina eius* in parabolis omnia fiunt" (p. 482, emphasis added). Because Matthew reported that the disciples had twice approached Jesus on this occasion (vv. 10, 36), the crowd, by contrast, was culpable. Bede used precisely this reasoning when commenting on Luke, equating "*ceteris*" to Mark's "*qui foris sunt*," and his revered opinion was the more influential because this passage in Luke had not been discussed by Origen in his homilies or Ambrose in his exposition: "qui appropinquant pedibus eius accipient de doctrina ejus . . . Recte itaque in parabolis audiunt et in enigmate qui clausis sensibus cordis neque intrare neque curant cognoscere ueritatem" (p. 175). Bede's formulation rests on the basic, scenic division of this episode into two groups, and places the entire crowd in the wrong: because it was tepid, Jesus spoke to it in parables.[14]

Two other positions on Jesus' deliberate obscurity must be mentioned. Chrysostom brings up the apparent contradiction that the Lord should speak at all, even in dark figures, to people whom he did not wish to enlighten, and explains this as proof of God's mercy even toward sinners. As the allusions to conversion and healing in his quotation from Isaiah reveal, Jesus used parables to provoke and incite, to hint that *if* the crowd were to change, it might yet be saved. Had Jesus not wished the ultimate salvation of the crowd, he would have kept silent.[15] In this manner Chrysostom harmonizes the notion of parables as devices of concealment with God's charity; it was not a very popular line of reasoning, perhaps because of the difficult idea that a set of utterances may serve two opposed ends, but it was incorporated under Chrysostom's name into the *Gloss* on Matthew 13:15 and very likely influenced Aquinas' formulation in the *Summa theologiae*, given his high regard for Chrysostom's homilies on Matthew.[16]

More widely repeated is a vindication of divine goodness found in the *Quaestiones septemdecim in Matthaeum*, which circulated as a work of Augustine. Although the Jews merited their incomprehension, one might nonetheless sympathize with them because of their exclusion from the Gospel and hence from salvation—"quis non exsurgat in defensionem Judaeorum, ut eos extra culpam fuisse proclamet, quod non crediderunt? Propterea enim non poterant credere, quia excaecavit oculos eorum" (col. 1372). Since one cannot impute fault to God, one must seek out his just intention in apparently denying Jews access to salvation. The key is provided by Acts 2:37–41, which narrates the extreme compunction and subsequent conversion of many Jews when Peter told them about the crucifixion and resurrection. The obscure language of parables was part of God's plan to convert Jews by the eventual, full understanding of their crime—"per obscuritatem sermonis excaecati, dicta Domini non intellexerunt, et ea non intelligendo, non in eum crediderunt, non credendo crucifixerunt eum; atque ita post ejus resurrectionem . . . majore criminis reatu compuncti sunt et prostrati ad poenitentiam . . . flagrantissima dilectione conversi" (col. 1373). Jesus spoke in parables, therefore, to veil his meaning, but did this with compassionate intent. The ensuing ignorance of the crowd was, paradoxically, a necessary step toward the justification of some—"illa caecitas ad conversionem, quae per linguam parabolarum fiebat" (ibid.). The author concludes with metaphors of medication, pointing out that affliction is often required for healing and that ointments for the eye necessarily obscure vision in order to cure. With its labored series of steps leading to the conversion of the relatively few Jews in question, this rationalization appears intrinsically weak. Carrying the authority of Augustine, however, it was endorsed by Rabanus (col. 943), by the Matthew commentary attributed to Bede (col. 66CD), by the *Gloss* on Matthew 13:13, by Zacharias (col. 231A), and by Aquinas (p. 430).

The medieval discussion we have presented thus far is an effort to explain Jesus' words about his use of parables in terms of separate and distinct audiences. However one interprets the transmitted details, Jesus seemed to be stating an intention to withhold his meaning by using parables, and this intention was corroborated by the fact that he explained to his disciples (but not to the crowd) the allegory of "The Sower." From Mark 4:34 ("Seorsum autem discipulis suis disserebat omnia") one might reason that Jesus explained *all* his parables to the disciples, although the Gospels do not transmit these explanations, which would support the concepts of the parables as enigma and of the chosen few.[17] Had the scriptural tradition of the parable theory consisted only of those verses that we have studied thus far, the medieval legacy would be a comparatively coherent set of ideas developed to clarify and rationalize the theory as set forth in Matthew, with important influences from the wording of Mark and Luke and with one major problem to which no fully satisfactory answer could be given: why should Jesus have preached in order not to be understood?

A separate line of discussion from Jerome onward is based on Matthew 13:1-3 and Mark 4:1-2, 33-34. This presents the parable as a pedagogical tool; its roots lie in classical rhetoric, and its affirmative theory of parabolic speech rests in uneasy proximity to the theory of obfuscation outlined above.

In his *Rhetoric*, Aristotle presented the parable as a device of persuasion within the general category of exempla.[18] He admitted that real examples had greater force than invented ones, but as the former were not always at hand, one could resort to the latter. In the parable two similar situations are compared, so that concessions made in the fictive case will also be made in the actual, and a clear connection of the two is essential. Although Aristotle's *Rhetoric* was not directly influential on medieval tradition, not being translated into Latin until the thirteenth century, it nourished the Ciceronian school of rhetoric, which was authoritative. Using the term *similitudo* (as a translation of *parabola*), the *Rhetorica ad Herennium* (attributed to Cicero) recommended this figure of speech "aut ornandi causa aut probandi aut apertius dicende aut ante oculos ponendi."[19] Quintilian, in the *Instituto oratoria*, explained the *parabola* as a comparison utilizing the *similitudo* for the sake of emphasis and clarity.[20] Seneca mentioned the parable as a benefit to those "qui simpliciter et demonstrandae rei causa eloquebantur,"[21] and the Ciceronian tradition is perceptible in numerous medieval treatises on grammar, rhetoric, or poetics that mention the parable, such as the *Ars poetica* of Gervase of Melcheley ("Apologus vel parabola est cum adducta rerum similitudine quod de uno dicitur de alio intelligitur").[22] Isidor of Seville treated the parable as one of the three kinds of similitude, commenting that it had served Solomon as a means of communicating "imagines veritatis," and his formulations were widely imitated.[23] This rhetorical tradition made all scholars in the period of our interest aware that the *parabola* or *similitudo*—terms that alternate in the Latin Bible as they do in related exegetical writings[24]— was a figurative device to facilitate, not to impede, communication and persuasion. The parable's essence was clarity in the figurative demonstration of truth.

The parable of "The Sower" is introduced by Matthew with the observation that Jesus told the crowd many things in parables ("et locutus est eis multa in parabolis," v. 3). The implication of this verse—that he used such figures of speech to demonstrate rather than to obscure his meaning—is decisively confirmed by Mark, who (as noted above) uses the verb *docere* twice and specifies the Lord's *doctrina* as the ideas communicated by means of parables: "Et iterum coepit docere ad mare . . . et docebat eos in parabolis multa / et dicebat illis in doctrina sua" (vv. 1-2). Chrysostom explains that Jesus used parables to arrest the attention of his listeners, to make his teaching more vivid, and to plant it more deeply in their memory.[25] Jerome regarded the plurality of parables as a concession to the diversity of individuals constituting the multitude: given the parable as a pedagogical tool, Jesus used many different ones to reach the greatest number of people.[26] Jerome compared this procedure to a host's offering of various foods to guests of differing tastes, and to the varying treatment of diverse injuries.[27] Both similes rest on a positive understanding of parabolic discourse, yet Jerome was bound to the idea that such figures of speech were difficult and puzzling. He stressed that Jesus used parables to communicate "non omnia . . . sed multa," since the crowd would have derived no profit from a purely parabolic address, and suggested that Jesus' plain speech stimulated his audience to seek the truths hidden in figures. This notion of the spiritual exercise provided by parables was popular throughout the Middle Ages.[28]

The single most influential remark on the parable as a teaching device was made by Gregory the Great in one of his homilies on the Gospels. His text is Matthew 13:44–52, comprising the parables of "The Buried Treasure," "The Pearl," and "The Seine." He observes that Jesus employs such mundane comparisons so the spirit will ascend from known and familiar things to the unknown.[29] Gregory's text in another homily includes the parable theory in Luke, but he does not discuss it. Hence the Gregorian contribution to the discussion of Jesus' teaching in parables is the positive concept of the parable as tool. Among the many authorities who repeat Gregory's idea of leading the mind through tangible likenesses to the comprehension of intangibles, Rupert of Deutz adduces as a parallel Paul's remark about milk and solid food (Hebrews 5:13–14). He thus places all men in the position of novices, when compared to the apostles, and presents the parable as an essential means of our spiritual edification: "nos autem populares siue plebei, quibus tanta non collata est gratia, coepimus . . . ex parabolis istis euangelicis eadem paulatim percipere mysteria regni Dei" (III, p. 1816). For Albert the Great, it lies in the cognitive faculty of ordinary men to require the assistance of comparisons for the grasping of spiritual truth. Jesus used the parable not as a convenience but a necessity:

"*Cui assimilabimus*," humano operi, "*regnum Dei*," qui in terra cognoscitur? "*Aut cui parabolae comparabimus illud?*" quia humanus et rudis intellectus ad coelestia non elevatur, nisi parabolicis sit adjutus similitudinibus. Omnis enim cognitio intellectiva fit ex his quae nota sunt nobis, et aliter doceri non possumus.[30]

When Albert comments on Mark 4:33–34, he interprets these verses as applying to the disciples as well as the crowd. Thus he finds the parable to have been an integral part of Jesus' discourse to all men; the disciples, however, were granted an explanation of each parabolic teaching because they were "capaciores," the explanations brought their finer spiritual understanding to higher levels. Albert explains the statement "sine parabola autem non loquebatur eis" by referring again to his theory of knowledge for common men: "Hoc est, sine humanis similitudinibus . . . quia divina simplicitas et pura spiritualia ab animalibus hominibus non possunt sine humanis similitudinibus intellegi" (XXI, p. 438).

The rhetorical tradition of the parable was thus given spiritual depth by Gregory and epistemological precision by Albert. It is the foundation of commentary on the opening verses of Mark 4 and Matthew 13, and on the verses that establish the customary nature of Jesus' teaching through parables (Mark 4:33-34; Matthew 13:34-35), but in the body of medieval comment there is little or no effort to integrate this tradition with the terms of the Markan parable theory. The less ambitious of our authorities transmit the two sets of remarks disjunctively, a procedure made easier to the degree they wrote as glossators—no unified understanding of the parable can be gained from the *Gloss* itself! Even the authors of more substantial essays on one or more of the Gospels—Origen, Jerome, Bede, Paschasius, Christian of Stablo, Bruno of Segni, Aquinas—leave the question unresolved, or suggest solutions that may be convenient but do not stand critical scrutiny, as the following comments will show.

We have already noted Origen's attempt to restrict the *parabola* as such to Jesus' public speech, contrasting its obscurity to the clarity of the *similitudo* used for the instruction of the disciples. Jerome repeats this idea ("Non discipulis sed turbis per parabolas loquebatur," I, p. 282) but he knows that parables were devices for teaching ("loquitur . . . in multis parabolis ut iuxta uarias uoluntates diuersas reciperent disciplinas," I, p. 264). Bede simply ignores the implications of Mark 4:2 ("et docebat eis in parabolis multa") when he analyzes the situation of Jesus separated from the crowd (pp. 479-80). Paschasius repeats Jerome ("eisdem loquitur multis in parabolis, ut . . . diversas reciperent disciplinas," col. 484B), but organizes his whole discussion around the exclusion from truth of those so addressed ("Quapropter rogemus Christum, ne et nobis loquatur cum turbis in parabolis," col. 498B). Christian of Stablo observes that parables were commonly used in Jewish culture at that time, implying that Jesus considered them an effective teaching device ("Consuetudo erat incolis illis cum similitudinibus loqui frequentius, idcirco Dominus morem quem audire soliti erant sequitur"),[31] but reverts to the notion of punishing the recalcitrant to explain why they were not effective ("Qui non vult esse discipulus, audit verba in turba et parabolis," col. 1375D).

Aquinas explains that the crowd was composed of two groups—one fathful and benign, the other unfaithful and malign—and that the parable was a way of revealing truth to the former while concealing it from the latter.

This distinction enables him to associate the positive tradition of the parable with revelation to the worthy ("homines, scilicet rudes, quando divina sub similitudinibus explicantur, melius capiunt et retinent," p. 425) and the negative tradition with the unworthy ("per hujusmodi parabolas absconduntur sacra ab infidelibus," ibid.). This was an ingenious solution, but the crucial analysis of the crowd lacked scriptural support: *all* the crowd had come to listen to Jesus, and in none of the Gospels is there a suggestion that the multitude was polarized in Aquinas's terms. Jerome had noted diversity, not dichotomy ("Turba non unius sententiae est sed diuersarum in singulis uoluntatum," I, p. 264). For whatever reasons, Aquinas abandoned the idea of worthy and unworthy components in the crowd when discussing Jesus' use of parables in the *Summa theologiae,* and abandoned with it all explicit reference to the positive tradition.[32] Nicholas of Lyra will admit only a superficial kind of teaching to be implied by the verb *docere* in Mark 4:33–34. He observes that there are many senses beneath the letter of Scripture, "quorum aliquii sunt potentiores et alii magis latentes." The understanding of the multitude was restricted to the "patent" meaning of parables, which were interspersed by Jesus into his preaching when he wished to conceal matters fit only for the disciples.[33]

Alone among the authorities under consideration, Albert the Great sets forth a fully integrated understanding of Jesus' use of parables. It is highly original, resting on an interpretation of key Scriptural passages for which tradition provided no hints, and employing the careful distinctions of scholastic moral theology on the premise of Jesus' uncompromised charity. As one would expect, Albert develops his ideas most fully in his commentary on Matthew, although certain formulations and emphases in the commentaries on Mark and Luke are useful in tracing his thought.

Three important points mark the lines of his exegesis. (a) Albert construes the crowd on the shore favorably. In this he follows the early scholastics, who had relinquished Hilary's censure (the sterility of the sands like that of the people) and taken a conciliatory view recalling Jerome, but Albert's discovery of specific virtues in the crowd has no precedent: "Turba enim non novit legem: et ideo necessaria fuit eis doctrina . . . 'Stabat', rectitudine corporis, parans se ad rectitudinem verbi auditi . . . 'In littore' stabilimenti virtutis et veritatis."[34] (b) The parable is a device for communicating spiritual truth to common men, as we have seen above ("pura spiritualia ab animalibus hominibus non possunt sine humanis similitudinibus intellegi"). (c) Christ never used a parable or likeness that he wished *not* to be understood, for it would be the act of a *praevaricator* to teach with such a desire.[35] Given these premises one must conclude that Jesus spoke to the crowd in parables in order to teach them, having chosen this rhetorical form as suited to the mental processes of this audience, and that is precisely Albert's belief. He explains that minds that have been elevated to a higher level of spirituality may comprehend through direct perception with or without the help of likenesses,[36] but he distinguishes the disciples from the crowd and stresses the necessity of teaching the latter figuratively.[37] As clear and cogent as Albert's reasoning may be, it places him in opposition to the parable theory as traditionally understood.

Albert solves this problem by a new reading of Matthew's phrases "videntes non vident / et audientes non audiunt" and their parallels. These phrases were customarily taken as negatives ("their senses seem to be working but actually aren't") that lead to the moral condemnation derived from Isaiah 6:9-10. Albert breaks this connection. He treats the words of Jesus reported by Matthew (vv. 11-13) separately from the words of Isaiah repeated by Jesus (vv. 14-15); he distinguishes the reference of "eis" in verse 13 from that of "eis" in verse 14; he connects the earlier verse to the immediate situation and to the disciples' question ("quare in parabolis loqueris eis," v. 10), but takes the latter as a general comment on spiritual perversity; and he thus unifies the charitable preaching of Jesus with a hard judgment on the *obstinati* of all times.[38] Albert explains that the crowd perceived truth veiled in similitudes while not perceiving it directly, a reading that easily accomodates the idea of "outsiders" that had traditionally been understood as moral censure:

"Illis autem," idiotis, *"qui foris sunt"* extra mysticum intellectum . . . *"in parabolis"* datum est praedicari divina: quia spiritualia intelligere non possunt, nisi in corporalium rerum similitudinibus . . . In figuris parabolarum, coelestia *"videant"* involuta . . . *"Et audientes"* in parabolis involuta, *"audiant,"* et sicut magna venerentur: *"et non intelligant"* involuta, quia intelligere talia non possunt.[39]

With these paradoxical verses thus clarified as expressing the greatest possible benefit for common men, it was of no consequence whether one followed Matthew or Mark and Luke in reading *"quia"* or *"ut"* as the introductory conjunction: the Lord taught as efficaciously as possible either "because" men learn as they do or "so that" they might learn as they do. At the end of his exposition of Matthew 13:13, Albert makes a very telling comment on the difficulty of following traditional interpretations, for it was obviously unworthy of the Lord to propound something to men "so that" they not understand and thus become yet more culpable.[40] It seems clear that Albert had worried about the Gospel's parable theory and the implications of the conjunction *ut* in Mark and Luke.

The prophecy of Isaiah, treated by Albert as the third section of Matthew 13:11-15, explains the condign punishment of men who obdurately turn from truth and shun grace. These are not the crowd, nor are they a clearly distinguished component of the crowd (cf. Aquinas on Matthew), but they are a moral type. For Albert, the prophet pointed ahead to men who would close their eyes and ears to the evidence of miracles and parables both in Jesus' day and later. He interprets the clauses following "nequando" as a series of aversions experienced by the obdurate that prevent Christ's truth from reaching them.[41] Thus the interest in noncommunication set forth in verse 15, which had been attributed since Origen to Jesus and justified by defects in his hearers, is transferred to a perverse human type that has nothing definitive in common with the *turba* of the episode. The Lord sought to teach all men, even those of the rudest intelligence, but among those who listened to him, as among those who hear Christian preaching at any time, some were and are prevented from understanding by their inner aversion from the light ("motus animi humani inhaerentis malo, et aversi a divino lumine").[42]

Although Albert's solution is not as satisfactory for Mark's text as for Matthew's, because in Mark the clause "nequando convertantur" immediately follows the paradoxes of vision and sight (v. 12), he no doubt thought this textual compression typical of Mark the *pedisequus* and *breuiator* of Matthew: with the text of Matthew analyzed, the work was essentially done. Albert dismisses the "nequando" clause in Mark with a single sentence ("Hoc de duris intelligitur, qui ex parabolis proficere nolunt," XXI, p. 428). The Universal Doctor admitted the two main difficulties of traditional response to the Gospels' parable theory—the question of the parable as a device of demonstration rather than obfuscation, and the theological problem of Christ concealing his message. By thinking through the relevant Scriptures afresh he was able to expound Christ's wisdom and charity, the character and limits of human understanding, and the perversity of those who turn away from the truth.

Thus far we have been concerned with a specific problem in the history of exegesis. At this point we will consider how this problem intersects larger issues in the study of the Middle Ages. The following remarks will have served their purpose if they draw attention to ways in which Scriptural interpretation may open new perspectives on questions of other disciplines.

The character of Bible study in the Latin West resulted (to oversimplify a complex matter) from the triumph of Origen and his method of spiritual exegesis, rooted in the allegorical traditions of Alexandria, over John Chrysostom and the historical–moral approach associated with Antioch. The parable theory is a result rather than a cause of the interest in allegorism in the early Church, but for medieval readers the theory, interlocking with "The Sower" and Jesus' allegory of this tale, could be taken as proof that all the Bible was to be searched for spiritual significance, even those apparently simple stories told by the Lord. The theory accused those "outside" of neither seeing nor hearing with the inner senses, which meant that neither the signs of Jesus nor his words were properly understood. Bede explains that both the miracles and the stories are parables, in the real sense of that term —"Notandum in his domini uerbis quia non solum ea quae loquebatur uerum etiam quae faciebat parabolae fuerunt, id est rerum signa mysticarum."[43]

I am not sure that the implication of the medieval parable theory for Christian hermeneutics have been fully appreciated.

It is the consensus of Biblical scholars that the early Christian community, rather than Jesus, originated the allegorical tradition associated with the parables and formulated the parable theory in Mark.[44] The theory is easily understood as an expression of militancy in the early Church. It explained why many people heard the preaching of the Gospel but did not believe and were not converted, and it rationalized the missionary failures of the first generations of believers in the same terms that explained the "failure" of Jesus himself to convince all those he addressed. At the same time it offered a means of discriminating the faithful from the rest, a method of self-definition. As Hilary of Poitiers said, only within the boat of the Church is there spiritual understanding; access to the Lord's parabolic teaching is reserved for true believers, hence one might describe the Christian community as those granted insight into the deep meanings of the parables.

We have seen that the parable theory was used to attack the wickedness (and resulting obtuseness) of the Jews. In principle it might be used against any unorthodox group. The most vigorous interpretations of the theory as a lesson in segregation and exclusion come from periods in Church history when Catholics were laboring to vindicate their faith in cultural settings where paganism, Judaism, and other Christian churches constituted significant alternatives. Hilary of Poitiers apparently wrote his commentary on Matthew in the first years of his episcopate (ca. 350–352), and the strength of his reading of the parable theory must be connected to the strength of his opposition to Arianism, which brought about his exile to Phrygia in 356. When Hilary wrote that the crowd on the shore was as sterile and useless as sand, he was certainly attacking the Arians of Gaul. It would be interesting to review Catholic polemics of the Middle Ages with the language and interpretive history of the parable theory in mind. Nicholas of Lyra, in the famous postils that were so widely admired as a masterpiece of scholarship, repeats the condemnation of the Jews that earlier authorities had found in Matthew 13:11–15 ("Sic enim crassitudo circa cor congregata suffocat et extinguit vitam corporalem, sic malicia Iudaeorum extinxit in eis vitam spiritualem"), and it is significant that Nicholas, interpreting the parable of "Tares Among the Wheat" (Matthew 13:24–30), returns to the perspective of Jerome by identifying the tares as heretics.[45] He believes that the servants' question to the lord, "vis imus et colligimus ea," refers to the excommunication of heretics followed by their destruction through the secular arm; he abandons the traditional hopes that, given time, heretics may be converted, and that they may even have an improving influence on the orthodox; if one can identify them, he says, and if they are powerless so that civil turmoil will not result, then the Church should turn them over to secular justice and so protect its purity.[46] This very militant reading of the parable is connected to

Nicholas's attack on the Jews in his explanation of the parable theory (which comes a few verses earlier in Matthew 13). Both theory and instance are made to serve the cause of orthodoxy.

The verses we have been studying were used in the process of self-definition of the early Church and as a polemical weapon against Jews and heretics. They were also used to help describe the religious life by at least one monastic commentator, the Benedictine abbot Gottfried of Admont, and I suspect that a review of monastic preaching on this passage would show his approach to be representative. In 1138 Gottfried went to the Styrian abbey of Admont from his position as prior at St. George in Swabia. He introduced the Hirsau reform, developed a fine scriptorium, and remained as abbot until his death in 1165.[47] In a homily for Sexagesima Sunday, based on a pericope from Luke including the parable theory, Gottfried explains that true seeing and true hearing entail the enacting of the word, i.e., the imitation of the apostolic life ("Nosse quidem mysterium regni Dei, nosse mysterium sacrae Scripturae nobis datum esse affirmat, non ut tantum sciamus, sed ut ea quae scimus, opere adimplere studeamus," col. 154D). Gottfried interprets the *videntes* as those who expound Scripture and the *audientes* as those who are taught; the failure of sight and hearing is the failure to experience and enact the message of Christ (col. 155A). He concludes his sermon by quoting Paul on the hardships of his life for the faith, then urges the imitation of this life so that he and his brothers will not be among those to whom the Lord speaks *in para-bola*. Gottfried is distinguishing cloistered persons from the secular; his homily is, in effect, a polemic for the life of the reformed Benedictine houses. His integration of the parable theory into this argument is nicely demonstrated by the sentence that Holy Scripture, which communicates the mysteries of the kingdom of God to spiritual men, is like a parable to the worldly.[48]

When Gregory the Great observed that the mundane, literal terms of parables helped raise our understanding toward unknown things, he was speaking as a preacher and a teacher of ordinary men. No sophisticated epistemology underlies his remark. This is not true, however, for the analysis some six hundred years later by Albert the Great, which would appear to reflect his immersion in the writings of Aristotle and the Aristotelian commentators. It is well known that Albert (and Aquinas after him) followed Aristotle in teaching that knowledge was attained by reason operating on information gained by the senses, and that the sphere of reason was thus to be distinguished from that of revelation. When Albert observes that the apostles and other perfect men might understand mysteries without the aid of material likenesses, he seems to except them from the general truth that the mind relies on the senses ("quia spiritualia intelligere non possunt, nisi in corporalium rerum similitudinibus"). Perhaps attention should be given to the understanding of parabolic teaching on the part of scholastics who, like Albert and Aquinas, followed the epistemological principle *nihil est in intellectu, nisi prius fuerit in sensu.*[49]

The parable theory formulates differences between audiences and corresponding differences in the manner of addressing them. To the degree that the rhetorical tradition of the parable as a means of communication was recognized and admitted—and we have seen that this varies considerably from source to source—we will agree with James Murphy that "it constitutes a rhetorical precept of great importance."[50] Murphy has suggested the theory's implications for preaching in the Middle Ages, and to conclude this essay I shall point out its likely relevance to medieval literature.

Alan of Lille, famed for his universal learning, taught in Paris and composed a variety of theological and pastoral works. He wrote his long quasi-epic poem "Anticlaudianus" between 1181 and 1184, furnishing it with two prologues, one in prose and one in verse; in the former he asserts that his poem has three levels of meaning, the literal, moral, and allegorical. Alan follows this statement, which obligates us to the same concern for levels of meaning that we bring to medieval exegesis, with the wish that a certain kind of audience be kept away from his poem, those readers who are content with the literal meaning alone and do not strive for the spiritual senses: "Let those be denied access to this work who pursue only sense-images and do not reach out for the truth that comes from reason, lest what is holy, being set before dogs, be soiled, lest the pearl trampled under the feet of swine be lost, lest the esoteric be impaired if its grandeur is revealed to the unworthy."[51] These ideas are unquestionably related to the general theory of scriptural communication set forth by Augustine in *De doctrina christiana*: readers must always seek a hidden, spiritual sense within a passage if the literal sense does not conduce to charity and dissuade from cupidity; those who fail to do this—"who pursue only sense-images," in Alan's words—are guilty of reading carnally, contenting themselves with the flesh of the letter where they should seek the spirit of meaning. Augustine's remarks have been presented as a systematic theory of medieval literature by D. W. Robertson, Jr., and Bernard F. Huppé, who have argued that Alan's prose preface to "Anticlaudianus" provides "a further illustration of the prevalence and continuity of the Augustinian tradition."[52] But one does not have to espouse the highly controversial "Augustinian tradition" of Robertson and Huppé to situate Alan's polemic in an ongoing discussion of literary meaning, for it has strong affinities with the theory of Jesus' parabolic speech; and given its place at the start of an elaborate literary invention, I believe it more likely that Alan was thinking of the Master's allegorical stories than of Holy Writ in general, inspired by the Holy Spirit, when wishing himself a perceptive audience. His citation of Matthew 7:6 certainly suggests this. We recall that Hugh of Saint-Cher stated as one of the reasons Jesus used parables "ut veritas indignis celetur" (in the introduction to his commentary on Matthew 13); Aquinas repeated this idea, "per hujusmodi parabolas absconduntur sacra ab infidelibus" (quoted above). When Alan discredits that part of his potential audience which is not adept at the kind of allegorical interpretation he wants, I hear commentators criticizing the Jews for the failure of their understanding to move beyond the carnal or literal level of parables, and as we have pointed out (note 12), Matthew 7:6 was cited in discussion of the parable theory.

Perhaps thirty years after Alan wrote "Anticlaudianus," Gottfried of Strassburg composed his romance of "Tristan und Isolt," introducing it with a prologue divided into two parts, one strophic and one in couplets. In the latter Gottfried says that he has written for a particular audience, kindred spirits often identified by Gottfried's term *edele herze* (noble hearts), and that he has sought out the true version of the Tristan story for the benefit of these particular persons: "And now I freely offer the fruits of my reading of this love-tale to all noble hearts." [53] A great deal has been written to elucidate Gottfried's comments on his audience, his complementary disparagement of others who may hear his poem ("What I have to say does not concern that world and such a way of life; their way and mine diverge sharply," p. 42), and the philosophical message in his re-telling of the old story that stands behind his insistence on having found "the true and authentic version" (p. 43). While I think it likely that Alan of Lille was consciously using locutions from medieval discussion of the parable theory to demand the allegorical reading of his poem, I do not think this is the case with Gottfried. Yet I think that his discrimination of audiences on the basis of their amenability to deeper understanding of his narrative, his praise of the spiritual superiority of some that makes them *capaciores* (to use Albert the Great's term for the disciples of Jesus), should be placed within the long tradition of story-telling, hearing, and understanding connected to the Gospel verses that we have studied. Although medieval authors would not have used this characterization, Jesus was the inventor of literary fictions and (for the Middle Ages) the source, both in precept and practice, of a method of their interpretation. The constant recurrence in medieval poetry of remarks on audience and the correct comprehension of literature may be attributable in part to Jesus' statements about his figurative stories and their reception. I find it fully appropriate that Jacques Ribard has prefaced his symbolic reading of the *Chevalier de la charrette* by Chrétien de Troyes, in which he concludes that the romance is an allegory of salvation, with a key verse from Jesus' commentary on his use of parables. [54]

NOTES

1. "He told them: 'To you the mystery of the reign of God has been confided. To the others outside it is all presented in parables, so that they will look intently and not see, listen carefully and not understand, lest

perhaps they repent and be forgiven' " (*The New American Bible* [New York, 1970]). Equivalent translations will be found in *The Jerusalem Bible* (New York, 1966); and *The New English Bible* (n.p.: Oxford University Press and Cambridge University Press, 1970). In this essay the Bible is quoted from *Biblia sacra iuxta vulgatam versionem*, ed. Robertus Weber et al., 2nd ed. (Stuttgart, 1975), where the verses in question read: "et dicebat eis / vobis datum est mysterium regni Dei / Illis autem qui foris sunt in parabolis omnia fiunt / ut videntes videant et non videant / et audientes audiant et non intelligant / nequando convertantur et dimittantur eis peccata."

2. See Rudolf Pesch, *Das Markusevangelium. I. Teil. Einleitung und Komkentar zu Kap. 1,1-8,26.* 3. Auflage (Freiburg, Basel, Wien, 1980). Pesch discusses the parable theory on pp. 236–41 and provides extensive bibliography. One should note that his translation of the final clause of verse 12 is crucially different from that of the modern English Bibles cited in note 1, and of the Vulgate: "daß 'sie sehend sehen und doch nicht erkennen und hörend hören und doch nicht verstehen; vielleicht werden sie umkehren und wird ihnen vergeben' " (p. 236).

3. Terms used respectively by Frederick C. Grant in *The Interpreter's Bible*, 12 vols. (New York and Nashville, 1952-57), vol. 7, p. 700; Vincent Taylor, *The Gospel According to St. Mark*, 2nd ed. (London, 1966), p. 257; and Ernst Haenchen, *Der Weg Jesu. Eine Erklärung des Markus-Evangeliums und der kanonischen Parallelen*, 2nd ed. (Berlin, 1968), p. 165.

4. Ed. Franciscus Weihrich (Vienna and Leipzig, 1904). The following quotation is from I. 2 (p. 4).

5. *PL* 186:15A.

6. Origen's commentary on Matthew in the anonymous Latin translation, ed. Erich Klostermann and Ludwig Früchtel (Leipzig and Berlin, 1933-55). Hilary of Poitiers, *In Matthaeum*, ed. Jean Doignon, 2 vols. (Paris, 1978-79); Sources Chrétiennes (hereafter: SC) vols. 254, 258. Jerome, *In Matthaeum*, ed. Emile Bonnard, 2 vols. (Paris, 1977-79), SC 242, 259. John Chrysostom's homilies on Matthew nums. 44–45—lacking an edition of the Latin translation of Burgundio of Pisa we must use that based on George of Trapezunt (*PG* 57:463-72 and *PG* 58:472-76). Pseudo-Jerome, commentary on the Gospels, *PL* 30:531-644. Pseudo-Augustine, *Quaestiones septemdecim in Matthaeum*, *PL* 35:1365-76. Peter Chrysologus, sermon 86, *PL* 52:469-71. Pseudo-Chrysostom, *Opus imperfectum in Matthaeum*, homily 31, *PG* 58:791-98. Gregory the Great, homilies 11 and 15 on the Gospels, *PL* 76:1114-18 and 1131-34. Bede, *In Lucae evangelium expositio. In Marci evangelium expositio*, ed. D. Hurst (Turnhout, 1960). Smaragdus of Saint-Mihiel, *Collectiones in epistolas et evangelia*, *PL* 102:13-552. Haimo of Auxerre, homily 22 on the seasons and homily 11 on the saints, *PL* 118:163-72 and 790-95. Rabanus Maurus, *In Matthaeum*, *PL* 107:729-1156. Pseudo-Bede, *In Matthaeum*, *PL* 92:9-131. Paschasius Radbertus, *In Matthaeum*, *PL* 120:31-994. Christian of Stablo, *In Matthaeum*, *PL* 106:1261-1505.

Geoffrey Babion, *Ennarationes in evangelium Matthaei*, PL 162:1227–1500. The *Gloss* by Anselm of Laon and his school, *Biblia sacra, cum glossa ordinaria . . . et postilla Nicolai Lyrani . . .* (Lyons, 1589). Bruno of Segni, *In Matthaeum*, PL 165:71–314. Rupert of Deutz, *De sancta Trinitate et operibus ejus*, 4 vols. (Turnhout, 1971–72). Zacharias Chrysopolitanus, commentary on the gospel harmony *In unum ex quattuor*, PL 186:11–620. Robert of Melun, *Quaestiones de divina pagina*, ed. Raymond M. Martin (Louvain, 1932). Hugh of Saint-Cher, commentary on the Gospels, vol. 6 of his *Opera omnia* (Lyons, 1645). Bonaventure, *Commentarius in Evangelium St. Lucae* in *Opera omnia* (Quaracchi, 1883–1902), vol. 7. Albert the Great, commentaries on Matthew, Mark, and Luke in *Opera omnia*, ed. Auguste Borgnet (Paris, 1890–99), vols. 20–23. Thomas Aquinas, *Super Matthaeum* in *Opera omnia*, ed. S. E. Fretté and P. Maré (Paris, 1871–80), vol. 19. Nicholas of Lyra, commentary on the gospels (see the *Gloss*, above). Ludolph of Saxony, *Vita Jesu Christi ex quatuor evangeliis* (Paris and Rome, 1865).

7. Jerome: "populus, nequaquam periculum sustinens nec temptationibus circumdatus quas ferre non poterat, stat in litore fixo gradu et audiat quae dicuntur" (I, p. 264); "Haec de his loquitur qui stant in litore et diuiduntur ab Iesu et, sonitu fluctuum perstrepente, non audiunt ad liquidum quae dicuntur" (I, p. 268). Bede, On Mark, p. 480: "Porro turba quae circa mare super terram posita uerbis domini auscultabatur ita ut nec fluctibus maris tangeretur nec cum illo in naui transcensis fluctibus sederet illorum aptissime gestat figuram qui nuper ad audiendum uerbum conuenerant. Et quidem pietate animi a reproborum amaritudine obscuritate instabilitate secreti sunt sed necdum caelestibus mysteriis quae desiderant imbuti." Repeated by Rabanus, col. 939AB. Cf. Geoffrey Babion, col. 1369B: "Turba . . . quae neque in mari, neque in navi erat, gerit figuram recipientium verbum Dei . . . a reprobis separatorum, sed necdum per gratiam baptismatis in Ecclesia intromissorum." See also the *Gloss* on Matthew 13:2, and Zacharias, col. 224C.

8. Jerome: "Quaerendum est quomodo accedant ad eum discipuli, cum Iesus in naui sedeat; nisi forte intelligendum datur quod dudum cum ipso nauem conscenderint et ibi stantes super interpretationem parabolae sciscitati sint" (I, p. 266). Repeated or paraphrased by Rabanus, col. 942CD; Paschasius, col. 485A; Christian of Stablo, col. 1372B; the *Gloss* on Matthew 13:10; etc.

9. Pseudo-Bede: "Nunc aperit apostolis quod ideo turbis in parabolis loquebatur, quia superba intentione se videntes et audientes aestimabant" (col. 66C). Christian of Stablo: "oculis corporis vident, et oculis cordis habere nolunt propter invidiam et incredulitatem" (col. 1372C). Zacharias: "Abundantia malitiae dicit incrassatum cor Judaeorum . . . averterunt prae invidia intuitum mentis" (col. 230C).

10. Frank E. Eakin, Jr., "Spiritual Obduracy and Parable Purpose," in *The Use of the Old Testament in the New and Other Essays. Studies in Honor of William Franklin Stinespring*, ed. James M. Efird (Durham, N.C.,

1972), pp. 99–100. Cf. Geoffrey Babion: "Legitur in Evangeliis, Christum locutum fuisse in parabolis, aliquando ad ultionem, quia qui audiebant mysteria Dei, indigni cognoscere erant" (col. 1369BC).

11. The Latin version of these passages (X, 4 and 16) has been lost. I have used Robert Girod's edition of Origen's commentary on Matthew (Paris, 1970), pp. 153–55, 213, and the introduction, pp. 83–86.

12. Hugh of Saint-Cher: the Lord used parables "ut veritas indignis celetur" (introduction to commentary on Matthew 13); Hugh quotes Matthew 7:6 re Matthew 13:11 and again re Luke 8:10. Quoted also by Aquinas, p. 425.

13. "Si dixisset, Ideo in parabolis loquor eis, ut videntes non videant: forsitan non esset culpa non intelligentium Judaeorum, sed Christi, qui sic loquebatur, ut non intelligeretur ab eis. Nunc autem dicit: *Ideo in parabolis loquor eis, quia videntes non vident.* Intelligitis ergo, quia non est culpa Christi, nolentis dicere manifeste, sed eorum qui audientes nolebant audire" (*Opus imperfectum,* col. 798).

14. Bede is repeated or paraphrased by Smaragdus of Saint-Mihiel (col. 110D), the *Gloss* on Mark 4:11 and Luke 8:10, Zacharias (col. 230A), Hugh of Saint-Cher on Luke 8:10, and Ludolph of Saxony, conflating Mark and Luke: "*Ceteris autem* qui foris sunt, qui clausis sensibus non curant intrare et cognoscere veritatem" (p. 283).

15. "Hoc autem dicit, ut illos attrahat incitetque, et ostendat, si convertantur, se ipsos sanaturum esse . . . Hoc porro dicit ostendens quomodo reconciliatus fuisset . . . Se enim noluisset eos audire et servari, silere oportebat, non in parabolis loqui: nunc autem hoc ipso incitat illos, quod obscure loquatur" (John Chrysostom *PG* 58:473).

16. *Summa theologiae* 3a. 42, 3, resp. "Et sic Christus quaedam turbis loquebatur in occulto, parabolis utens ad annuntianda spiritualia mysteria, ad quae capienda non erant idonei vel digni: et tamen melius erat eis, vel sic sub tegumento parabolarum spiritualium doctrinam audire quam omnino ea privari" (vol. 53 of the Blackfriars edition [New York-London, 1971], p. 98. Aquinas quotes from one of Chrystostom's homilies on Matthew later in this article of the *Summa.* On his esteem for them, see Beryl Smalley, *The Study of the Bible in the Middle Ages* (New York, 1952), p. 337.

17. Albert the Great on Mark: "Ex hoc autem patet, quod parva pars evangelicae sapientiae descripta est: quia de interpretationibus parabolarum non est scripta nisi una, cum tamen hic expresse dicatur, quod Dominus omnia dicta parabolica per seipsum disseruit" (XXI, p. 438). Ludolph of Saxony: "Unde patet quod non solum parabolas, de quibus eum interrogabant, sed etiam alias ibidem eis exposuit, licet de aliarum expositione mentio non fiat" (p. 283).

18. *The 'Art' of Rhetoric,* ed. and trans. John Henry Freese (Cambridge, Mass., and London, 1926), II. 20 (pp. 273–79). I am aware of no thorough presentation of the parable as a rhetorical form in classical and medieval culture, but see Adolf Jülicher, *Die Gleichnisreden Jesu,* 2.

Aufgabe (Tübingen, 1910: repr. Darmstadt, 1976), pt. 1, pp. 69–73; and M.-J. Lagrange, "La parable en dehors l'évangile," *Revue biblique*, vol. 6 (1909), pp. 198–212 and 342–67, esp. 208–10.

19. Ed. Harry Caplan (Cambridge, Mass., and London, 1954), p. 376.

20. Ed. H. E. Butler, 4 vols. (Cambridge, Mass., and London, 1921–22): "Praeclare vero ad inferendam rebus lucem repertae sunt similitudines . . . In omni autem parbole aut praecedit similitudo, res sequitur, aut praecedit res et similitudo sequitur," VIII. 3. 72, 77 (III, pp. 250–54).

21. Quoted by M.-J. Lagrange, *Evangile selon Saint Marc* (Paris, 1947), p. 101.

22. Quoted by Fritz Peter Knapp, *Similitudo*, I (Vienna and Stuttgart, 1975), p. 82. See Knapp's reference to the *parabola* in his section "Die drei Arten des Vergleichs" (pp. 66–76 passim).

23. Isidor, *Etymologiarum sive originum libri XX*, ed. W. M. Lindsay (Oxford, 1911), sections I. 37. 33, VI. 2. 18, VI. 8. 13. Bede: "*Parabola* est rerum genere dissimilium comparatio" ('Liber de schematibus et tropis' in *Rhetores latini minores*, ed. Karl Halm [Leipzig, 1863], p. 618). Pseudo-Jerome: "Parabola est natura discrepantium rerum sub alia similitudine facta comparatio" (col. 603AB), repeated by the *Gloss* on Mark 4:10, Zacharias (col. 224C), and Hugh of Saint-Cher on Matthew 13:1. Bruno of Segni: "Est autem parabola similitudo, in qua aliud dicitur aliud rationabiliter intelligitur" (col. 191C). Geoffrey Babion: "comparatio ex dissimilibus, id est comparativa similitudo, eo quod in ipsa comparativa similitudine figuras verborum et imagines veritatis ostendit" (col. 1374D). Robert of Melun: "Parabola est rerum dissimilium naturarum inter se collectio" (p. 35). Ludolph of Saxony: "[parabola] graece, *similitudo* dicitur Latine, per quam veritas demonstratur, et in qua aliud dicitur, et aliud rationabiliter intellegitur" (p. 282).

24. Pseudo-Jerome: "[parabola] Graeco vocabulo dicitur similitudo" (col. 603B). Repeated by Rabanus (col. 939B), the *Gloss* on Mark 4:10, and Ludolph of Saxony (see n. 23).

25. "Nam quia aenigmatice praedicaturus erat, auditorum animum primo per parabolam excitat . . . Nec ideo solum in parabolis loquitur, sed ut majore cum emphasi verba faceret, et magis memoriae imprimeret, resque sub aspectum poneret" (John Chrysostom, *PG* 57:467). Hugh of Saint-Cher (introduction to Matthew 13) and Aquinas (p. 425) repeat the idea of parables as an aid to memory.

26. I, p. 264. Often repeated, as by Rabanus (col. 939), Paschasius (col. 484B), and the *Gloss* on Matthew 13:3.

27. Jerome, I, pp. 276, 280. Cf. Ludolph of Saxony, p. 277.

28. Jerome: "Perspicua miscet obscuris ut per ea quae intellegunt prouocentur ad eorum notitiam quae non intellegunt" (I, p. 264), paraphrased by Paschasius (col. 484B). Pseudo-Jerome: "Et ideo in parabolis loquitur eis, ut requirerent quod non intelligerent" (col. 603A). Peter Chrysologus: "nunc vero cum petit anima, mens pulsat, quaerit sensus, sperat pietas, fides exigit, meretur intentio, apparet et sudantis fructus . . . Hinc est quod doctrinam suam Christus parabolis velat" (col. 469CD). Hugh of

Saint-Cher: Jesus spoke in parables "ut studiosi exerceantur" (introduction to Matthew 13).

29. "Coelorum regnum . . . idcirco terrenis rebus simile dicitur, et ex his quae animus novit surgat ad incognita, quaetenus exemplo visibilium se ad invisibilia rapiat, et per ea quae usu didicit, quasi confricatus, incalescat, ut per hoc quod scit notum diligere, discat et incognita amare" (Gregory the Great, cols. 1114D–15A). Gregory's words are quoted or paraphrased by virtually all later authorities.

30. Albert the Great, On Mark 4:30 (XXI, p. 436).

31. Christian of Stable, col. 1371C. Repeated by Bonaventure (p. 190) and Hugh of Saint-Cher (introduction to Matthew 13).

32. "Turbis Dominus in parabolis loquebatur . . . quia non erant digni, nec idonei nudam veritatem accipere, quam discipulis exponebat" (3a. 42. 3 ad 3).

33. "In parabolis Christi turbae capiebant sensum magis patentem non autem latentem, sed de tali intellectu docebat Christus apostolos ad partem ideo subditur *Seorsum autem discipulis*" (Nicholas of Lyra on Mark 4:33–34). Nicholas says that Jesus used plain speech to tell the crowd what it needed to know and, when speaking of the future Church, used parables to restrict comprehension of his remarks to its founders ("aliqua etiam interponebat parabolice, qua scilicet pertinebant ad secreta ecclesiae," on Matthew 13:34–36).

34. Albert the Great, On Matthew, XX, p. 549. Cf. XX, p. 556: "isti qui sic ad Doctorem veritatis veniunt, ignorantes spiritualia et dubitantes de doctrina, sed admirantes veniunt . . . jam ignorantiam fugere desiderantes."

35. "Nec ist intelligendum quod Dominus aliquas similitudines proposuerit, vel aliquas parabolas dixerit, quas nullo modo intelligi voluerit. Quia hoc esset praevaricatoris, quod doceret et nollet intelligi" (Albert the Great, On Luke, XXII, p. 537).

36. The disciples have received Gifts of the Spirit: *intellectus* and *sapientia* (XX, p. 555; XXII, p. 536).

37. " '*Quare in parabolis loqueris eis?*' Adhuc enim carnales discipuli nesciverunt distantiam inter parvulos et perfectos, nescientes quod parvuli instrui non possunt nisi manducati per similitudines corporalium ad doctrinam spiritualium" (Albert the Great, On Matthew, XX, p. 554).

38. "Per Isaiam probat, quod meritum excaecationis obstinatorum ad signa et parabolas venit ex duritia cordis eorum, et non ex Deo aliquid operante ad caecitatem" (ibid., p. 557).

39. Albert the Great, On Mark, XXI, p. 427. Cf. On Matthew, XX, pp. 556–57, and On Luke, XXII, p. 536.

40. Albert the Great, On Matthew, XX, p. 557: "Nisi autem iste locus sic exponatur, videtur sequi inconveniens: quia etiam parum intelligenti frivolum videtur, si Dei sapientia proponat aliquid hominibus ad hoc *ut* non videant, et *ut* ex hoc magis condemnentur" (emphasis added).

41. Albert the Great, On Matthew, XX, p. 558: *aversio ab inducentibus ad gratiam, aversio a veritate inducente ad gratiam, aversio a consensu veritatis, aversio a gratia convertente, aversio ab effectu.*

42. *Summa theologiae* 1a. 2ae. 79, 3 resp.

43. Bede, *On Mark* (see note 6), p. 482, incorporated into the *Gloss* on Matthew 13:11 ("Nota non solum verba domini, sed et facta, parabolas esse: id est, signa mysticarum rerum, quae non intelligebant multi qui foris sunt").

44. Pesch, p. 276: "Die große Lehrrede Jesu, der erste größere Redeabschnitt in Mk-Ev, ist keine Komposition aus einem Guß, sondern, eher locker gefügt und nicht spannungsfrei, Produkt einer längeren Traditions- und Redaktionsgeschichte, in der thematische verwandte Saat- und Wachstumsgleichnisse mit einer allegorischen Auslegung des ersten und zwei Spruchfolgen sowie einer 'Parabel- bzw. Verstockungstheorie' . . . verbunden wurden" (parenthetical citations omitted). Joachim Jeremias, *The Parables of Jesus. Revised Edition*, trans. S. H. Hooke (New York, 1963), p. 66: "The primitive Church had applied many parables to its own situation . . . One of the expedients made use of by the Church in the process of reinterpreting the parables was the allegorical method of interpretation."

45. Jerome, *In Matthaeum* (see note 6), I, pp. 286–88. A broader, moral interpretation of the tares was offered by Augustine in sermon 73 (*PL* 38:470-72), and a different one by Rabanus Maurus in his commentary on Matthew (*PL* 107:946-47).

46. The hopes of conversion and good influence were first advanced by Jerome (ibid.), then repeated by many authorities (e.g., the *Gloss*). Nicholas comments on verse 29: "Ex quo patet, quod dominus non vult haereticos permitti vivere absolute, sed in casu tantum scilicet quando non possunt separari a fidelibus sine periculo fidelium . . . ubi autem non occurrerunt ista pericula, sunt separandi ab ecclesia et iusticiae seculari relinquendi, ut exterminentur per mortem, ne per eos totum corpus ecclesiae currumpatur."

47. Johann Wilhelm Braun, "Gottfried von Admont," in *Die deutsche Literatur des Mittelalters. Verfasserlexikon*, 2nd ed., ed. Kurt Ruh et al. (Berlin and New York, 1978–), III, cols. 118–23. The homily by Gottfried to be discussed is printed in *PL* 174:153D–58B.

48. "Sancta Scriptura, quae spiritalibus loquitur regni Dei mysteria, saecularibus hominibus est quasi *parabola*" (col. 154D).

49. Quoted from David Knowles, *The Evolution of Medieval Thought* (New York, 1962), p. 261.

50. *Rhetoric in the Middle Ages* (Berkeley, Los Angeles, London, 1974), p. 279.

51. Alan of Lille, *Anticlaudianus*, trans. James J. Sheridan (Toronto, 1973), p. 41.

52. Huppé and Robertson, *Fruyt and Chaf. Studies in Chaucer's Allegories* (Princeton, 1963: repr. 1972), p. 13.

53. Gottfried von Strassburg, *Tristan*, trans. A. T. Hatto (Harmondsworth, 1960), p. 43.

54. Jacques Ribard, *Chrétien de Troyes. Le Chevalier de la Charette. Essai d'interprétation symbolique* (Paris, 1972), citing Matthew 13:13.

Heathen Sacrifice in Beowulf and Rimbert's Life of Ansgar

THEODORE M. ANDERSSON

A perennial crux in *Beowulf* is the passage in which the Danes, in despair over Grendel's depredations, make sacrifice to heathen idols (175–88):[1]

> Hwilum hie geheton æt *hæ*rgtrafum[2]
> wigweorþunga, wordum bædon,
> þæt him gastbona geoce gefremede
> wið þeodþreaum. Swylc wæs þeaw hyra,
> hæþenra hyht; helle gemundon
> in modsefan, Metod hie ne cuþon,
> dæda Demend, ne wiston hie Drihten God,
> ne hie huru heofena Helm herian ne cuþon,
> wuldres Waldend. Wa bið þæm ðe sceal
> þurh sliðne nið sawle bescufan
> in fyres fæþm, frofre ne wenan,
> wihte gewendan! Wel bið þæm þe mot
> æfter deaðdæge Drihten secean
> ond to Fæder fæþmum freoðo wilnian![3]

At times they made sacrifices [devotion to idols] at heathen temples, prayed with words that the soul-slayer might lend them help against the great calamity [dire distress of the people]. Such was their custom, the hope of the heathens; they recalled hell in their spirits [their minds reverted to hell], they had no knowledge of the Creator, the Judge of deeds, they did not know the Lord God, nor indeed did they know to praise the Lord of the heavens, the Ruler of glory. Woe to him who, through horrid enmity, will thrust his soul into the embrace of fire, have no expectation of solace, in no way relent! Well off is he who, after his death, may seek out the Lord and desire peace in the embrace of the Father.

The passage causes difficulty because it appears not long after the "Song of Creation" (vv. 90–98), which is a paean of praise to the almighty Creator and would seem to establish firmly the Christianity of the Danes. It therefore comes as a surprise when vv. 180–81 state that the Danes did not know God.

Medievalia et Humanistica, New Series, Number 13 (Paul Maurice Clogan, ed.). Rowman & Allanheld, Totowa, NJ. 1985.

Various remedies have been suggested. Fr. Klaeber guardedly accepted the idea that the Danes reverted to pagan ways, with the understanding that "Metod hie ne cuþon" should not be taken literally to mean that they did not know God, but only that they did not know Him fully, as the almighty Helper.[4] He supported a possible apostasy on the part of the Christian Danes with a number of passages from Bede's *Ecclesiastical History*. Thus, in II. 15 King Eorpwald of the East Anglians is converted, but relapses into paganism through the advice of his wife and certain counselors. In III. 30 an onset of plague causes King Sighere of the East Saxons to revert to paganism and restore the worship of idols. In IV. 27 plague causes a return to idolatry among the common people. Klaeber's edition, however, also made allowance for the idea that the poet, mindful of the pagan setting in sixth-century Denmark, momentarily "failed to live up to his own modernized representation" (p. 135). Klaeber further suggested that the poet was influenced by the idol worship of the Babylonians in the Old English *Daniel* (p. xci, citing various verbal parallels in *Daniel*, vv. 170–233).

Hoops proposed that since the Danish prayers go unfulfilled, it was necessary to deflect them from an efficacious Christian God, who might be expected to respond, to inefficacious pagan gods, who would by definition turn a deaf ear to such entreaties.[5] Tolkien quarreled with the theology underlying such an interpretation and surmised that vv. 180–88 have been tampered with.[6] They originally meant not that the Danes were unaware of God, but that "they *forsook* God under tribulation, and incurred the danger of hell-fire" (p. 102). Dorothy Whitelock believed that a more radical solution was required and declared vv. 175–88 to be an interpolation.[7] She attributed the interpolation to "a man of the Viking Age, who could extract some comfort from the thought that, while the Danes were ravaging his country, they were bound straight for hell" (p. 78). In the event that the reader finds this solution too radical, Whitelock offered the alternative explanation that the passage is designed to show the futility of such appeals to superstition, and she adduces "ecclesiastical documents which are directed against the paying of honour to wells, or stones or other natural objects, a practice which may include the making of propitiatory offerings to the powers believed to inhabit such things."[8] Norman E. Eliason again reviewed the controversy and took the view that the *Beowulf* poet intended that his Christianization of the Danes should be "understood as a fictional device."[9]

The most extensive commentary was provided by Arthur G. Brodeur.[10]

If . . . nearly all the inconsistencies of *Beowulf* can be disregarded as irrelevant to a judgment of its artistic quality, one remains which cannot be ignored: the sharp incongruity between the poet's representation of the Danish court in generally Christian terms, together with his attribution to Hrothgar of sentiments monotheistic if not specifically Christian; and his characterization, in lines 175-188, of the Danes as pagans, who offer sacrifice to heathen idols for deliverance from Grendel. Hoops justly refers to this contrast as "diese unleugbare Inkonsequenz"; it has plagued generations of scholars [pp. 186-87].

Brodeur (p. 197) rejected Tolkien's theory of revision and his thought that: "If it [the passage] is original, the poet must have intended a distinction between the wise Hrothgar, who certainly knew of and often thanked God, and a certain party of the pagan Danes—heathen priests, for instance, and those that had recourse to them under the temptation of calamity—specially deluded by the *gastbona*, the destroyer of souls" (Tolkien, p. 101). Furthermore, he rejected the idea that the Danes have relapsed into idol worship on the evidence of the unequivocal lines "Swylc wæs þeaw hyra, / hæþenra hyht / . . . / Metod hie ne cuþon"; the Danes are heathen plain and simple. But, Brodeur argued, having made the Danes heathen under the pressure of history, the poet proceeded to depict them as redeemable heathens (pp. 216-17): "The author must have intended his hearers to think of both Hrothgar and Beowulf as not beyond the saving grace of God." Larry D. Benson also broke with the theory of a relapse into heathen ways.[11] He suggested that the poet's tone is compassionate, inspired by pity for pagans who know no better and not aimed at apostates who know better and deserve no mercy. Such compassion is seen in terms of the doctrine of the noble heathen and the sympathetic view of the Christian English toward their unconverted cousins on the Continent. What Brodeur and Benson failed to come to terms with is the evidence of Danish Christianity elsewhere in the poem.

None of these commentaries on Danish idolatry in *Beowulf* has produced an adequate parallel from early medieval literature. In the hope of filling this gap, I submit the following episode in Rimbert's *Life of Ansgar*.[12] It occurred about the year 842.

At almost the same time it happened that a certain king of the Swedes named Anund, driven from his realm, was an exile among the Danes. Wishing to return once more to his former realm, he began to seek aid from them, hoping that if they followed, many gifts might accrue to them. He proposed to them a town named Birka because there were many wealthy merchants there and an abundance of goods and a great hoard of treasure. He therefore promised that he would lead them to that town, where they might then enjoy many things needful to them without damage to his forces. Delighted by the promised gifts and eager for the acquisition of treasure, they settled with him on an expeditionary force and embarked on twenty-one ships. He himself had eleven ships of his own. Leaving Danish territory, they came quite unexpectedly to the aforementioned town. And it happened that their king was absent at a considerable distance and the leader and general population could not be assembled. Only the aforementioned Herigarius, the prefect of that place, was present with the people and the merchants who were staying there.

Thus placed in great peril, they fled to the town that was nearby (Sigtuna). They also began to promise and bring many offerings and sacrifices to their gods, or rather evil spirits, that they might come to their aid in such danger. But because the town itself was not very well defended and there were few to resist, they sent messengers to them requesting a pact and truce. The aforementioned king demanded that they should pay a hundred pounds of silver for the ransom of their town so that they might have peace. They immediately sent what was demanded and it was received by the king already mentioned. Then the Danes, ill content with this agreement because they had not intended that it should be done in this way, wished to overrun them suddenly and plunder and burn the place to the ground, saying that any one of the merchants there possessed more than had been surrendered to them [the Danes] and declaring that in no way did they wish to tolerate such an evasion. As they treated of these things among themselves and prepared themselves to take the town in which the others [inhabitants of Birka] had sought refuge, this also became known to the latter [the Danes].

Once again gathered in assembly, since they had by no means the power to resist and there was no hope of refuge, they urged each other to greater offerings and sacrifices to their gods. In wrath the faithful servant of the Lord, Herigarius, spoke to them: "May your offerings and sacrifices together with your idols be cursed by God. How long do you wish to serve evil spirits and, to your own detriment, reduce yourselves to poverty with empty offerings? Lo, you have sacrificed much and vowed even more. In addition you have surrendered a hundred pounds of silver. What has it availed you? They now come to seize everything that you have. They will take your wives and children captive, they will set fire to city and town and destroy you with the sword. What do your idols profit you?" Terrified by his voice and uncertain what to do, they replied as one: "Let our salvation and our counsel rest in your hands and whatever you suggest to us, we will do without doubt." He replied to them: "If," he said, "you wish to make offerings, make your vows and offerings to almighty God, who reigns in heaven and whom I serve with pure conscience and righteous faith. He is the Lord of all and all things are subject to His will and there is no one who can resist His dominion. If therefore you ask His aid with all your heart, you will recognize that His omnipotence will not fail you." Having accepted his advice, they all went into a field, as was their custom, willingly and with a single purpose, and vowed fasting and alms to Christ for their liberation.

In the meantime, the aforementioned king began to submit to the Danes that they should inquire by divination whether it was the will of the gods that they should destroy the place. He said: "There are many great and powerful gods there, similarly a church formerly built in that place, and the worship of Christ is exercised there by many Christians, and he is the strongest of the gods and is able to help those who hope in him in any way he wishes. It is therefore necessary to inquire whether we are urged to this act by the will of the gods." This they could by no means reject because it was the custom among them. Inquiry was therefore made by divination and it was discovered that they could by no means carry this out to their benefit, nor was the place given over to their plundering by God. Again inquiry was made as to where they should turn to gain money, lest they be thwarted by vain hope and return home empty-handed. The inquiry fell out to the effect that they should go to a certain distant city in the territory of the Slavs. They, that is the Danes, believing this to be virtually a divine command, withdrew from the aforementioned place and hastened directly to that city. Bursting in unexpectedly on the inhabitants, who were dwelling in peace and security, they took the city by arms, and, having seized many spoils and treasures in it, returned home.

That king, who had come to plunder them, made peace with them, restored the silver he had formerly received from them, and resided with them for a certain time, wishing to be reconciled with his people. Thus the grace of the Lord, liberating the people of that place from the attack of the enemy because of the faith of His servant Herigarius, restored their property to them. When this was done, Herigarius himself submitted the matter in a public assembly of the people and admonished them to observe attentively who God was: "Lo, wretches," he said, "now you well understand how vain it is to ask help from evil spirits who cannot aid their worshippers. Receive the faith of my Lord Jesus Christ, whom you have proven to be the true God, and who gave you the comfort of His mercy when you had no refuge. Do not exercise any longer superstitious worship and do not propitiate your idols with worthless sacrifices. Worship the true God who rules all things in heaven and on earth, submit to Him, and worship His omnipotence."

The gist of the story is that the residents of Birka, under the threat of imminent attack by their exiled king Anund and his Danish allies, begin to make sacrifices to their gods. Having tried in vain to ransom their town, they meet a second time and urge one another to even greater sacrifices. At this point the leader of the Christian party, Herigarius, intervenes to curse their sacrifices and idols and denounce their worthlessness. "What do your idols profit you?" He urges them to petition God instead and their prayers are answered by a miraculous reprieve. The episode concludes with a triumphant exhortation of the people thus liberated from peril: "Nolite ultra culturam superstitiosam quaerere et inani sacrificio idola vobis placare. Verum Deum, qui omnium quae in caelis et in terris sunt dominatur, colite."

The situations in *Beowulf* and the *Vita Anskarii* are analogous. A people whose homes are imperiled by an attack takes refuge in sacrifice to heathen idols. In *Beowulf* the situation is unclear because the reader has been led to believe that the Danes are Christian. In the *Vita Anskarii* there is no such difficulty because the reader has been informed on the religious situation in Birka. Chapter 11 has related how Ansgar first came to Birka (829), was well received by King Bern (Bjørn), and persuaded many to accept baptism, including the prefect Herigarius. In chapter 19 we learn that Birka remains without the service of a priest for seven years after Ansgar's departure, but that Ansgar then dispatches a hermit named Ardgarius to prosecute the mission. Ardgarius is welcomed with open arms by the Christian community and by Herigarius, who has stoutly maintained his faith (and even vindicated it with minor miracles) in the teeth of heathen ridicule during the intervening seven years. On one occasion when he suffered from pains in his leg, the heathens urged him to sacrifice to the gods, but he rejected "empty idols" and, addressing his prayers to God, was immediately cured of his malady.

In Birka there are two religious factions, a pagan party and a Christian party. These parties are in open conflict, as we learn in chapter 17, when the heathen party bands together to drive Bishop Gauzbertus out of the land (ca. 835), although this occurs explicitly without the sanction of the king. What we must imagine therefore is a semi-converted community in which the king, the prefect Herigarius, and some of the people subscribe to Christianity, while others remain heathen. This situation is in perfect agreement with the politics of conversion in the north, according to which the mission began at the top of the social ladder and worked down.[13]

Does the situation in Birka shed any light on Heorot? If we imagine a semi-converted community in and around Heorot, it seems to me that the puzzle is solved. The critics have been baffled by Hrothgar's obvious Christianity and the heathenism of the Danes, but this split is explained by the state of semi-conversion. Hrothgar, like the Swedish king Bern and his prefect Herigarius, is a good Christian, but many of his people are still unregenerate. They have been exposed to Christianity, but have not embraced it. They either continue to sacrifice to their idols as they are accustomed or they return to a suspended usage with renewed zeal because of the threat posed by Grendel. Such a split between elite Christianity and popular paganism is perhaps implied in Bede's *Ecclesiastical History* IV. 27, in which the common people specifically revert to idolatry in time of plague.

One further analogy between the episodes in *Beowulf* and the *Vita Anskarii* requires comment. In *Beowulf* the report of heathen sacrifice is followed by a moral exhortation (vv. 183–88: "Wa bið . . . Wel bið") contrasting hellbound pagans to heaven-bound Christians. This is also the case in the *Vita Anskarii*. After the vanity of heathen sacrifice has been proven and the efficacy of prayer brilliantly vindicated, Herigarius assembles the throng once more to state the case: "iam nunc intellegite, quod vanum sit a daemonibus auxilium petere. . . . Suscipite fidem domini mei Iesu Christi." And again: "Nolite . . . inani sacrificio idola vobis placare. Verum Deum . . . colite." The *Beowulf* text is more elliptical, but Rimbert filled in the obvious moral of the story: it is useless to appeal to idols—the only recourse in time of peril is to God. The rhetoric is similar enough to suggest a common underlying theme in the sermon tradition contrasting the worthlessness of heathen worship to the efficacy of Christian prayer. This scheme is visible in the Ælfric texts cited by Dorothy Whitelock.[14] In both of these texts the prohibition against heathen sacrifice is followed by an exhortation to pray.

Traces of such conversion rhetoric survive in the thirteenth-century accounts of Saint Olaf's conversion activity in Norway. Chapters 37–38 of the so-called *Legendary Saga of Saint Olaf* (= *Heimskringla*, chap. 113) relate how Olaf undertook to convert the chieftain Guðbrandr of Gudbrandsdal and his people.[15] The resistance is intense, and the heathens bring out their idol of Thor all decked in gold and silver to overawe the Christians, whose paltry god is not even visible. Guðbrandr delivers a menacing speech recommending that Olaf and his followers not try Thor's patience further and restore his worship forthwith. King Olaf whispers to his retainer Kolbeinn, instructing him to strike Thor with a mighty blow of his club as soon as the heathens look away from their idol. Then Olaf rises to address the crowd. He announces the imminent arrival of his own god and ridicules a god like Thor who is both blind and deaf, can save neither himself nor others, and cannot move unless he is dragged by others.[16] He bids everyone look to the east where his god fares with great brilliance. At this moment the sun rises, riveting the eyes of the beholders, and Kolbeinn splits Thor with his club, thus releasing a host of resident mice, vipers, toads, and snakes. The heathen are terrified and flee in all directions, but when they are reassembled, Olaf rises to address them once again: "Now you can see what your god was capable of when you brought your gold and treasures, food and provisions. Now you saw what creatures had the benefit, mice and snakes and vipers and toads.[17] Now they are worse off who believe in such things and persist in their folly. Now take your gold and treasures, strewn on the field here, and bring them home to your wives and never again bring them to stocks and stones." Guðbrandr is chastened and replies: "We have had a great disgrace with our god. And now because he could not help us, it appears to me that your god is more powerful and our god isn't worth much as soon as he does not have to deal with us alone, and now we will reward him by withdrawing all worship from him and we will now worship the god whom you praise and devote all our faith to him."

This conversion anecdote has the same form as the anecdote told by Rimbert. Christian and heathen gods are matched against each other, the Christian God triumphs (by a real or mock miracle), and the leader of the Christian party draws the obvious conclusion for the benefit of the astonished pagans. There is even a minor coincidence of theme in the idea that sacrifices involve a gratuitous wasting of substance. Olaf points out that the sacrificed gold and treasure might better be brought to the idolators' wives, and Herigarius chides them for reducing themselves to poverty: "How long do you wish to serve the evil spirits and, to your own detriment, reduce yourselves to poverty with empty offerings?"

In *Beowulf* this homiletic scheme appears to be partial because the failure of heathen sacrifice is only implicit and the Christian counterpoise is less obvious. But we may argue that the scheme is not so much abbreviated as it is extended and elaborated. Heathen sacrifice fails, and Beowulf, who is introduced in verse 194 just after the passage on sacrifice, is himself the Christian counterpoise. That Beowulf and his men are good Christians emerges on their arrival in Denmark from their thanksgiving to God for an easy passage (vv. 227-28). That Beowulf operates as God's instrument emerges from his declaration (vv. 435-41) that he will meet Grendel without sword or shield and trust in God's judgment. The contest thus becomes a kind of ordeal to be determined by God's direct intervention. Hrothgar acknowledges this conception of the contest in his reply when he states that God can easily put an end to Grendel's deeds (vv. 478-79). Wealhþeow also acknowledges God's primacy and thanks God for giving her hope (vv. 625-28). When Beowulf begins his watch in Heorot, the reader is told that it is God who has posted him there (vv. 665-67):

> Hæfde Kyningwuldor
> Grendle togeanes,   swa guman gefrungon,
> seleweard aseted.

And Beowulf concludes his "gylp-word" by placing the outcome in God's hands (vv. 685-87):

> ond siþðan witig God
> on swa hwæþere hond   halig Dryhten
> mærðo deme,   swa him gemet þince.

The poet tells us that no one expected him to survive, but that God decided otherwise, and he invokes God's name no fewer than three times (vv. 696b, 701a, 706b). Grendel is just as clearly presented as God's antagonist: he bears God's wrath (711b), is God's enemy (786b), feuded with God (811b), and his heathen soul is swallowed up by hell (v. 852). Hrothgar begins his speech of gratitude with thanks to God (v. 928) and goes on to name God four more times (vv. 930b, 940a, 945a, 955b). Finally, Beowulf's response contains one additional acquiescence to God's will (v. 967b) and an anticipation of God's judgment on Grendel (977b-79).

Thus the whole Grendel episode in *Beowulf* may be considered an extension of the moral formulated by Rimbert. The depredations of Grendel (like the attack of Rimbert's Anund) are opposed first by an unsuccessful appeal to heathen idols and then by the successful intervention of God's elected champion Beowulf (like Rimbert's Herigarius). *Beowulf*, no less than the *Life of Ansgar*, dramatizes the defeat of the gods and the victory of God. The heathen sacrifice of the Danes is not a lapse, a digression, or an afterthought, but an antithetical preface designed to set off God's triumph in the person of Beowulf.

In conclusion, I believe that the apparent contradiction between the pagan sacrifice of the Danes and the Christianity of Hrothgar's court can be resolved by the assumption of a divided community. King, queen, and noblemen are Christians, but the Danish people have not yet been won over to the new faith. They either persist in their heathen customs or practice sacrifice with redoubled zeal in times of crisis. This situation is readily comprehensible in terms of northern conversion history, since we know that royalty converted first and the people were sometimes slow to follow. I thus revert to the idea that Tolkien regarded as second best, namely that the poet "intended a distinction between the wise Hrothgar . . . and a certain party of the pagan Danes—heathen priests, for instance, and those that had recourse to them under the temptation of calamity."[18] In my view, however, the distinction is not so much between royalty and a pagan priesthood as between upper-class Christianity and a firmly entrenched popular religion.

NOTES

1. A good review of the problem may be found in Howell D. Chickering, Jr., *Beowulf: A Dual-Language Edition* (Garden City, N.Y., 1977), pp. 288–90.
2. The MS reads "hreargtrafum." Kemble commented on the passage in a letter to Jakob Grimm: "Hrearg-trafum, Beów. 15, must it not however be hearg, because I don't recognize Hrearg? The word wig-weorðung (id.), i.e., *ministerium in templis adhibitum*, seems preferably to be adapted to heathen or pagan service. Also in the legend of St. Juliania [*sic*] in Cod. Exon. 68, it is called weoh-weorðing, concerning the pagan worship. The Haruc etc., makes good sense but what should hrear mean?" Cited from *John Mitchell Kemble and Jakob Grimm: A Correspondence 1832-1852*, ed. and trans. Raymond A. Wiley (Leyden, 1971), p. 31.
3. From Fr. Klaeber, ed., *Beowulf and the Fight at Finnsburg*, 3rd ed. (Boston, 1950), pp. 7-8.
4. "Die christlichen Elemente im Beowulf," *Anglia* 35 (1912):134–35. Klaeber refers to James W. Bright only by name and to James Edward Routh, Jr., "Two Studies on the Ballad Theory of the Beowulf" (Ph.D. dissertation, Johns Hopkins University, 1905), p. 54, note 1. The latter is not available to me.
5. Johannes Hoops, *Kommentar zum Beowulf* (Heidelberg, 1932), p. 39.
6. J. R. R. Tolkien, "*Beowulf*: The Monsters and the Critics," 1936; reprinted in *An Anthology of Beowulf Criticism*, ed. Lewis E. Nicholson (Notre Dame, Ind., 1963), pp. 51-103 (specifically 101-103).
7. *The Audience of Beowulf* (Oxford, 1951), pp. 77-79.
8. Her references (p. 79) are to: Ælfric, *The Sermones Catholici*, vol. I ed. Benjamin Thorpe (London, 1844), p. 474 ("Passio Sancti Bartholomei Apostoli"); Ælfric, *Lives of Saints*, ed. Walter W. Skeat, EETS, 76 (London, 1881), pp. 372-74; Agnes Jane Robertson, ed. and trans., *The Laws of the Kings of England from Edmund to Henry I* (Cambridge, 1925), pp. 176, 352.

9. "Beowulf Notes," *Anglia* 71 (1953):442-15.

10. *The Art of Beowulf* (Berkeley, 1959; rpt. 1971), esp. pp. 186-88, 196-99, 216-19.

11. "The Pagan Coloring of *Beowulf*" in *Old English Poetry: Fifteen Essays*, ed. Robert P. Creed (Providence, 1967), pp. 193-213, esp. 201-2. The more recent textual commentaries shed no new light on the passage. Else von Schaubert, ed., *Heyne-Schückings Beowulf, 2. Teil: Kommentar* (Munich, etc., 1961), passes over the problem in silence; Gerhard Nickel, ed., *Beowulf und die kleineren Denkmäler der altenglischen Heldensage Waldere und Finnsburg, 2. Teil: Einleitung, Kommentar*, etc. (Heidelberg, 1976), p. 12, merely restates the problem.

12. *Vita Anskarii auctore Rimberto*, ed. Georg Waitz, Scriptores Rerum Germanicarum in Usum Scholarum (Hannover, 1884; rpt. 1977), pp. 41-43 (my translation). On Ansgar, see W. Lammers in *Reallexikon der germanischen Altertumskunde*, Vol. 1 (Berlin and New York, 1973), pp. 346-48 (with bibliography).

13. E.g., Helge Ljungberg, *Den nordiska religionen och kristendomen: Studier över det nordiska religionskiftet under vikingatiden*, Nordiska texter och undersökningar, 11 (Stockholm, 1938), pp. 77-78.

14. See note 8 above.

15. *Olafs saga hins helga, efter pergamenthaandskrift i Uppsala Universitetsbibliotek Delagardieske samling nr. 8*[II], ed. Oscar Albert Johnsen (Kristiania, 1922), pp. 33-34.

16. Cf. Ælfric, *Lives of Saints* (reference in footnote 8), pp. 372-74: "Sume men synd swa ablende þæt hi bringað heora lác to eorðfæstum stane and eac to treowum and to wylspringum, swa swa wiccan tæcað, and nellað under-standan hu stuntlice hi doð, oððe hu se deada stán oððe þæt dumbe treow him mæge gehelpan oððe hæle forgifan þone hi sylfe ne astyriað of þære stowe næfre" ("Some men are so blinded, that they bring their offerings to an earth-fast stone, and eke to trees, and to wellsprings, even as witches teach, and will not understand how foolishly they act, or how the dead stone or the dumb tree can help them, or give them health, when they themselves never stir from the place").

17. The naiveté of the heathen Scandinavians in supposing that their gods accepted the offerings of food that were in reality consumed by animals is noted by Ibn Fadlan, trans., in Albert Stanburrough Cook, "Ibn Fadlān's Account of Scandinavian Merchants on the Volga in 922," *JEGP* 22 (1923):58: "Upon this, he [the merchant] takes a number of cattle and sheep, slaughters them, gives a portion of the meat to the poor, and carries the rest before the large statue and the smaller ones that surround it, hanging the heads of the sheep and cattle on the large piece of wood which is planted in the earth. When night falls, dogs come and devour it all. Then he who has so placed it exclaims: 'I am well pleasing to my lord; he has consumed my present.'"

18. Tolkien, "*Beowulf*," p. 101.

Issues in Natural Philosophy at Paris in the Late Thirteenth Century

EDWARD GRANT

THE DETERMINATION OF SIGNIFICANT ISSUES

To identify, with any reasonable degree of fidelity, the issues in natural philosophy that were of major concern in the late thirteenth century at Paris, it is first necessary to determine what constituted an "issue" in natural philosophy.[1] In the broadest sense, every *questio* among the *questiones* on the natural books of Aristotle represented an issue in natural philosophy, as did many of the *questiones* on the second book of Peter Lombard's *Sentences*, where Peter considered problems on the creation. From this standpoint, literally hundreds of issues in natural philosophy were regularly discussed, concerning which there were differences of opinion.[2] Obviously, they were not all of equal significance. But how can one determine which among them were judged significant in the late thirteenth century; that is, which proved sufficiently controversial to transcend their immediate subject matter and assume general importance? Because both important and unimportant questions that were formulated for a particular treatise were routinely included and presented in a rather standardized, impersonal format, the questions themselves, with perhaps a few exceptions, are not likely to reveal any sense of their own significance.

In truth, no certain criteria are readily available that would permit us to select with any reasonable degree of confidence all the issues that the theological and arts masters themselves would have ranked as the most momentous and controversial. But if we are unable to determine all the dominant issues, we can surely identify some that were of undoubted significance. In this category belong those questions that were deemed crucial because of their perceived relevance to theology and faith. They are identified for us in such works as the *Errores philosophorum* of Giles of Rome (Aegidius Romanus),[3] the *De quindecim problematibus* of Albertus Magnus[4] and, most important of all, the lists of articles condemned by the bishop of Paris in 1270 and 1277. Of the issues discussed here, all but one were of direct theological significance. The sole exception—the problem of celestial matter—had separate treatises devoted to it, thus providing a reasonable measure of its importance.

75

Medievalia et Humanistica, New Series, Number 13 (Paul Maurice Clogan, ed.). Rowman & Allanheld, Totowa, NJ. 1985.

THE WORKS OF ARISTOTLE AND THE
UNIVERSITY OF PARIS IN THE
THIRTEENTH CENTURY

For the University of Paris, the thirteenth century was a period of intellectual excitement accompanied by contention and often bitter controversy. During this century, the masters struggled successfully to assert their supremacy over the Chancellor of the Cathedral of Notre Dame and, in concert with the students, won significant economic and legal rights from the municipality and townspeople of Paris. In the intellectual sphere, however, the masters were not pitted against an outside foe, but against each other: arts masters against theologians; theologian against theologian; and arts master against arts master.

The intellectual turmoil that rocked Paris in the thirteenth century derived from the introduction of the philosophical and physical works of Aristotle and the commentaries thereon of his greatest commentator, Averroes. Aristotelian principles and assumptions about the world were not easily subordinated to theology. To the contrary, Aristotelian physics, metaphysics, and philosophy formed not only a reasonably cohesive worldview, but were found useful for the analysis of problems in theology and Holy Scripture. There was thus genuine fear that Aristotle's concepts and principles would eventually dominate theology and become the arbiter and validator of theological dogmas. During the first forty to fifty years of the thirteenth century, Christian authorities at Paris agonized over the degree of acceptability that might be accorded to the works of Aristotle. By the 1250s, however, efforts to control access to the Aristotelian corpus were abandoned, and that powerful body of philosophical and physical literature became firmly entrenched at the University of Paris, where it formed the basis of the arts curriculum.[5]

A second phase of the struggle developed in the 1260s when an intensive effort was made to guarantee that the new pagan and Arabic learning would not subvert the body of traditional theological doctrines and interpretations. Inspired by St. Bonaventure, conservative theologians attempted to stem the tide by outright condemnation of ideas they considered dangerous and offensive. When it was apparent that repeated warnings about the perils of secular philosophy were of no avail, the traditional theologians, many of whom were neo-Augustinian Franciscans, appealed once again to the bishop of Paris, Etienne Tempier, who had responded to an earlier appeal in 1270 with the condemnation of thirteen propositions. This time, in 1277, Tempier's response was to issue a massive condemnation of 219 propositions, which could henceforth be held or taught only under penalty of excommunication.[6]

Although the condemned articles were drawn up in haste without apparent order and with little concern for consistency or repetition,[7] a number of them were relevant to science and natural philosophy. The condemnation of an article, however, does not of itself indicate that it was the center of controversy in natural philosophy. Its danger may have been exaggerated by the authorities, or it may have been included because of a perceived threat if it should be openly discussed. By virtue of its inclusion, however, and its association with the truly controversial articles, it acquired a degree of importance that it might not otherwise have had. The Condemnation of 1277 is thus a reasonably reliable gauge that points to some of the weighty issues in natural philosophy at the University of Paris in the latter part of the thirteenth century.

Because, rightly or wrongly, the condemned articles were deemed theologically and doctrinally offensive, the articles relevant to natural philosophy may be appropriately categorized as problems falling within the area of the interrelations between science and religion. It is thus hardly surprising that the major issues in natural philosophy at Paris during the late thirteenth century were those that had strong theological implications, the consequences of which could not be ignored. In their efforts to carve out an area of competence in natural philosophy, some Parisian arts masters apparently involved themselves in theological issues. To forestall a confrontation with the theologians, the conservative majority of the arts faculty voted, on April 1, 1272, to forbid their members from determining or disputing theological questions.[8] As a consequence, attempts by arts masters to inject theological issues into questions and commentaries on Aristotle's treatises on natural philosophy were opposed by the theologians, as we learn from complaints made by John Buridan, perhaps the greatest Parisian arts master of the fourteenth century.[9] By contrast, theologians who wrote questions and commentaries on Aristotle's physical treatises, or *libri naturales*, could introduce theological material as they pleased, as we find in Nicole Oresme's French commentary on Aristotle's *De caelo*.[10] Curiously, the real threat to theology from the arts masters came not from an aggressive desire to inject theological matters into their discussions of natural philosophy, but from an opposite tendency: a general refusal to allow theology into their deliberations. Those principles and conclusions of natural philosophy that conflicted with the truths of faith were usually characterized as the best that could be achieved by the unaided reason, although they were readily conceded to be false by the standard of revealed truth. Well aware that natural philosophy and theology were an explosive mixture, arts masters made no effort to reconcile the two, choosing, for the most part, to leave theology to the theologians. As we shall see, this move enabled philosophy to enhance its credibility at the expense of theology.

THE ETERNITY OF THE WORLD

What, then, were some of the major issues of natural philosophy that agitated the University of Paris toward the end of the thirteenth century? Beyond any doubt, the most significant was the eternity of the world, which was to the relations between science and religion in the Middle Ages what the Copernican theory was to the sixteenth and seventeenth centuries and the Darwinian theory to the nineteenth and twentieth centuries. As one of the major physical and cosmological assumptions in Aristotle's natural philosophy, the eternity of the world was a powerful threat to the creation account in *Genesis*. A full awareness of this threat is manifested in the Condemnation of 1277, where it was denounced in some fifteen to twenty separate articles. That so many were required is perhaps a reflection of the numerous guises under which the eternity of the world masqueraded.[11] For example, article 9 asserted that "there was no first man, nor will there be a last; on the contrary, there always was and always will be the generation of man from man."[12] In article 98 we read that "the world is eternal because that which has a nature by [means of] which it could exist through the whole future [surely] has a nature by [means of] which it could have existed through the whole past." Finally, in article 107, the claim that the elements are eternal but that "they have been made [or created] anew in the relationship which they now have" is also condemned. Some articles declared the eternity of the world in a more straightforward manner, while others are less direct, as, for example, in those articles that proclaimed the eternity of the world by appeal to the eternity of the celestial motions or celestial substances. Thus article 101 declared that "an infinite [number] of celestial revolutions have preceded which it was not impossible for the first cause [that is, God] to comprehend, but [which is impossible of comprehension] by a created intellect," while article 93 asserted that "celestial bodies have eternity of substance but not eternity of motion."

With some fifteen to twenty articles specifically condemning the eternity of the world in its various forms, we might plausibly expect that belief in the world's eternity was widespread. In fact, no one has yet been identified who held this heretical opinion unqualifiedly. Since the bishop of Paris and his advisors could hardly have been unaware of this, why, we may well ask, did they emphasize the eternity of the world more than any other theme? Why were some fifteen to twenty articles condemned to prevent the dissemination of a proposition that no one explicitly advocated?

The answers to these questions probably lie in the nature of the responses about the eternity of the world. Arts masters like Boethius of Dacia and Siger of Brabant, both of whom wrote separate treatises on the eternity of the world, argued that from the standpoint of reason, the creation of the world is not demonstrable.[13] In his *Quæstiones super libros Physicorum*, Boethius even argued for the eternity of matter when he considered the question "whether prime matter was made anew [that is, created]."[14] He concluded that prime matter was not created but was co-eternal with the "first principle," God. Because prime matter could not be generated by nature without a pre-existent matter, it followed, according to Boethius, that prime matter is "the direct effect of the first principle." Thus although God created prime matter, it was yet co-eternal with Him, a position similar to that suggested by Thomas Aquinas (see below). Boethius believed that the eternity of matter was a conclusion that followed logically from the application of reason (*per rationem*).

By stipulating that his conclusion was proper for reason, rather than faith, Boethius left open the possibility that faith could provide the *real* truth. In his *De aeternitate mundi*, written at approximately the same time as his questions on the *Physics*, Boethius made this explicit when he declared that no philosopher could demonstrate that a first motion came into being or that the world was created.[15] But if human reason was incapable of demonstrating the creation of the world, neither could it demonstrate its eternity. As far as the eternity of the world was concerned, there was no contradiction between the Christian faith and philosophy. Opting for the faith, Boethius concluded that

the world is not eternal, but was created anew, although . . . this cannot be demonstrated by arguments, just as may be said about other things that pertain to the faith. For if they could be demonstrated, they would not belong to faith, but to science. . . . There are many things in the faith which cannot be demonstrated by reason, as [for example] that a dead person comes to life again numerically the same as he is now, and that a generable thing returns without generation. And who does not believe these things is a heretic; [and] whoever seeks to know these things by reason is a fool.

Siger of Brabant argued in a similar fashion. The world and its species cannot have been created, because no species of being could be actualized from a previous state of potentiality and thus must have been in existence previously.[16] To protect himself against possible heresy charges, Siger justified such conclusions by insisting that "we say these things as the opinion of the Philosopher, although not asserting them as true."[17] Where the pronouncements of faith conflicted with Aristotle's conclusions, the former were assumed true.[18] Under such circumstances, Aristotle's conclusions, which were the product of reason based on sense experience, must be judged inadequate, although they were the best that could be achieved with the unaided reason.[19] This attitude was typical of many arts masters of the late thirteenth century and is fully exhibited in the early fourteenth century by the famous and controversial arts master John of Jandun.[20] When theological and church doctrine conflicted directly with the conclusions of Aristotelian natural philosophy—as it did in the question of the eternity of the world— the arts masters yielded to theology and faith. But they often did so in a manner that left the theologians disquieted because the arts masters implied or explicitly stated that the truths of natural philosophy, based on the application of reason to sense experience, could not be reconciled with the truths of faith. Under these circumstances, the faith was upheld but in a manner that left the truths of natural philosophy virtually intact and even implied their superiority over faith.[21]

Although no arts masters have yet been discovered who believed literally in the infamous doctrine of the double truth, most probably believed in a doctrine of a higher and lower truth. The former was the domain of faith, which was indubitable but unintelligible to the unaided reason; the latter, based on reason and sense experience and therefore imperfect, was nonetheless the best that human understanding could achieve. By default, then, it became the practical, usable and, in some sense, even superior truth to the publicly and universally acknowledged "higher" truth of theology. John of Jandun exemplified this attitude when he declared that

I concede that everything which follows necessarily from them [doctrines of faith] is possible by divine power. If anyone knows how to prove this and to make it accord with the principles of philosophers, let him rejoice in this possession, and I will not grudge him, but declare that he surpasses my ability.[22]

With the prevalence of such attitudes during the late thirteenth century at Paris, it comes as no surprise that many theologians were convinced that Boethius of Dacia, Siger of Brabant, and others actually believed in the eternity of the world even as they proclaimed their fidelity to the Christian dogma of creation.

If the good bishop of Paris was suspicious of arts masters like Boethius of Dacia and Siger of Brabant, he and his partisans were hardly delighted with Thomas Aquinas, who, in his treatise on the eternity of the world (*De aeternitate mundi*), also argued that the world might be eternal. Unlike St. Bonaventure, Aquinas denied that any demonstrative proof could be formulated in favor of creation. "That the world had a beginning is an object of faith, but not of demonstration or science."[23] God could have willed the existence of creatures without a temporal beginning. If He did, then God had chosen to will the coeternality of created things with Himself. For Thomas, the coeternality of the world with God was nonetheless a creation because the world was totally dependent on God. To the bishop of Paris and like-minded traditional theologians, the arguments proposed by Aquinas, Siger, and Boethius of Dacia must have appeared suspicious. They seemed to confer respectability on belief in the eternity of the world even as they seemed to undermine confidence in its creation. Such arguments would have been sufficient to convince the bishop and his colleagues that their proponents were true believers in the eternity of the world.

During the fourteenth century, and undoubtedly with the Condemnation of 1277 in mind, scholastics would, when "speaking naturally" (*loquendo naturaliter*), assume the hypothetical eternity of the world. Although that hypothesis could produce strange consequences, it was permissible to reason from such an assumption. Albert of Saxony, for example, assumed the eternity of the world and a fixed quantity of matter. Over an infinite time, this limited and fixed quantity of matter would have formed an infinite number of bodies which would have required an infinite number of souls. On the day of resurrection, when every soul receives its material body, the same finite quantity of matter would be received by an infinite number of human souls—a clearly heretical consequence, since one and the same body would necessarily receive a plurality of souls. To resolve the dilemma and avoid theological entanglements, Albert replied that "the natural philosopher is not much concerned with this argument because when he assumes the eternity of the world, he denies the resurrection of the dead."[24] By such appeals to the hypothetical, medieval natural philosophers could consider almost any condemned and controversial proposition. But, as we have seen, most natural philosophers who were arts masters sought to avoid theological questions. Thus Marsilius of Inghen dismissed the same question by insisting that the world had a beginning and would come to an end.[25] Whether, on the assumption of the eternity of the world, an infinity of souls would receive the same matter was, for Marsilius, a theological question and of no relevance to a work on natural philosophy. Although he sought to avoid the question, Marsilius did allow that God could, if He wished, assign one matter to many men. Marsilius had thus invoked God's absolute power to achieve a naturally impossible effect.

THE REACTION AGAINST DETERMINISM: GOD'S ABSOLUTE POWER

Whatever the source of Marsilius's appeal to God's absolute power, the *concept* of God's absolute power (*potentia Dei absoluta*) played a significant role in the Condemnation of 1277 and was destined to shape attitudes toward many problems in natural philosophy. Many of the articles condemned in 1277 were damned in order to preserve God's absolute power, a power that natural philosophers were thought to have restricted as they eagerly sought to interpret the world in accordance with Aristotelian principles. Under Aristotle's influence, natural philosophers had regularly denied the possible existence of other worlds and therefore, by implication, had denied that God could create other worlds. By condemning the opinion that God could not create other worlds, article 34 made it mandatory to concede that He could indeed create them, and create as many as He wished.[26] Although no one was required to believe that God had created a plurality of worlds—indeed no one in the Middle Ages did so believe—the effect of article 34 on natural philosophy was to encourage speculation about the conditions and circumstances that would obtain if God *had* indeed created other worlds. Beginning with Richard of Middleton in the thirteenth century and continuing with authors of the stature of William of Ockham, John Buridan, and Nicole Oresme in the fourteenth century, the possible existence of other worlds was rendered intelligible, as was the idea that void space, the existence of which was denied in Aristotelian physics, might exist between two or more worlds.[27]

Article 49 denied to God the power to move the outermost heaven, and indeed the world itself, with a rectilinear motion because such a motion would leave behind a vacuum when the world departed its present position.[28] After its condemnation in 1277, scholastics routinely conceded that God could indeed move the world rectilinearly. From this assumption, some, like Jean de Ripa, inferred the existence of imaginary void spaces beyond our world in which bodies or angels could be received. Without such empty spaces, no places would exist into which God could move the world with a rectilinear motion.[29]

Articles 139, 140, and 141 condemned the seemingly self-evident principle that an accident could not exist without a subject in which to inhere and, more important, also condemned the opinion that not even God could create such a subject-independent accident.[30] Articles 139 and 141 further condemned the Aristotelian axiom that no quantity or dimension could exist independent of a material body, since this would make it a substance, and denounced the equally basic Aristotelian principle that two or more dimensions could not exist simultaneously in the same place. God was thus denied the power to achieve these feats if He wished.[31] It became fashionable to introduce these naturally impossible conditions into discussions of natural philosophy and to investigate what might happen if such conditions actually obtained. Thus Walter Burley argued that as in the Eucharist God makes a quantity devoid of corporeal substance, so also could He make a quantity devoid of inhering qualities. Such a distinct and separate qualityless quantity, or dimension, would indeed be a vacuum through which light and heavy bodies could move as if in a material medium.[32] In this manner Burley linked the condemned articles on the supernatural separation of accidents from their subjects, or attributes from their substances, with the much-discussed medieval problem of motion in a separate space.

Because the concept of a regular, lawful, and deterministic world had appeal for both strict Aristotelians and astrologers who followed Greek tradition as represented in Stoic accounts of the world, a number of articles were directed against deterministic astrology and the idea that God could not intervene in the natural order by creating new effects. The denial of new effects, which would have eliminated miracles and particular providence, and the assumption of deterministic astrology were embodied in the Stoic concept of a Great Year, which assumed the recurrence of identical sequences of all celestial configurations over fixed periods of time, usually 36,000 years, a value based on the Ptolemaic estimation for precession of the equinoxes of one degree in 100 years.[33] Because it was assumed that each particular configuration of celestial bodies caused a particular effect on some or all bodies in the terrestrial region, it followed that the same configuration in successive worlds would produce the same effect. Since the same configurations in the same sequences were held to recur in every successive world, each world would be an exact replication of its predecessor.[34]

The bishop of Paris undoubtedly had the Great Year in mind when, in article 6, he condemned the belief "That when all celestial bodies have returned to the same point—which will happen in 36,000 years—the same effects now in operation will be repeated."[35] Nicole Oresme, who considered the Great Year an error in philosophy and faith,[36] used elaborate mathematical arguments based on the probability that the celestial motions were mutually incommensurable to refute the Great Year and its inevitable consequence of an exact repetition of events.[37]

Where article 6 implicitly denied to God the possibility of causing new effects in the world, article 48 made it quite emphatic by declaring "That God cannot be the cause of a new act [or thing], nor can he produce something anew."[38] The substance of this article was frequently repeated and was ascribed to Aristotle by Giles of Rome in the form "That nothing new can proceed directly from God."[39] As he did with the Great Year, Nicole Oresme sought to demonstrate mathematically that God could indeed produce new effects, and Oresme provided numerous hypothetical examples. Again based on the assumption of the incommensurability of the celestial motions, he argued that celestial events are inherently unique and non-repetitive. Because medieval scholastics universally assumed that celestial motions influenced terrestrial events and further assumed that in the natural course of events, the same cause always generated the same effect, the incommensurability of the celestial motions guaranteed that the same celestial configuration could not occur twice in precisely the same part of the sky. It followed that the same cause and its effect could not occur twice. All events were thus unique. God's ingenious creation was planned to yield an ever-flowing pattern of unique, though closely related, events. Thus was the world made more interesting than if celestial and terrestrial events were regularly repeated.[40] Oresme's extraordinary intellectual effort was an extreme response to an old problem rooted in the thirteenth century and manifested in the Condemnation of 1277.

No area of natural philosophy was affected more by the Condemnation of 1277 and its major emphasis on the concept of God's absolute power than was the Aristotelian notion of vacuum. Not only did articles 34 and 49 concern the vacuum, but so also did article 201, which condemned the idea that God required a vacuum in which to create the world.[41] Although no articles of the Condemnation of 1277 were specifically concerned with vacua within the cosmos itself, the great emphasis on God's absolute power made it appear obvious that God could, if He wished, create vacua anywhere He pleased. And so it was that God was frequently imagined to annihilate all or part of the matter within the material plenum of our world.[42] Within such empty spaces, all manner of conditions and circumstances were imagined after 1277, and the questions that were raised came to be commonly discussed in the large literature on the nature of vacuum and the behavior of bodies placed within it. A variety of "thought experiments" were imagined and analyzed in terms of Aristotelian principles, even though the conditions imagined were often "contrary to fact" and impossible within Aristotelian natural philosophy. Indeed, the annihilation of matter would become a principle of analysis in the seventeenth century in much the same manner as in the late Middle Ages. Thomas Hobbes paid unwitting tribute to his scholastic predecessors when he declared that "In the teaching of natural philosophy, I cannot begin better (as I have already shewn) than from *privation*; that is, from feigning the world to be annihilated,"[43] a process that, among other things, enabled him to formulate his concepts of space and time.

Events of the late thirteenth century had made God's absolute power a vehicle for the introduction of subtle and imaginative questions,[44] which generated novel replies. Although these speculative responses did not replace or cause the repudiation of the Aristotelian worldview, they did challenge some of its fundamental principles.

ARE SPIRITUAL SUBSTANCES IN A PLACE?

Many of the condemned articles that were relevant to natural philosophy concerned space, vacuum, and motion, but embraced spiritual as well as material substances. Three of them—articles 204, 218, and 219—were concerned with whether a separate, spiritual substance, such as a celestial intelligence or an angel, is locatable in a specific place.[45] Two major positions were condemned in the three articles. The first is that a spiritual substance is in a place solely because of its substance, that is, it is coextensive with its place just as a body is. It was theologically objectionable to treat a spiritual substance as if it were a three-dimensional body. The second dangerous interpretation held that a spiritual substance was locatable solely by reason of its operations or actions, and not by its substance, from which it followed that an angel, for example, could act anywhere by a mere act of the will. It could move from the celestial region to the earth instantaneously without moving successively and continuously through the intervening space. Theological objections to the second interpretation were based on the clear implication that if an angel, for example, chose not to act, or exercise its will, it was nowhere since it was locatable only when it chose to act. The theologically safe explanation was to follow Peter Lombard and concede that although a spiritual substance could be said to occupy a specific, finite, and bounded place, it was not coterminous with that place.[46] Indeed, the whole of a spiritual substance was assumed capable of occupying any part of its place, however small that part might be.[47]

The condemnation of the articles concerning the place of spiritual substances was very likely promulgated with at least Thomas Aquinas, Siger of Brabant, and Boethius of Dacia in mind.[48] Although Aquinas had died three years prior to the Condemnation of 1277, his works contained opinions that were clearly in violation of the condemned articles.[49] With respect to location and movement, Aquinas had treated spiritual substances radically different from bodies. For Aquinas, a body is in place by the contact of its volume with the innermost surface of the containing body that surrounded and touched it at every point. But an angel is not a corporeal volume, which led Aquinas to conclude that it could not occupy a place in the manner of a body. Indeed it could not—or at least did not—occupy a place at all; rather, it acted in places by its will, or desire, and not by the presence of its substance. Thus, an angel if it wished could act on, and in, a distant place by its power alone without actually moving to it by a continuous motion.

John Duns Scotus upheld the condemnation of article 204.[50] He was critical of those who, like Thomas Aquinas, insisted that an angel could act anywhere by its will alone. How could a finite creature with limited power act as if it were omnipresent and yet not occupy any places? Such powers were appropriate only to God, not to the beings He had created. It also appeared absurd to Scotus that if an angel were to pass from heaven to earth, it should be able to do so without passing through, or acting on, the intermediate places. Scotus, and those who supported the condemnation, rejected action at a distance for separate substances other than God; they held instead that an angel could act in a place only by "occupying" it and must pass through all the intervening points between a *terminus a quo* and a *terminus ad quem*. Despite some disagreements, the Scotistic position was upheld by a number of fourteenth-century scholastics, such as Peter Auriol, William of Ockham, Thomas of Strasbourg, and John Baconthorpe.

THE PROBLEM OF CELESTIAL MATTER

Of the many issues and questions judged of importance for natural philosophy in the late thirteenth century that were not manifestly theological, one at least appears worthy of special mention because of its fundamental cosmic significance: Is there matter in the heavens? Questions about the existence of celestial matter and its probable nature represented a significant aspect of medieval natural philosophy. Discussions appear in commentaries and *questiones* on Aristotle's *De caelo* (for example, by Aquinas and John Buridan),[51] in commentaries on the *Sentences* of Peter Lombard (for example, by St. Bonaventure, Aquinas, and Peter Auriol),[52] and occasionally in separate treatises, which usually bore the title *De materia celi* (Hervaeus Natalis and Giles of Rome).[53] The issue retained its significance well into the seventeenth century, until the consequences of the Copernican heliocentric cosmology finally made the centuries-long distinction between the terrestrial and celestial regions untenable.

Why should medieval natural philosophers have been so intensely concerned with whether the heaven with all its planets and stars possessed matter? Was it not obvious that the planets and stars were composed of matter? In the context of Aristotelian natural philosophy, it was far from obvious. Aristotle's division of the world into radically different celestial and sublunar parts thrust the problem onto the Middle Ages. The celestial region was filled with an unchanging ether, a very special entity that moved eternally with a natural, circular motion and changed only its position. By contrast, the sublunar realm was a place of continual change, where generations and corruptions proceeded without interruption. Because Aristotle had denied the occurrence of generation and corruption in the heavens and because he had also argued that only things subject to generation and corruption could possess matter, many scholastics concluded that Aristotle, and Averroes, had denied the existence of matter in the heavens. In some sense, then, the heaven had to be simple, for if it were a composite of matter and form, it would be generable and corruptible. The issue was often formulated in terms of an option between a heaven that was conceived as a composite of matter and form or a heaven that was an absolutely simple entity. Supporters of Aristotle and Averroes defended some version of the second alternative and were definitely in the minority.

Most scholastic natural philosophers opted for a heaven that was composed of matter and form, although differences arose over the properties and characteristics of the celestial matter as well as of the form with which it was associated. Thomas Aquinas, and many who followed him, argued that celestial matter differed radically from terrestrial matter.[54] The former suffered no substantial transmutations, whereas the latter did incessantly. Others, notably Giles of Rome, although accepting the substantial immutability of the heavens and the incessant mutability of the terrestrial region, denied any distinction between their matters,[55] insisting that if all forms were removed from heaven and earth, the matter remaining in the two regions would be identical. On closer inspection, however, the proclaimed identity disappears, for Giles agreed with his colleagues in denying that generation and corruption could occur in the heavens. The celestial ether lacked the capacity, that is, the potentiality, to take on different substantial forms. The matter of the heavens was joined permanently to a single form. Thus, despite an alleged identity between celestial and terrestrial matter, Giles allowed that celestial matter had greater actuality than terrestrial matter and was therefore more perfect. With such a major difference between them, their declared identity was little more than rhetorical.

Finally, there were those who placed a strict interpretation on Aristotle's association of substantial change with matter. Godfrey of Fontaines in the thirteenth century and Peter Auriol and John Buridan in the fourteenth believed that if substantial change occurred only in the terrestrial region, matter could exist only there and not in the heavens, where all were agreed that substantial changes did not occur.[56]

THE INTELLECTUAL ENVIRONMENT FOR DEBATE OF THE ISSUES

The issues in natural philosophy identified and described here were all of major importance in late thirteenth-century Paris, although some did not achieve their most significant impact until the fourteenth century. To conclude, it seems appropriate to inquire about the intellectual climate in which all issues, great and small, were contested. Under what circumstances and conditions of intellectual freedom were issues such as the nature of the celestial ether and the host of other questions in natural philosophy debated?[57] Those without theological implications appear to have been discussed with complete freedom, restricted only by the limitations imposed by the intellectual *Zeitgeist*. Where theological concerns were central, or strongly implied, matters were somewhat different. Efforts to ban and expurgate the physical works of Aristotle during the first half of the thirteenth century bear witness to theological fears of uncontrolled disputes in natural philosophy. The Condemnation of 1277 marked the culmination of theological efforts to contain and control natural philosophy. The bishop of Paris and his supporters sought to restrict, by penalty of excommunication, categorical claims for a number of ideas in natural philosophy. It was forbidden, for example, to deny creation and assert the eternity of the world, to deny the possibility of other worlds, and to deny that God could create an accident without a subject in which to inhere.

Although these restrictions fell equally on masters of arts and theologians at the University of Paris, the arts masters were far more seriously affected. Not only were they obliged to comply with the Condemnation of 1277, but, in the absence of professional credentials in theology, they had been required since 1272 to swear an oath that they would avoid disputation of purely theological questions and were generally discouraged from introducing theological matters into natural philosophy. True, many arts masters were quite content to leave theological problems to the theologians; but those who were not so inclined were undoubtedly frustrated.[58]

No such obstacles hindered the theologians, who were trained in both natural philosophy and theology. They were permitted a remarkable degree of intellectual freedom and, for the most part, did not allow theology to obstruct their inquiries into the structure and operation of the physical world, a subject which for many was inextricably linked with theology. Indeed, the theologians used the doctrine of God's absolute power to speculate about the nature of a world that was often assumed to possess features that were contrary, and even impossible, in the Aristotelian cosmos. While these speculations did not lead to the abandonment of the Aristotelian world-view, they generated some of the most daring and exciting discussions of the Middle Ages.[59]

NOTES

1. Although natural philosophy (or natural science, as it was also called) in the late Middle Ages was broadly conceived and difficult to define, it was usually, and at the very least, identified with Aristotle's "natural books" (*libri naturales*), which, for the most part, were concerned with mobile bodies and the various changes to which they are subjected. Sometimes it was taken to include much more, as in a thirteenth-century guidebook for Parisian arts students where natural philosophy is said to include metaphysics, mathematics, and physics. See C. H. Lohr, "The Medieval Interpretation of Aristotle," in *The Cambridge History of Later Medieval Philosophy*, ed. Norman Kretzmann, Anthony Kenny, and Jan Pinborg (Cambridge, 1982), pp. 84–85.

2. For a sampling of such questions from the fourteenth century, *Questions on the Physics, On the Heavens,* and *On Generation and Corruption,* see Edward Grant, ed., *A Source Book in Medieval Science* (Cambridge, Mass., 1974), pp. 199–210.

3. *Giles of Rome Errores Philosophorum,* ed. Joseph Koch; English trans. John O. Riedl (Milwaukee, 1944). The "errors" were drawn by Giles from the works of Aristotle, Averroes, Avicenna, Algazel, Alkindi, and Maimonides and were presented in that order sometime between 1268 and 1274.

4. For the text, see Pierre F. Mandonnet OP, ed., *Siger de Brabant et l'Averroïsme Latin au xiiime siècle,* part 2, unedited text (Louvain, 1908), pp. 29–52. The fifteen problems were sent to Albertus by his student Giles of Lessines, perhaps between 1273 and 1276 (see John Wippel, "The Condemnations of 1270 and 1277 at Paris," *Journal of Medieval and Renaissance Studies* 7 [1977]:182). In a brief statement preceding the questions, Giles explains to Albert that these questions were proposed by the greatest masters in philosophy who teach in the schools at Paris ("*Articulos quos proponunt magistri in scolis Parisius, qui in philosophia maiores reputantur.*" Mandonnet, *Siger de Brabant,* p. 29. See also Fernand van Steenberghen, *Siger de Brabant d'après ses oeuvres inédites,* 2 vols. [Louvain, 1931, 1942], vol. 1, p. 719). The first thirteen propositions repeated the thirteen propositions condemned

in 1270 by Etienne Tempier, the bishop of Paris. Wippel observes ("The Condemnations," p. 180) that "many of the errors condemned in 1270 had already been denounced by Bonaventure in his conferences of 1267 (*Collationes de decem praeceptis*) and 1268 (*Collationes de donis Spiritus Sancti*)."

5. Wippel ("The Condemnations," pp. 172-73) argues that the first phase of the struggle between arts and theology ended around 1230. During this period, the restrictions placed upon Aristotle's natural books at Paris were absent from Oxford.

6. The Latin text of the 219 condemned articles appears in Heinrich Denifle and Emil Chatelain, *Chartularium Universitatis Parisiensis*, vol. 1 (Paris, 1889), pp. 543-55; for a rearrangement of the articles, see Mandonnet, *Siger de Brabant*, pp. 175-91. For references to translations and discussions, see Edward Grant, "The Condemnation of 1277, God's Absolute Power, and Physical Thought in the Late Middle Ages," *Viator* 10 (1979):212 n. 1; and Wippel, "The Condemnations," p. 169 n. 1. Although part nine of Etienne Gilson's *History of Christian Philosophy in the Middle Ages* (London, 1955), pp. 387-427, is titled "The Condemnation of 1277," Gilson says little about the Condemnation itself, concentrating instead on Siger of Brabant, Boethius of Dacia, and Thomas Aquinas.

7. Wippel, "The Condemnations," pp. 171, 195.

8. Ibid., p. 184. The statute further declared (see Grant, *Source Book*, p. 45) that any question that touched both faith and philosophy could not be resolved contrary to the faith; indeed, if a question even appeared to undermine the faith, the master had to refute the arguments against it or declare them erroneous.

9. See Grant, *Source Book*, pp. 50-51.

10. *Nicole Oresme: Le Livre du ciel et du monde*, ed. Albert D. Menut and Alexander J. Denomy; trans. and intro. Albert D. Menut (Madison, Wis., 1968). Because most theologians wrote their *questiones* on Aristotle's natural books while they were arts masters and before they became theologians, theological discussions are rarely found in such treatises. Oresme himself exemplifies this tendency . Prior to his theological degree and the French commentary on Aristotle's *De caelo*, Oresme had written a Latin *questiones* on the same treatise in which theology plays an insignificant role. See Claudia Kren, "The 'Questiones super De celo' of Nicole Oresme," Ph.D. dissertation, University of Wisconsin, 1965.

11. See Roland Hissette, *Enquête sur les 219 articles condamné à Paris le mars 1277* (Louvain/Paris, 1977), pp. 147-60. Prior to the Condemnation, Giles of Rome had already accused six of the greatest non-Christian philosophers of holding these errors (see the *Errores philosophorum*).

12. My numbering follows that of the *Chartularium Universitatis Parisiensis*. For Giles of Rome's attribution of this error to Aristotle, see *Errores philosophorum*, pp. 11, 13.

13. Hissette (*Enquête sur les 219 articles*, p. 314) identified thirty of the 219 condemned articles as directed against Siger of Brabant (with thirteen

more probably directed against him) and thirteen (with three more as probable) against Boethius of Dacia.

14. Boethius of Dacia, *Quaestiones super libros Physicorum*, in *Boethii Daci Opera*, vol. 5, pt. 2, ed. Géza Sajó (Copenhagen, 1974), p. 186. The question extends over pp. 186–88.

15. Boethius of Dacia, *De aeternitate mundi*, in *Boethii Daci Opera, Topica-Opuscula*, vol. 6, pt. 2, ed. Nicolaus Georgius Green-Pedersen (Copenhagen, 1976), p. 355. My references are to pp. 355–57.

16. This is the theme of Siger's *De aeternitate mundi*. See *St. Thomas Aquinas, Siger of Brabant, St. Bonaventure, On the Eternity of the World* (De aeternitate mundi), trans. Cyril Vollert, Lottie H. Kendzierski, and Paul M. Byrne (Milwaukee, 1964), pp. 12, 91–93.

17. Ibid., p. 93.

18. See Gilson, *History of Christian Philosophy*, pp. 398–99, where he also presents a plausible hypothetical representation of the attitude that sincerely religious masters of arts, including Siger, may have adopted.

19. See Stuart MacClintock, *Perversity and Error: Studies on the "Averroist" John of Jandun* (Bloomington, Ind., 1956), pp. 72, 164 n. 10.

20. Ibid., pp. 73–88; for Jandun, pp. 88–99.

21. Technically, this tactic was in conformity with the statute of 1272. Even before 1272, arts masters were reluctant to harmonize natural philosophy and religion. Lohr observes (*The Cambridge History of Later Medieval Philosophy*, pp. 89–90) that arts masters "identified the viewpoint of the theologians with the truth" and saw their own mission as devoted to a full explanation of Aristotle's judgments and opinions. As Siger put it in his *Questions on the Metaphysics* (bk. 3, qu. 15, trans. Lohr, ibid., p. 90): "It should be noted by those who undertake to comment upon the books of the Philosopher that his opinion is not to be concealed, even though it be contrary to the truth." But perhaps just as important was the fact that by refraining from reconciling the principles and conclusions of Aristotle with the truths of faith where these conflicted, the arts masters were subtly advancing the cause of Aristotle.

22. MacClintock, *Perversity and Error*, p. 95. The passage is from Jandun's *Quaestiones de anima*, bk. 3, qu. 29.

23. *Summa Theologiae*, pt I, qu. 46, art. 2, as translated in *St. Thomas Aquinas, Siger of Brabant, St. Bonaventure, On the Eternity of the World*, p. 66.

24. From Albert of Saxony, *Questiones De generatione et corruptione*, as quoted in Anneliese Maier, *Metaphysische Hintergründe der spät-scholastischen Naturphilosophie* (Rome, 1955), pp. 39–40.

25. Ibid., p. 40.

26. "34. That the first cause could not make several worlds." Grant, *Source Book*, p. 48. See also Giles of Rome, *Errores philosophorum*, pp. 5, 13, where Giles ascribes this error to Aristotle.

27. For an excellent account of the arguments, see Steven J. Dick, *Plurality of Worlds: The Origins of the Extraterrestrial Life Debate from Democritus to Kant* (Cambridge, 1982), pp. 23–37.

28. "49. That God could not move the heavens [that is, the world] with rectilinear motion; and the reason is that a vacuum would remain." Grant, *Source Book*, p. 48.
29. Not only Jean de Ripa, but also Thomas Bradwardine and Nicole Oresme proclaimed the real existence of an infinite, extracosmic void space. All three identified that space with God's infinite immensity. For a detailed study, see Edward Grant, *Much Ado About Nothing: Theories of Space and Vacuum from the Middle Ages to the Scientific Revolution* (Cambridge, 1981), pp. 119, 129-44. Hissette (*Enquête sur les 219 articles*, pp. 118-19) has accused Pierre Duhem of a misinterpretation of article 49. Instead of a rectilinear motion of the whole world itself through space, Hissette believes the article was concerned only with a rectilinear motion of the sides of the heavenly spheres toward the center of the world. Although some scholastics discussed the collapse of the celestial spheres toward the center of the universe, those discussions do not appear to have provoked article 49. Scholastics like Richard of Middleton, Walter Burley, Jean de Ripa, John Buridan, and Nicole Oresme leave no doubt that article 49 was concerned with the rectilinear motion of the whole spherical cosmos through space and not with the rectilinear fall of the spherical surfaces toward the center of the world. For the details, see Grant, "The Condemnation of 1277," pp. 226-32.
30. "139. That an accident existing without a subject is not an accident, except equivocally; and that it is impossible that a quantity or dimension exist by itself because that would make it a substance.

    140. That to make an accident exist without a subject is an impossible argument implying a contradiction.

    141. That God cannot make an accident exist without a subject, nor make several dimensions exist simultaneously [in the same place]." From Grant, *Much Ado About Nothing*, p. 339 n. 45 (the Latin texts are included). See also Grant, "The Condemnation of 1277," pp. 232-35. The error that God could not make an accident without a subject was charged to Aristotle and Maimonides by Giles of Rome (*Errores philosophorum*, pp. 9, 13, 63, 67).
31. The thirteenth error attributed to Aristotle by Giles of Rome accused the former of denying that God could make two bodies exist in the same place (*Errores philosophorum*, pp. 11, 13).
32. See Grant, "The Condemnation of 1277," pp. 233-34.
33. For a lengthy discussion of the Great Year, see *Nicole Oresme and the Kinematics of Circular Motion: Tractatus de commensurabilitate vel incommensurabilitate motuum celi*, ed. and trans. Edward Grant (Madison, Wis., 1971), pp. 103-24.
34. It is obvious that the Great Year is a peculiar version of the eternity of the world where the endless sequence of temporally finite, but identical and successive, worlds constitutes, in effect, a single eternal world without beginning or end.
35. Grant, *Source Book*, p. 48.
36. In the fourth chapter of his *De proportionibus proportionum*. See

Nicole Oresme "De proportionibus proportionum" and "Ad pauca respicientes", ed. and trans. Edward Grant (Madison, Wis., 1966), p. 307.

37. For a brief summary of the manner in which Oresme mathematically justified the conclusion that most physical magnitudes, including the celestial motions, are probably incommensurable, see Grant, *The Kinematics of Circular Motion*, pp. 73–76 n. 113.

38. Grant, *Source Book*, p. 48.

39. Hissette, *Enquête sur les 219 articles*, p. 55; Giles of Rome, *Errores philosophorum*, p. 13.

40. See Grant, *The Kinematics of Circular Motion*, pp. 311–21.

41. "201. That whoever generates [or believes in the creation of] the whole world assumes a vacuum because a place necessarily precedes what is generated in that place; therefore, before the generation of the world there existed something without a thing located in it, which is a vacuum." See Grant, *Much Ado About Nothing*, p. 326, n. 37.

42. For illustrations, see the pages cited under "God: annihilates all or part of the material world" in ibid., p. 445.

43. From Hobbes's *De corpore* (1655), as cited in Grant, *Much Ado About Nothing*, p. 390 n. 169.

44. Other condemned articles relevant to determinism and God's absolute power are cited by Hissette, *Enquête sur les 219 articles*, pp. 43–70, 117–47.

45. "204. That separated [that is, spiritual] substances are somewhere by operation; and that they cannot be moved from extremity to extremity, nor in the middle, unless they wish to operate in the middle, or at the extremities. [This is] an error if it is understood that the [separated] substance is not in a place and that it cannot move from place to place without operation [that is, without choosing to operate there].
    218. That an intelligence, or an angel, or a separated soul, is nowhere.
    219. That separated substances are nowhere according to substance. [This is] an error if it is understood [to mean] that a substance is not in a place. However if it is understood that substance is the reason for being in a place, [then] it is true that they are nowhere according to substance." The Latin texts and an analysis of the three articles are given in Hissette, *Enquête sur les 219 articles*, pp. 104–10.

46. Such a place was called an *ubi definitivum* and stood in contrast to an *ubi circumscriptivum*, wherein the body and the place are coterminous. See Grant, *Much Ado About Nothing*, pp. 129–30 and 342–43 n. 64–67.

47. For this "whole in every part doctrine", see ibid., pp. 143, 350 n. 127.

48. Hissette, *Enquête sur les 219 articles*, pp. 105–6.

49. For references, see Hissette, ibid., pp. 105–6, n. 7 and Grant, "The Condemnation of 1277," p. 236, nn. 95, 96.

50. *Quaestiones in lib.II sententiarum*, dist. 2, qu. 6 ("An locus angeli sit determinatus, punctualis, maximus, et minimus?") in *Opera omnia*, vol. 6, pt. 1 (Lyons, 1639; repr. Hildesheim, 1968), p. 189.

51. Aquinas, *Commentary on De caelo*, I, 1. 6 n. 63. To gauge the true measure of importance that the problem of celestial matter held for

Thomas, it is essential to know that he considered the issue in at least thirty-six separate places in a wide range of works. For the texts and references, see Thomas Litt, *Les corps célestes dans l'univers de Saint Thomas d'Aquin* (Louvain/Paris, 1963), pp. 54–80. For Buridan, see Ernest A. Moody, ed., *Iohannis Buridani Quaestiones super libris quattuor De caelo et mundo* (Cambridge, Mass., 1942), bk. 1, qu. 11 ("Utrum caelum habeat materiam"), pp. 49–54.

52. For Bonaventure, see his *Opera Omnia*, ed. College of St. Bonaventure (Quaracchi, 1882–1901), vol. 2 (1885), bk. 2, dist. 12, art. 2, qu. 1 ("Utrum caelestium et terrestrium una sit materia quantum ad esse"), pp. 302–3; for Aquinas, see R. P. Mandonnet, O. P., ed., *S. Thomae Aquinatis Scriptum super libros Sententiarum magistri Petri Lombardi*, vol. 2 (Paris, 1929), bk. 2, dist. 12, qu. 1, art. 1 ("Utrum omnium corporalium sit eadem materia"), pp. 301–4; and for Auriol, see *Petri Aureoli Verberii, Ordinis Minorum . . . Commentariorum in primum [-quartum] librum Sententiarum pars prima [-quarta] . . . 2* vols. (Rome, 1596-1605), vol. 2 ("Utrum, secundum sententiam Aristotelis et Commentatoris sui, caelum sit natura simplex non composita ex materia et forma"), pp. 186–89.

53. *Quolibet Hervei. Subtilissima Hervei Natalis Britonis . . . Tractatus VIII videlicet: De beatitudine; De verbo; De eternitate mundi; De materia celi; De relationibus; De pluralitate formarum; De virtutibus; De motu angeli* (Venice, 1513; repr. Ridgewood, N.J., 1966), fols. 33r–53v. For Giles, *Gaetani expositio in libro De celo et mundo. Cum questione Domini Egidii De materia celi nuperrime impressa et quam diligentissime emendata* (Venice, 1502), fols. 78r–84r. The 1552 (Venice) edition of Giles's *Metaphysicales Quaestiones* also contains the *De materia celi* (under the title *De coeli materiali compositione contra Averroem*).

54. For a passage from Aquinas's commentary on *De caelo*, see Litt, *Les corps célestes*, p. 79. Litt cites numerous other passages from works by Aquinas that also emphasize the differences; see also John Wippel, *The Metaphysical Thought of Godfrey of Fontaines: A Study in Late Thirteenth-Century Philosophy* (Washington, D.C., 1981), pp. 285–87.

55. For example, see Giles's *De materia celi*, fol. 81v.

56. References and analysis are supplied by Wippel, *The Metaphysical Thought of Godfrey of Fontaines*, pp. 288–91. For Auriol, see *In primum [-quartum] librum Sententiarum*, vol. 2, p. 189, col. 1. For Buridan, see *Quaestiones super libris De caelo*, p. 51.

57. Two works concerned with problems of intellectual freedom are Mac-Clintock, *Perversity and Error*, and Mary Martin McLaughlin, *Intellectual Freedom and Its Limitations in the University of Paris in the Thirteenth and Fourteenth Centuries* (New York, 1977).

58. If we can judge from remarks made in his *Questions on the Physics*, bk. 4, qu. 8, John Buridan should be counted among the frustrated. For a translation of the passages and references to the Latin edition, see Grant, *Source Book*, pp. 50–51. On pp. 51–52, Luis Coronel discusses Buridan's complaint.

59. Although the negative aspects of the Condemnation of 1277 are frequently emphasized, it is well to remember that it also inadvertently encouraged cosmological speculation under the guise of God's absolute power. Some of these speculations have been mentioned here but are described in detail in Grant, "The Condemnation of 1277."

From Roman de la Rose *to* Roman de la Poire*: The Ovidian Tradition and the Poetics of Courtly Literature*

SYLVIA HUOT

In modern studies of the *Roman de la Rose*, the poem by Jean de Meun often receives more attention and more acclaim than that of Guilllaume de Lorris.[1] It is generally felt that it was Jean's *Rose* that so excited the imagination of fourteenth- and fifteenth-century readers; certainly it was his text that inspired the famous *querelle*. In their enthusiasm for this clearly great poet, some critics almost seem to lose sight of the fact that Jean himself was, first and foremost, responding to Guillaume de Lorris. It is important to bear in mind that Guillaume's *Rose* is itself a seminal text, and that Jean de Meun was not the first poet to be inspired by it. A study of early responses to Guillaume de Lorris—those which pre-date Jean's work—can help us to understand the importance of Guillaume's work for his contemporaries. The present study will focus on one such response: Tibaut's *Romanz de la Poire*, generally dated 1250.[2]

The *Poire* is a text of approximately 3,000 lines, in which the narrator relates how he fell in love with a certain lady; how Amors took his heart and sent it to this lady; how she in turn fell in love and sent him her heart; how the lovers communicated through an exchange of refrains sung by allegorical personifications; and how he decided to write down the story of their love and have it read to her. The title is based on the opening episode, in which the narrator's lady hands him a pear from which she has eaten; one bite of it causes him to fall in love (404 ff.). Distinguishing features of the *Poire* text are its versification and its use of acrostics. The octosyllabic couplets of the narrative are interrupted not only by the numerous refrains, but also by the section immediately following the Prologue (21–283), which is composed in stanzas of four twelve-syllable lines each, with internal and end rhyme.[3] These form a series of first-person monologues spoken, in order, by Amors; Lady Fortune; Cligés; the *Poire* narrator; Tristan; Pyramus; the *Poire* narrator and his lady, in dialogue; Paris, and the narrator with reference to Paris; the

95

Medievalia et Humanistica, New Series, Number 13 (Paul Maurice Clogan, ed.). Rowman & Allanheld, Totowa, NJ. 1985.

narrator. In MS *A* (Paris, Bibl. Nat. fr. 2186, dated ca. 1275), each speech is accompanied by a full-page miniature portraying the speaker and the event to which he alludes.[4] This section functions as a kind of extended Prologue to the narrative proper, introducing the characters and the motifs that will be developed later. The acrostics, finally, are formed by the initials of the refrains, and spell out the name of the lady (ANNES—one letter has been omitted to preserve her anonymity), the name of the narrator (TIBAUT), and the word AMORS. Analysis of these acrostics by the narrator and his lady attributes considerable significance to the configuration of letters they present. The lady's name begins and ends with the same letters as 'Amors," proof of her worthiness for love (2785-9); both lover and lady have six letters and two syllables in their names, proof of the bond between them (2730-33); the name "Tibaut," if spelled backwards and the "b" inverted, yields the Latin phrase "tua sit," further proof that the lady belongs to him (2735-41).

That Tibaut was influenced by Guillaume de Lorris has long been recognized. Friedrich Stehlich, in the Introduction to his edition of the *Poire*, identifies a number of verbal echoes of the *Rose*;[5] Ernest Langlois, in the Introduction to his edition of the *Rose*, mentions several more.[6] Both texts are narrated in the first person and dedicated to the narrator's lady; both feature allegorical personifications of courtly virtues; both describe the birth of love. The *Poire* protagonist's encounter with Amors, in particular, is strongly reminiscent of the *querole* scene in the *Rose*. First the young hero meets a series of singing and dancing allegorical personifications (806 ff.); he then meets Amors, who is surrounded by songbirds and musicians, and wears a robe made of flowers (1,117 ff.). As in the *Rose*, Amors lectures his new vassal about the proper and improper comportment of lovers (1,234 ff.). Also as in the *Rose*, the young lover has a conversation with Lady Reason, who tries unsuccessfully to dissuade him from what she perceives as folly (2,016 ff.).

These similarities are clear and relatively straightforward, and serve to establish Tibaut's knowledge of the *Rose*. Langlois indeed states that the number of verbal echoes "donne l'impression que l'auteur de la *Poire* aurait pu réciter de mémoire la première partie du Roman de la Rose."[7] Given this close relationship, it would seem reasonable to suppose that Tibaut may have gotten more from the *Rose* than descriptive details, elements of plot, and a few elegant turns of phrase. A close reading of both texts reveals a more profound affinity, which suggests that the *Poire* can be understood as a response to the particular crystallization of poetic elements offered by the *Rose*. To demonstrate this, I will focus on the setting for Guillaume's *Rose*—the Garden, its inhabitants, and its Fountain of Narcissus—showing first how these textual figures serve to formulate a model of vernacular poetics, and then how this formulation is accepted and modified in the *Poire*.

*   *   *

Guillaume's allegorical Art of Love begins with the personifications of anti-courtly qualities represented on the wall surrounding the Garden of Delight. It is a commonplace of *Rose* criticism that this series of personifications is to be read in opposition to the characters of the *querole* scene inside the Garden.[8] The whole is in effect a visual representation of the *art d'aimer*, explicitly verbalized in Amors's instructions at the textual midpoint, where the same pattern of opposition between negative and positive qualities is followed. In addition to this didactic opposition is the contrast between the wall—an illuminated text that the dreamer must read before entering the Garden, with "maintes riches escritures" identifying the "ymages" and "pointures" appearing there (113-34)—and the intensely lyrical *querole*, a veritable theatrical performance of *fin'amors*. This contrast indicates the dreamer's growing involvement with the spectacle of the Garden, and also reflects a dichotomy inherent in courtly literature itself: its dual existence as text and performance. The dreamer's exploration of the Garden is his encounter with the idealized world of courtly literature, an encounter that involves reading, looking, listening, and ultimately participating. From this experience is produced a new courtly romance, the *Romance of the Rose*. This romance is explicitly a written text: the narrator states,

> Tote l'estoire veil parsuivre,
> ja ne m'est parece d'escrivre . . .
> (3,487-88)

At the same time, as Evelyn Vitz has stated, the development of the poem is characterized by "the increasing dominance of quotations (direct discourse) over narration as such: the romance takes on the quality of a dramatic dialogue."[9] Thus the new romance itself comprises both textual and theatrical qualities.

How has this aspect of the *Rose* been interpreted by the author of the *Poire*? Certainly, the Garden itself is almost totally lacking from Tibaut's text—the *vergier* where the pear tree incident occurs receives very little description, and is of minimal importance to the narrative as a whole. But the *Poire* does exemplify the textual qualities figured by the Garden. To be sure, the *Rose* itself draws on a set of conventions and expectations defined by the Old French courtly romance tradition, and available to Tibaut through numerous sources. Yet the compositional and structural principles operating in the *Poire* suggest that Tibaut's reception of this tradition is filtered through the lens of the *Rose*: that the *Poire* offers a response to its particular focusing of poetic issues.

As mentioned earlier, the *Poire* opens, after a short Prologue, with a progression of exemplary figures, juxtaposed in a non-narrative sequence. Each visual image, in MS *A*, is identified by its accompanying text: "Je sui le diex

d'amors" (21), "Je ai a non Fortune" (41), "Je sui Cliges li amoreus" (61),
etc. This set-up is reminiscent of the series of images on the Garden wall,
and has a similar structural position. In the *Rose*, the dreamer must walk
along the wall, studying all of its images, before gaining entrance to the
Garden. Similarly, the exemplary images at the opening of the *Poire* are the
necessary prelude to its narrative. It is here that the themes are presented;
here, that the narrator and his lady take their place among the famous lovers
of romance tradition. In the final speech of this section (264–83), the narrator
presents his lady with a book: their book, the romance of which they are the
subject. Only then, having laid the necessary groundwork, does the narrator
allow us to pass from the introductory section into the narrative itself.

The figures at the opening of the *Poire*, as opposed to those on the Garden
wall, represent positive rather than negative exempla. The lessons they offer,
however, do concern the dangers posed to lovers by the outside world. Each
offers himself and his *amie* as examples of true, loyal lovers, defined in
contrast to love's enemies, at whose hands they suffer. Tibaut has abandoned
Guillaume's careful separation of his characters into positive and negative
qualities, presenting an initial series of teachings in which both sides are
represented.

The *Poire* narrator's encounter with Amors's allegorical entourage parallels
Guillaume's *querole* scene; and just as the *querole* personages contrast with
those on the wall, so the vibrant lyricism of this passage in the *Poire* contrasts
with the romance tradition represented in the first section. If Guillaume's
didactic oppositions have been submerged in the *Poire*, it is in order to high-
light a different set of distinctions operant in both texts: the complex
dialectic between literature and experience, romance and lyric, text and
performance. In the *Poire*—with its lyricization of romance characters, its
use of sung refrains to create acrostics, its creation of a romance about
a specific individual, and its emphasis on both its oral and its written aspects
—Tibaut responds to Guillaume's codification of these central issues of
vernacular courtly poetry.

After the *querole* breaks up, the dreamer of the *Rose* comes upon the
Fountain of Narcissus. This important and complex passage continues to
exploit the textual processes identified above. Central to any reading of this
passage is an interpretation of the Fountain itself, with its "deux pierres de
cristal." Numerous critics have read the crystals as the eyes of the dreamer;[10]
others, following C. S. Lewis, have seen the crystals as the lady's eyes.[11] These
readings agree in seeing the crystals and their powers as a metaphor for the
psychological phenomenon of Love.[12]

A somewhat different reading of the crystals as a model for textual processes
operant in the *Rose* has been suggested by Michelle Freeman.[13] This interpretation takes into account the dynamics by which the crystals function: the
light of the sun is broken down into its primary colors and reconstituted in

the image of the Garden; the smallest details become visible, while the whole is reduced so as to appear completely within the tiny stones. These processes figure the rhetorical principles of articulation and *conjointure*, amplification and abbreviation. That only half the Garden is visible from any one vantage point suggests the two perspectives—those of narrator and protagonist— that the text offers on the central experience. According to this interpretation, the mirror provided by the crystals is the mirror the text holds up to reality. Lyric experience is broken down into its component parts, which are then reintegrated according to narrative patterns.

These readings of the crystals are not mutually exclusive; indeed, the complementary perspectives they offer can help to explain the intricate workings of the passage in question. Guillaume tells us that the crystals reproduce an exact image of the Garden. But what is the Garden itself, if not the elaboration of a literary *topos*, an artfully constructed *locus amoenus*? As focal point and image of the Garden, the crystals offer not so much a representation of the love experience, as a working model for the re-creation of this experience through conventionalized imagery and rhetorical figures.

If the *Poire* is to be understood as a response to the *Rose*, what has become of the fountain and its crystals? This crucial passage surely would not be ignored by any careful reader of the *Rose*. Imagery of fountain or mirrors is itself absent from the *Poire*, but Tibaut has reused the poetic possibilities of the crystals in a central feature of the *Poire*: the acrostics formed by the refrain initials. The similarities between the crystals and the acrostics begin, quite simply, with the basic function of each as a mirror. The crystals depict the Garden of Delight; more specifically, they offer an image of lover and beloved, and they inspire love in anyone who beholds them. The acrostics in turn spell out the names of lover and lady and the word "Amors": they too are a mirror for the love relationship, and their formation as messages is meant to ensure the permanent establishment of this love. The various truths that the narrator and his lady find expressed in the number and arrangement of letters and syllables in these names allows this three-word text to be truly a mirror of the larger text that contains it. In MS *A*, the acrostics mirror the text in a second manner as well: the initials forming them are historiated, and so provide a running visual representation of the narrative. The first acrostic —significantly, the one providing the name of the lady—is formed in the passage (806 ff.) that combines echoes of Guillaume's *querole* scene and of Amors's instructions to Amant. These in fact are the two passages framing the scene at the Fountain. The passage containing the first acrostic in the *Poire* can thus be seen as an abbreviated reworking of this entire section of the *Rose*. The scene with Fountain and Rose has been suppressed; but its narrative function—the young hero's unexpected and fateful vision of the love-object, shortly before he enters the service of Amors—is suggested by the image of the lady's name generated from the performance of Amors's entourage.

More important, the processes by which the acrostics are formed are analogous to those by which the crystals form their images. The acrostics emerge from the lyric passages of the *Poire*. To decipher them, the reader must first extract the initial letter of each refrain, then re-assemble these to form the new text. This process of fragmentation and reconstitution is that figured by the action of the crystals on sunlight: the processes of *translatio* and *junctura* by which new texts are formed out of old ones. The crystals in the Fountain are the tangible presence, in Guillaume's Garden, of previous texts: not only Chrétien's *Cligés*, but also Ovid's *Metamorphoses* and the Old French *Narcissus*, to name a few. And, through his experience of this dense textual locus, the dreamer himself becomes a participant in the romance world. What we witness, in effect, is the regenerative power of literary tradition. The careful reader, discovering an image of his own experience in the archetypes of courtly literature, synthesizes from various sources a new text of which he is both author and subject. This process is repeated, and rendered more explicit, in the use of popular refrains to create the highly personal text of Annes and Tibaut.

The specific manner in which this is accomplished in the *Poire*—i.e., through the use of lyric insertions—calls to mind a second highly influential text of the early thirteenth century: the other *Roman de la Rose ou de Guillaume de Dole*, by Jean Renart.[14] As has recently been shown by Norris Lacy, a major theme of this *Rose* is the imitation of courtly literary models by its characters.[15] The Emperor Conrad, listening to a romance recited by his resident minstrel, longs to live in a world populated by knights and ladies adhering to literary ideals. In particular, he wishes to be a romance hero himself, with an *amie* embodying all the traditional qualities. Upon hearing that Lïenor fits this description, he falls in love with her, and immediately sets in motion the negotiations for their betrothal and marriage. Later, he expresses his new-found role by singing appropriate selections from the currently popular corpus of courtly lyric. It is the appropriateness of these songs to their new context that Jean stresses in his Prologue:

> s'est avis a chascun et samble
> que cil qui a fet le romans
> qu'il trovast toz les moz des chans,
> si afierent a ceuls del conte.
>
> (26–29)

In other words, Jean is a good poet because he is a good reader. In the highly conventional and artificial language of these songs, he is able to discern the possibility of specificity: a certain moment in the experience of an individual. By exploiting this possibility, he creates both a new romance and a new understanding of these songs as expressions of emotion. Guillaume, on the other hand, portrays himself, as a textual persona, in an encounter with the motifs of courtly literature; this encounter too results in a new romance. Finally, Tibaut—through his own careful reading of both *Roses*—recognized this process at work and created a new text, in which a synthesis of key features of both sources served to make the entire process more explicit.

We must now turn to the issue raised earlier and deferred: the story of Narcissus. Although of central importance for the *Rose*, Narcissus is not even mentioned in the *Poire*. How does this affect our comparison of the two texts? To answer this question, let us first review Guillaume's presentation of the Narcissus story and its function within the text.

It is often said that in their reworking of the Narcissus story, medieval authors suppress the mythological elements of the story. Echo and Narcissus do not metamorphose, respectively, into a disembodied voice and a flower; they simply die. The *Rose* is no exception to this general rule. But is there not perhaps a suggestion of a different kind of metamorphosis? True, when the dreamer approaches the fateful fountain, he does not find the narcissus flower that would presumably have been left there. But he does find something quite interesting and, I believe, significant: a written text. As the narrator tells us:

> Dedenz une piere de mabre
> ot Nature par grant mestrise
> soz le pin la fontaine asise;
> si ot desus la pierre escrites
> el bort amont letres petites,
> qui disoient, ilec desus
> estoit morz li biau Narcisus.
> (1,430–36)

For the second time in the story, the dreamer reads a text before advancing to the next phase of the experience. This particular text, through the words "ilec desus," incorporates the surrounding area into its frame of reference. After reading the Garden wall, the dreamer entered the world of allegorical abstractions; here, he has entered the story of Narcissus, which he is warned not to repeat. It is upon discovery of this inscription that the modified version of the Narcissus story is recounted. This is not the first translation of the Narcissus story into French. At the time that the *Rose* was composed, the story of Narcissus already circulated in a French redaction of the twelfth century and, as motif, had received even further transformations in other vernacular texts.[16] Through its complex of associations, the Narcissus story evokes the dialectic between lyric and narrative poetry, and the regenerative power of the vernacular with regard to the Latin tradition. From his reading of, and meditation upon, the Narcissus story, the dreamer draws a lesson that he applies to his own experience, which allows him to modify the story in his reenactment of it. This reenactment is itself a rewriting: Guillaume's rewriting of the Narcissus story in the *Rose*.

To appreciate fully the importance of the inscription, we must read this passage in conjunction with a passage from the Ovidian text:[17]

> adstupet ipse sibi vultuque inmotus eodem
> haeret, ut e Pario formatum marmore signum . . .
> (*Met.* III, 418–19)

"Signum" here carries the sense of "statue," one of its standard meanings. The word, however, could also have the meaning of "sign" in a more general sense. The Ovidian Narcissus takes on the aspect of a marble statue or sign; the *Rose* protagonist finds a marble sign or inscription announcing Narcissus's death. There is thus a subtle suggestion, in Guillaume's reworking of the story, that his Narcissus was actually transformed not into the flower symbolizing his story, but into the text commemorating it. The story of Narcissus develops around the tension between the simultaneous identity and distinction of self and image of self. To resolve this tension, Narcissus must either extend his sense of self to include his image, or dissolve his sense of self entirely to become only the image. This latter possibility is suggested by the transformation of person into text. In the written word "Narcissus," the many "I's", "you's," and "he's" of Narcissus's impassioned discourse are at last united— but in a third-person, rather than a first-person, subject. Narcissus has become an artifact, one which does not merely refer to him, but actually is him, or all that is left of him.

How is this interpretation of Narcissus relevant to the *Rose*? The first-person narrative of the *Rose* creates a similar fragmentation of the self, the "I" of the narrative referring to both the present narrator and the past protagonist. The two personae are distinguished by the space of five years said to have elapsed between dream and narration (46). The use of preterite tenses for the narration, and of *passé composé*, present, and future for comments on the narrative act, serves further to distinguish these two roles. As the story progresses, there is an increased use of *passé composé* and present tenses for the narrative itself, suggesting that protagonist and narrator are becoming less distinct.[18] In the final lament with which the poem ends, preterites have disappeared entirely. Narrator and protagonist have become one and the same: the final transformation of Amant/Narcissus into the artifact/text.

It is interesting that the voice remaining at the end is not that of the narrator, but that of the dreamer. There is no conclusion in which the dreamer wakes up and writes the story down, so identifying himself with the narrator; nor is there an Epilogue in which the narrator leaves aside the dream world to speak once again of the lady to whom the text is dedicated. Rather, the resolution of the two "I's" is entirely within the textual world; it is as though the narrator has been swallowed up by his own text. It is this that gives the *Rose* its peculiar, unfinished quality. Vitz found this resolution of the two "I's" "odd."[19] Perhaps it will seem a little less odd if we understand it as an interpretation of Narcissus's transformation. Again, the resolution of self and image of self is entirely in favor of the image.

The crucial difference between Amant and Narcissus—the "correction" of Narcissism offered by the *Rose*—is of course the oft-mentioned fact that Amant does not fall in love with his own reflection, but with the Rose. Thus the doubling that takes place here is more complicated than that of Ovid's Narcissus. The attempts of Amant to possess the Rose are themselves the mirror of the narrator's attempts to impress the lady who "doit estre Rose clamee" (44). These two quests merge in the course of the narration, which —since the events prefigured by the dream presumably include the narrator's encounter with this lady—actually refers simultaneously to both. Neither quest is fully achieved: Amant remains cut off from the *Rose*, while the disappearance of the narrator as a separate persona suggests that he can never complete his message to the lady called Rose. The resolution of the two "I's" in the textual subject is paralleled by the conjoining of the two Roses in the title of the text: *Roman de la Rose*.[20] Just as the reconstitution of Narcissus's fragmented self-image is effected only in the creation of the sign, so the relationship between "I" and Rose is realized only in the textual artifact itself, as the relationship between subject and object of the discourse it embodies.

What, then, in the *Poire* corresponds to the Narcissus story in the *Rose*? Although Narcissus himself is absent, we do find another Ovidian story, that of Pyramus and Thisbe. Like the story of Narcissus, the story of Pyramus and Thisbe circulated as early as the twelfth century as an independent vernacular text; indeed, all three surviving manuscripts of the Old French *Piramus et Tisbé* also contain the *Narcissus*.[21] The story of Pyramus and Thisbe was also, of course, a frequent motif in courtly narrative.[22] We can thus assume that the figures of Narcissus and Pyramus, while not equivalent, may have been perceived in a somewhat similar light as prime examples of the vernacularization of Ovidian material. Moreover, the stories themselves represent two complementary poles of love poetry: the terrifying isolation of Narcissus, consumed with himself, and the perfect reciprocity of the love shared by Pyramus and Thisbe. Both *Poire* and *Rose*, then, offer a reading of an Ovidian subtext; but the texts in question have certain fundamental differences. Let us examine the role of Pyramus and Thisbe in the *Poire* to see just how their story operates within the text, and how it differs from the story of Narcissus as a poetic model.

The story of Pyramus and Thisbe as presented in the opening section of the *Poire* (161–80) is a lyric *complainte* in the present tense, in which Pyramus describes his attempts to communicate with Thisbe through the chink in the wall; this distinguishes his speech from those of Cligés, Tristan, and Paris. Cligés and Tristan both relate events in the preterite tense (the doctors' investigation of Fenice's feigned death; Mark's discovery of Tristan and Iseut in the Cave of Lovers). Both have thus become narrators of their own stories, and in so doing speak from some undetermined point outside the story itself.[23] The story of Paris is not even recounted by him at all, but is told in the third person, with Paris himself speaking only in the last three lines (238–40). Pyramus, however, speaks of an ongoing situation: he and Thisbe are even now imprisoned in the tower, sending words and kisses through the wall. Their story is not so much narrated as performed. This gives the story of Pyramus and Thisbe a sense of lyric immediacy equalled only by that of the *Poire* couple, who of course also speak in the present and *passé composé*: their story is only now unfolding.

A second feature links the presentation of the story of Pyramus and Thisbe with that of the *Poire* couple: these are the only figures of the opening section whose stories are continued in the later narrative. Moreover, Pyramus and Thisbe are the only figures of this section whose miniature in MS *A* depicts an event not referred to by the accompanying text. Like most of the illustrations in this part of the *Poire*, that for Pyramus and Thisbe consists of two scenes. The upper medallion shows Pyramus and Thisbe attempting to speak through the wall; the lower one shows their death.[24] The visual representation of their death scene—clearly something that cannot be recounted in the first person—reminds us that their story is in fact closed and circulates as a text independent of them. This death scene is narrated several hundred lines later (717–41); here, the tone is quite different. The narrator tells us that the story of Pyramus and Thisbe is from the Latin tradition, stressing its bookish quality. He introduces the tale as

> . . . l'essemple d'un jovencel
> Qui jadis fu en Babyloine,
> Si com la lestre nos tesmoine.
> (717–19)

Several lines later, he claims that the story of the mulberries' color-change is true,

> A tesmoig d'Ovide, .I. preudome,
> El quart livre de la grant somme.
> (736–37)

If we read the two Pyramus passages together, as we are encouraged to do by the illustration of both on a single page, we find that the story as a whole embodies the various oppositions identified earlier: lyric and narrative, performance and book, vernacular and Latin. As in the *Rose*, we have a model of the vernacularization of Latin material. Again, this process exploits the tension—a creative tension—between theatrical and textual aspects of both lyric and narrative compositions.

As I have said, the story of Pyramus and Thisbe already carried these associations through its circulation in both Latin and vernacular forms. The vernacular treatment of the story is quite different from the Latin text, in that the speeches of Pyramus and Thisbe are developed into long lyric *complaintes* and dialogues. The Old French *Piramus* itself thus comprises both lyric and narrative discourse and versification (octosyllabic couplets for the narrative, other forms for the monologues and dialogues), and—since direct discourse far outweighs narrative—lends itself to dramatic presentation. The *Piramus* offers an analogy for the *Poire*, with its use of different verse forms and its blend of lyric and narrative discourse. It seems likely that Tibaut's reading of the vernacularization of Pyramus and Thisbe was a source of inspiration for the *Poire*, just as Guillaume's reading of the vernacularization of Narcissus provided inspiration for the *Rose*.

Three aspects of the Pyramus and Thisbe story are stressed in the *Poire*: their attempts to communicate, the reciprocity of their love, and the miraculous transformation of the mulberry as a sign of this love. All three aspects are important for the story of the *Poire* as well. Much of the narrative of the *Poire* is devoted to the communication between the narrator and his lady, which is accomplished by means of the refrains, by the letter sent to the narrator from his lady, and by the nightingale he sends her. Also, the *Poire* itself is intended as the narrator's message to his lady, whereby he hopes to make his love known to her and elicit a favorable response. Communication between separated lovers, then, is a theme shared by both stories.

Related to this is the reciprocity of love represented in the story of Pyramus and Thisbe. This is most dramatically expressed in the double suicide, emphasized in the *Poire* account with the juxtaposition of the rhymes *ocis* and *ocise* (725, 727).[25] Throughout the story, though, both play an equally active role. Thisbe is far from the passive, distant ladies often depicted in courtly poetry. She arrives first at the proposed meeting place; in the *Metamorphoses*, it is she who prays that the mulberries, darkened with the blood of Pyramus, be an eternal monument to their love. In the Old French *Piramus*, Tisbé first discovers the wall crevice and proposes the furtive meeting outside the city. Similarly, the *Poire* lady repeatedly affirms her love for the narrator; she takes the initiative in dispatching messages to him, inviting him to join in the formation of the third acrostic, and requesting that he come read her the poem he has written for her. This contrasts markedly with the reception afforded Amant in the *Rose*: the response of his lady, as figured by the various allegorical personifications, is mixed and ambiguous. While certainly offering a modification of pure Ovidian Narcissism, the *Rose* still exploits the dynamic tension of a love which, if not entirely unrequited, is still uncon-summated. In the final lament, Amant's isolation, his inability to make contact with Bel Acueil or the Rose, does approach that of Narcissus. The *Poire*, however, celebrates mutual love.

The transformation of the mulberry receives considerable emphasis in the *Poire*, where it is recounted twice:[26]

> Li sans qui chut des plaies fors
> Del vallet et de la meschine
> A si bien teinte la racine
> Del morier qui sor els estoit,
> Que li fruiz blans qui s'aparoit,
> Des mores en devint toz noirs.
> (729–34)

> Li rain del morier et des mores
> Devindrent noires qui deslores
> Avoient esté totes blanches.
> (738–40)

The darkened mulberries are the monument to the love of Pyramus and Thisbe, and as such parallel the flower at the end of the Narcissus story. There is, however, an important difference. Narcissus himself became the flower; while the mulberry is an external sign created by Pyramus and Thisbe, and referential to them, but yet distinct from them.

In the story of Pyramus and Thisbe, the problematic relationship between self and image of self so crucial for Narcissus has been replaced by the rela-tionship between self and other. It is this that makes the story so different from that of Narcissus. For example, Narcissus laments that, although only a sheet of water separates him from the object of his love, he is unable to cross this barrier to touch the youth that he sees there or exchange words with him. Pyramus and Thisbe, on the other hand, are separated by a stone wall, yet find a way of sending words through it. As a couple, they represent a reciprocal, rather than a one-way, relationship. This same reciprocity is expressed in their relationship, as a couple, to the monument commemo-rating their love. Where Narcissus's body disappeared, their bodies (or rather their ashes) remain, united in a single vessel. Thus even in death, their physical existence continues, providing a tangible referent for the mulberry symbol.

This same reciprocal relationship between sign and referent is operant in the *Poire*. Unlike the *Rose*, it is a text which declares itself to be com-plete. It closes with an Epilogue in which the narrator states:

> Ci voudrai mon cuer arester.
> Ne voil pas matire emprunter
> Qui se descort de la premiere.
>   (2,978–80)

After a short diatribe against the *mesdisant*, he closes the text by dispatching it into the world as a finished product:

> Saches, tant com durra cist mondes
> Sera en boche et en memoire
> Toz jorz "Li Romanz de la Poire".
>   (3,021–23)

The *Poire* is thus presented as a text with distinct boundaries. The very establishment of these boundaries suggests the existence of an extra-textual world, in which the *Poire* will exist as an artifact and to which it will bear some relationship. And indeed the text does point to the existence of its protagonist couple as members of this world. The narrator's constant references to the process of poetic composition, and to his plan to have the finished romance read and shown to his lady, remind us that this "I" does not refer exclusively to a textual persona. It also corresponds to an extra-textual persona who creates the text and uses it for a specific purpose—someone who belongs not to the text, but to its context. The same thing is of course implied by the similar statements made by the *Rose* narrator, but the *Rose* narrator does not maintain his separate identity through to the end of the poem.

The identity of the *Poire* lady is equally intriguing. She contributes materially to the construction of the poem by providing one acrostic and part of another. The narrator, however, suggests that the lady of the text is in fact distinct from the "real" lady: the persona with whom he interacts and builds the acrostics is not actually this lady, but the "veraie semblance" (2,004, 2,255) that Amors conjures up in the lover's imagination. This persona, who becomes one of the voices of the text, is the image of the lady to whom the text will eventually be presented. This becomes most explicit in her final speech, in which she invites her lover to come and read the poem to her. Again, this statement refers outside the text itself to the context of its composition and performance, and reminds us that the couple within the text is to be understood as the image of the extra-textual couple of poet and audience.

CONCLUSION

The *Poire*, as a reading of the *Rose*, goes beyond the use of allegorical person-ifications and verbal echoes of descriptive passages, to a realization of the textuality figured by Guillaume's Garden. While movement between the poles of lyric and narrative, text and performance, vernacular and Latin is characteristic of Old French literature in general, contrast and conflation of these poles is made explicit in the *Rose*. Tibaut recognized in the *Rose* a model of vernacular poetics, which he used as the basis for his own text. In its format and structure—an enumeration of exemplary figures who serve as the vehicle for sermonizing about love and its enemies, a lyric celebration of love, textual creation of the images of lover and beloved—the *Poire* also imitates the format and arrangement of the Garden as a textual artifact.

Both *Poire* and *Rose*, through the use of first-person narrative discourse, present a dialectic between textuality and experience. The central action of both is the creation of a new text out of a synthesis of previous texts and personal experience. This process is handled somewhat differently, however, in the two texts. The *Rose* illustrates the transformation of the self into art. References to external context are eliminated as the *Rose* progresses; the textual artifact acquires a reality of its own, which subsumes that of its referent. There results the isolation of the textual world, and the impossibility of bridging the gap between textual and empirical realities. This is dramatized in the narrator's disappearance into the fictional "I"; he is unable to complete the poem and step back out of it. The sense of isolation and the impossibility of fulfillment are expressed, in narrative terms, in the unfulfilled desire of Amant for the eternally receding Rose.[27] The myth lying at the basis of this construct is that of Narcissus.

The *Poire*, on the other hand, illustrates the creation of a work of art that is the image for the self, but does not completely subsume the reality of its referent. The text consistently reminds us that it refers to some external context; both the narrator and his lady are able to complete the poem and step outside of it. In narrative terms, this is figured by the reciprocity of the love relationship. The central myth of this story—like that of Narcissus, one that offers a complex model for the vernacularization of Ovidian material—is that of Pyramus and Thisbe.

The unfinished quality of the *Rose* made it a text that invited completion by its readers. While the continuation by Jean de Meun is by far the most famous such response, there is at least one other anonymous continuation that also allows the dreamer to pluck the Rose and wake up.[28] The *Poire* is a different sort of response to the incompleteness of the *Rose*. By incorporating verbal echoes and poetic and structural principles of the *Rose* and handling these in a new manner, Tibaut proposes a solution to the literary problems raised by Guillaume's text and its Ovidian model.

NOTES

1. Guillaume de Lorris and Jean de Meun, *Le Roman de la Rose*, ed. Félix Lecoy, CFMA (Paris, 1973–75), 3 vol. All references will be to this

edition. Pierre-Yves Badel, in his recent study of the reception of the *Rose*, expresses this attitude: "Le *Roman de la Rose* a été longtemps reçu comme un tout et l'ensemble porté au credit de Jean de Meun. . . . Le succès de la continuation due à Jean de Meun a servi l'oeuvre de Guillaume de Lorris qui, sans son imposante suite, n'aurait pas eu un sort posthume beaucoup plus enviable que le *Roman de la Poire* de Thibaud." (*"Le Roman de la Rose" au quatorzième siècle: Etude de la réception de l'oeuvre*, Publications Romanes et Françaises, no. 153 [Geneva, 1980], p. 331.)

2. Messire Thibaut, *Li Romanz de la Poire*, ed. Friedrich Stehlich (Halle, 1881). A new edition by Christiane Marchello Nizia is forthcoming in the series SATF (Paris). For discussion of the *Poire* in the context of the courtly allegory exemplified by the *Rose*, see Marc-René Jung, *Etudes sur le poème allégorique en France au moyen âge*, Romanica helvetica, no. 82 (Bern, 1971), pp. 310–17; Arié Serper, "Thèmes et allégorie dans le 'Romaine de la Poire' de Thibaut," in Gaetano Macchiaroli and John Benjamins, eds., *Atti del XIV Congresso Internazionale di Linguistica e Filologia Romanza* (Naples, 1974), pp. 397–403.

3. There are two exceptions to this pattern: the first stanza of the piece spoken by Cligés (61–64) has sixteen-syllable lines, and the section "Jente de corps, simple de vis" (241–63) consists of octosyllabic verses arranged according to the rhyme scheme aabaab.

4. Because of the close relationship between text and illustration in this manuscript, and because the illustrations are virtually contemporary with the poem, I include them in my discussion of the *Poire*. For descriptions of the miniatures, see Stehlich, *Poire*, pp. 20–23. For discussion of the style and format of *Poire* MS *A*, see Robert Branner, *Manuscript Painting in Paris during the Reign of Saint Louis: A Study of Styles* (Berkeley, Los Angeles, London, 1977), pp. 102–7; Allison M. Stones, "Secular Manuscript Illumination in France," in Christopher Kleinhenz, ed., *Medieval Manuscripts and Textual Criticism*, University of North Carolina at Chapel Hill, Department of Romance Languages, Symposia 4, 1976, pp. 83–102.

5. Stehlich, *Poire*, pp. 9–10.

6. Ernest Langlois, ed., *Le Roman de la Rose*, Guillaume de Lorris and Jean de Meun, SATF (Paris, 1914), vol. I, pp. 6–8.

7. Ibid., p. 7.

8. For a discussion of the oppositions and pairings operating between the figures on the wall and those within the Garden, see Douglas Kelly, *Medieval Imagination: Rhetoric and the Poetry of Courtly Love* (Madison, Wis., 1978), pp. 58–84.

9. Evelyn B. Vitz, "The *I* of the *Roman de la Rose*," Genre 6 (1973):64.

10. See, for example, D. W. Robertson, *A Preface to Chaucer* (Princeton, 1962), p. 95; John Fleming, *The "Roman de la Rose": A Study in Allegory and Iconography* (Princeton, 1969), pp. 93 ff. For a general discussion of the various interpretations of the crystals, see Larry H. Hillman, "Another Look into the Mirror Perilous: The Role of the Crystals in the *Roman de la Rose*," Romania 101 (1980):225–38.

11. C. S. Lewis, *The Allegory of Love* (Oxford, 1936), pp. 125 ff.; Jean Frappier, "Variations sur le thème du miroir, de Bernart de Ventador à Maurice Scève," *Cahiers de l'Association Internationale des Etudes Françaises* 11 (May 1959):134–58; Erich Köhler, "Narcisse, la fontaine, et Guillaume de Lorris," *Journal des Savants*, April/June 1963, pp. 86–103.

12. In this light, see Daniel Poirion, "Narcisse et Pygmalion dans 'Le Roman de la Rose,'" in *Essays in Honor of Louis Francis Solano* (Chapel Hill, 1970), pp. 153–65. For Poirion the crystals do not represent eyes, but simply the magical qualities of love itself.

13. Michelle Freeman, "Problems in Romance Composition: Ovid, Chrétien de Troyes, and the *Romance of the Rose*," *Romance Philology* 30 (1976):158–68.

14. Jean Renart, *Le Roman de la Rose ou de Guillaume de Dole*, ed. Félix Lecoy, CFMA (Paris, 1962). On the relationship between this text and Guillaume's *Rose*, see Michel Zink, *Roman rose et rose rouge: "Le Roman de la Rose ou de Guillaume de Dole" de Jean Renart* (Paris, 1979).

15. Norris J. Lacy, "'Amer par oïr dire': *Guillaume de Dole* and the Drama of Language," *The French Review* 54 (1981):779–87.

16. *Narcisse: Conte ovidien français du XIIe siècle*, ed. Martine Thiry-Stassin and Madeleine Tyssens, Bibliothèque de la Faculté de Philosophie et Lettres de l'Université de Liège, fasc. 211 (Paris, 1976). See Frederick Goldin, *The Mirror of Narcissus in the Courtly Love Lyric* (Ithaca, 1967), for a discussion of various vernacularizations of the Narcissus story, including the *Rose*. Freeman, "Problems in Romance Composition," discusses the influence on Guillaume of Chrétien's reworking of the Narcissus story in *Perceval*.

17. Ovid, *Metamorphoses*, Loeb Classical Library (Cambridge, Mass., and London, 1971).

18. See Vitz, "*I* of the *Roman de la Rose*," for an analysis of the verb tenses used in the *Rose*.

19. Ibid., p. 64.

20. In this regard, see David F. Hult, "Vers la société de l'écriture: *Le Roman de la Rose*," *Poétique* 50 (1982):153–72.

21. *Piramus et Tisbé*, ed. C. de Boer, CFMA (Paris, 1921). On the manuscript tradition, see pp. iii–iv. On manuscripts of the *Narcissus*, see Thiry-Stassin and Tyssens, *Narcisse*, pp. 17–19.

22. See Foster E. Guyer, "The Influence of Ovid on Chrestien de Troyes," *Romanic Review* 12 (1921):97–134, 216–47; Cesare Segre, "Piramo e Tisbe nei Lai di Maria di Francia," in *Studi in onore di V. Lugli e D. Valeri* (Venice, 1961), vol. 2, pp. 845–53; Franz Schmitt-von Mühlenfels, *Pyramus und Thisbe: Rezeptionstypen eines Ovidischen Stoffes in Literatur, Kunst, und Musik* (Heidelberg, 1972).

23. Tristan in fact speaks of himself as one who has already entered literary tradition:

> Mes ge si sui Tristan   et ci m'amie Yseut
> Dont meinz biax moz dit an . . .
>
> (102–3)

24. This illustration has been published by the National Gallery of Ottawa, *Arts and Courts* (Ottawa, 1972), vol. 2, pl. 6.

25. It is interesting that two other couples of the *Poire* sequence are themselves "versions" of Pyramus and Thisbe in this respect: Cligés's reaction to the near death of Fenice, and the misunderstandings that result in the deaths of Tristan and Iseut in Thomas d'Angleterre's poem, are both reworkings of the Pyramus and Thisbe death scene. Indeed, Pyramus and Thisbe might seem a rather dangerous model of love—certainly one requiring modification if a happy ending is to be achieved. The poetic possibility of such modification is suggested in the *Poire* by the prominent presence of Cligés, whose story is an explicit avoidance of the fates of both Pyramus and Tristan.

26. In this way the *Poire* account parallels that of the Old French *Piramus*, where the color-change is also narrated twice in rapid succession (787–92).

27. For an interesting discussion of the implications of the eternally unfulfilled desire in the *Rose*, see Paul Verhuyck, "Guillaume de Lorris *ou* La Multiplication des cadres," *Neophilologus* 58 (1974):283–93.

28. See Langlois, *Rose*, pp. 3–4.

Vestiges of Paradise: The Tree of Life in Cursor Mundi and Malory's Morte D'Arthur

JAMES DEAN

I am concerned in this essay with identifying and briefly outlining a significant medieval tradition, with literary ramifications, which I shall term "vestiges of paradise." I refer to the interest expressed by medieval writers in objects that have their origin in the earthly paradise. This tradition achieved prominence in the Middle Ages chiefly through two legends, of Seth and of the Holy Grail, and through the cycle of Alexander romances. But vestiges of paradise appear in other guises as well, notably in the submerged form of relics such as the true cross, since the cross, according to legend, originated from a tree or trees once in paradise.[1] The vestiges tradition is an offshoot of what H. R. Patch in 1950 characterized as "Journeys to Paradise," an aspect of medieval concern with the "other world."[2]

Medieval writers drew a consistent moral from the various manifestations of the vestiges tradition. For although the fascination with relics from the earthly paradise was rooted in curiosity with the literal, physical site and its artifacts, the tradition suggests that the true means of access to paradise is not a physical but a moral or interior voyage, sometimes a visionary, anagogical glimpse, as in Seth's peek (*Cursor Mundi*) or Dante's dream. The vestiges are just that—traces, relics, shadows, simulacra. The wholeness of garden innocence has departed from the world, and its dream has become broken and fragmented. Medieval writers, especially after the twelfth century, took delight in mulling over the shards, so to speak, of that dream.

The context within which the vestiges of paradise tradition existed in medieval literature was another idea or topic, that of the world grown old (*senectus* or *senium mundi*).[3] According to this nearly universal medieval scheme, the world began to grow old like a man at the moment of Adam's fall, and it has continued to decline physically through six great historical ages because of mankind's increasing moral corruption.

In medieval historical and theological writings, man grew away from garden innocence, but he never forgot his origins. This concern for the archetypical world has been characterized as medieval nostalgia for paradise.

Medievalia et Humanistica, New Series, Number 13 (Paul Maurice Clogan, ed.). Rowman & Allanheld, Totowa, NJ. 1985.

In my judgment it was not nostalgia but curiosity that inspired so many medieval writers to dwell upon the return to paradise or upon objects that allegedly derived from Eden. In the literature of *curiositas*, as Christian Zacher has shown, medieval writers focused attention on the by-ways of pilgrimage—on the objects and human customs encountered along the pilgrimage routes.[4] Zacher makes the point that Mandeville was motivated by love for this world and its curiosities. I would add that many of the world's curiosities, as Mandeville understood them, are just those material objects and places in which the physical and metaphysical spheres, and past and present times, may be said to join. In Mandeville's *Travels*, the supernatural realm seems to hover just beyond the verge, and primitive historical events still exert influence on the present. Still, there is a disjunction between then and now. "Like the relics and shrines of the Holy Land or the peoples and creatures of the East," Donald Howard has written, "all things to be seen in the world [of Mandeville's *Travels*] bespeak a past age from which the world has declined."[5] By all medieval accounts, the terrestrial paradise is remote, but theologians and historians nonetheless thought it still existed, albeit in a far-off eastern site and perhaps, as in Dante, on an island mount, in mid-ocean, where it escaped the flood waters.[6]

Like other writers in the travelbook and related genres, Mandeville was especially concerned with holy shrines of the faith and with orient locales, where he reportedly encountered vestiges of paradise. Some of these vestiges may be traced back to the earthly paradise, while others seem to represent figures or tropes that recall the original garden in a vague way. Among the former are the Nile River, which Mandeville identifies as the paradisiacal Gyson (chapter 6);[7] Golgotha, where Adam's head was buried, having been recovered after Noah's flood (chapter 10); and the great Chan's chariot, which was constructed of wood from the terrestrial paradise (chapter 25). Among the tropological remembrances of Eden are the apple tree of Adam, an Egyptian species, which bears marks similar to bites on two sides of its trunk (chapter 7), and the "apples" of paradise (bananas) which, when cut open crosswise, disclose a tiny cross (chapter 7),[8] as if slicing these "apples" offers a lesson in botanical semiotics. There are other examples of vestiges in Mandeville, such as the "vale of Mambree" (chapter 9), or valley of tears, where Adam is said to have wept one hundred years for the murder of Abel by Cain; the field of Damascus, where God reportedly made Adam before transferring him to paradise (chapter 9); and a great lake in Ceylon, where Adam and Eve are said to have sorrowed for a hundred years after their exile from Eden (chapter 21).

Few medieval writers claimed to have visited the earthly paradise or even to have come near it; nevertheless, the original garden made its presence felt in medieval literature. It provided an item or topic for contemplation. Despite the obstacles to return—animals, deserts, huge mountains, a terrible darkness, waters rushing from a mountain's crest—Seth reportedly managed to locate paradise, in the first world age, though he did so with God's blessing; and Alexander sailed up the Ganges to the moss-covered walls, where he received an eye or stone that taught him a moral lesson about human limitation.[9] (Alexander's journey to paradise is by no means the only fabulous element in the Alexander cycle, and there appears to be a connection between his journey and these other wonders, such as the flight with griffons, the well of life, the talking trees of sun and moon, and the descent to the bottom of the sea.)[10] Moreover, according to medieval legend, Adam and Eve carried off a few artifacts from their first homeland. Skins from animals that browse along the "river of paradise" provide the border for Briseida's cloak in the *Roman de Troie.*[11] Occasionally wood, such as *lignum aloes*, spice-scented leaves, "fragrant apples," "grauel in þe grounde" (*Floris and Blancheflour*), or other material tumbles out of paradise born along on the rushing waters.[12] A tropological vestige or sign is the well of oil—fulfillment of Seth's quest for the oil of mercy—that gushes in Rome at Christ's birth in þe deuelis parlement, a fourteenth-century life of Christ from a satanic perspective.[13]

Mandeville represents the late medieval concern for vestiges in the travel-book genre, but the vestiges tradition appears often in imaginative literature as well. The remainder of this essay will focus upon two distinct though related examples of vestiges, the first in the early fourteenth-century anonymous verse chronicle, *Cursor Mundi,* and the second in Malory's *Le Morte Darthur* by way of the thirteenth-century *Queste del Saint Graal.* The vestiges are (a) the withered grass from Adam and Eve's footsteps as they left paradise, traces that Seth followed as he made his way back to the first garden; and (b) the three spindles, white, red, and green, from the tree of knowledge, discovered by Galahad on the ship of Faith.[14] In context of the world grown old, these vestiges suggest both what mankind has lost, and what remains behind. These vestiges and the two related legends through which they were transmitted are well known to medievalists, notably through the work of Patch and Quinn;[15] but their relation to the specific context of worldly decline is not so well known. My concern here is to set these legends in their proper context of worldly degeneration and to relate them to the larger context of the vestiges tradition.

I

The Seth legend receives special attention in the *Cursor Mundi.* The heading of leaf 9 of the Cotton MS reads "De fine Adae & oleo misericordiae."[16] In brief the story is as follows: When Adam was nine hundred years old, he became weary of his toiling, sorrowful life. He instructed his third-born son Seth to return to Eden to inquire of the guardian cherubim when Adam should die and to ask for the promised oil of mercy. Seth does as his father bids, following the withered tracks to paradise, and he learns that his father will die in three days. When Seth asks about the oil of mercy, the angel tells him to look into but not actually to enter paradise. Seth sees a vision or tableau representing Adam's fall and Christ's incarnation. Adam understands that he ultimately will achieve salvation and dies peacefully.

Seth reaches the terrestrial paradise by backtracking along the "fallow slough" produced by Adam and Eve as they quit Eden. The formerly green grass recoiled from Adam's tread, as if sorrowing with or shrinking from the first pair, and it never recovered its former hue. The footprints are important because they constitute the first tangible evidence of the world's decline after Adam's fault. Those vestiges point both outward toward the post-Edenic existence, the wide world, and back to the garden. If these traces could be located by postdiluvian men, they would provide testimony that the earthly paradise still existed, and that Adam and Eve took their solitary way out of it in such-and-such a place. For the author of *Cursor Mundi*, the important point is that Seth found the sere traces, the vestiges, and that he actually traversed the ground to the green gate. More than this, Seth also peered into Eden, although his body was not given access. His reasonable part, that is, could enter, as if in a dream or vision, but his fleshly part was denied since his body participated in the corruption resulting from the fall.

In his glimpse into Eden, Seth beholds the Eden familiar in hexaemeral literature—the garden, the spring from which gushes all the external world's water source—but also a barren tree: the dry tree associated with the tree of knowledge in medieval literature.[17] Seth reflects:

> O þe steppes vmthogt he þan
> þat welud war for sin of man;
> þat ilk schil did him to min
> þis tre was dri for adam sin.
> (1325–28)

This is the tree of knowledge, which has dried up like the grass outside Eden in token of original sin. The bare tree also discloses to Seth the entire course of salvation history, from Abel's dead body, in hell, at the tree's roots, to the infant Christ bouncing at its crown. It is an atemporal, anagogic vision, apprehended in time's "plenitude," which ratifies Seth's claim—or rather the claim made for him—to be patriarch of the city of God.

Seth carries away three pippins from the apple tree, as the tree of knowledge is now identified (1367–68), and plants them under Adam's tongue, from which pippins will grow cedar, cypress, and pine trees. These trees allegorically signify Father, Son, and Holy Ghost, respectively; and from them, or at least from one of them, the cypress, the cross shall be fashioned (cf. Mandeville, chap. 2). The progress of the pippins from seeds to saplings to trees, finally to a single tree in David's reign before it is cast into a pool in Solomon's time, forms the outline of the spindle legend that appears in Malory's *Morte Darthur.*

II

Malory's tale of three spindles on the ship of Faith is central in establishing Galahad as the true Christian knight and in preparing for Lancelot's relapse into sin with the queen. These vestiges, like the withered footsteps and the three pippins of the Seth legend, span historical ages, and we may understand them fully in context of the world grown old.

The tale of spindles in Malory constitutes an apparent digression within the interlaced, allegorical story of how Percival, Bors, and Galahad end up on the ship of Faith (Books XV–XVII), and specifically of how Galahad achieves the marvelous sword of Solomon (XVII. 3–7). Percival's sister, the daughter of Pellinore, relates the story of the spindles. When God banished Adam and Eve from paradise, she recounts, Eve carried out with her a bough from the tree of knowledge (XVII. 5).[18] This bough was especially green, and it reminded Eve of paradise, so she planted it as a token of her former blissful estate.[19] Because she was then a virgin, the plant grew up as a white tree. But she united sexually with Adam under the same white tree, and it turned green as a sign of God's blessing upon their fertility. When Cain slew Abel under the green tree, it turned red and its plants died, although the trunk thrived in its red hue. During Solomon's reign, Solomon's wife, identified as evil (XVII. 5),[20] asked a carpenter to manufacture a spindle from this tree. He at first demurred: " 'A, madam,' seyde he, 'thys ys the tre which oure firste modir planted' " (XVII. 6). Eventually Solomon's wife caused three spindles to be made from the three trees (which were yet one tree), of the three colors, and she attached them to the canopy of the bed that rested in the ship of Faith.

Perhaps unwittingly Malory creates from the number of spindles a theological mystery (three from one). Malory was probably unacquainted with the versions of the holy rood legend in which David cast the three rods of cypress, cedar, and pine into a pool, whence they grew together to form a single tree from which the cross was later fashioned.[21] In the *Queste del Saint Graal* the different colored spindles originate from offshoot twigs planted by Eve during the three states of the tree's existence. At the time of the spindles' manufacture, the main tree was red and, as in Malory, it dripped blood when cut into by the carpenters. Smaller trees, white and green, provided the wood for the other spindles. In his reduction of the *Queste* story, Malory neglects to mention the derivative trees, an omission that imparts to his version a quality either of mystery or confusion.[22]

The spindles are especially appropriate in conjunction with the bed because of their association with women and with the punishments consequent upon the fall. In the grail portion of the *Morte Darthur*, individual women are either wholly good, as is Percival's sister, or utterly evil, as is the gentlewoman whom Bors should love or else slay Launcelot (XVI. 11). Solomon's wife is wicked, although her handiwork, the spindles, find their way onto the ship of Faith as symbolic ornamentation. They remain in that ship as a twofold reminder: both as a remembrance of paradise—what mankind once was—and as a memorial, almost a *memento mori*, of the penalties of Eve, which include spinning. The distaff or spindle was a powerful iconographic emblem of fallen womanhood throughout the Middle Ages.[23] The spindle evokes woman's loss of the blissful, a-technic life to which Christ alludes in the sermon on the mount when he says: "Consider the lilies of the field, how they grow: they labour not, neither do they spin. But I say to you, that not even Solomon in all his glory was arrayed as one of these" (Matt. 6:28-29; Rheims). The three spindles, white, green, and red, represent the clerical history of womanhood in little, from her innocence, to her sexual experience, to her later fallen estate (women such as Solomon's wife). All of this is embodied atop the canopy of the bed on the ship of Faith, a ship that recognizes women in some way, but that subtly indicts them in the process. Were it not for sinful Eve, these spindles suggest, mankind might enjoy the whole tree rather than particolored man-made products of that tree.

Two further points should be made concerning the bed and its fittings. First, recent students of Malory and of Malory's source for his grail sequence, the *Queste del Saint Graal*, have tended to understand the bed on Solomon's ship as something other than a bed. Yet, considered as an historical object, the bed, which Pauphilet, Locke, and Quinn have glossed as a prefiguration of the cross, contains an unmistakable erotic element. This erotic component of the ship and of the grail sequence should not be ignored or minimized. It may on some level symbolize the cross, but it is primarily a bed with magical or semi-magical properties, with rich appointments, and it enhances the atmosphere of mystery in the grail section, which must be appraised as a chivalric romance as well as a doctrinal allegory. Inspiration for the bed, after all, comes from the same woman who, we are told, often outwits her proverbially wise husband and who in general causes trouble for him. Like the withered imprints and the spindles on the bed's canopy, the bed evokes the loss of paradise and particularly woman's emotional role in that loss. The second point, related to the first, is that Malory translates the *Queste*'s words *fuissel* or *fuissiax* as "spyndle" or "spyndles."[24] The Middle French word, which derives from Latin *fusus* (spindle), can mean "wand," "rod," "small piece of wood" (cf. *baguette*), "post," or "bedpost" as well as spindle. The bed fittings might make better sense as posts or rods, and one translator of the *Queste* renders them as "posts."[25] In Langland's garden of Charity passage from *Piers Plowman* the equivalent objects become "thre pyles" (B. xv. 23), or "shides" or "plaunkes"—all "of o lengthe, / And of o kynne colour · and o kynde" (C. xix. 20-21)—which underprop the tree and preserve it from the

three temptations.[26] But Malory insists on spindles, objects intimately identified with medieval womanhood and woman's fall.

In Malory the spindles harmonize decorously with the congeries of images
and symbols that recur in Malory's grail section. For if the spindles should
be understood in context of the world grown old, as I think they should, they
also belong with the images of the pelican, of diseased old age restored to
youth (Galahad manifests, as has been said, "a theology of health"),[27] of
the waste land (trope for the world grown old),[28] and of the sangreal itself,
which has healing, restorative properties as well as "goostli" Christian powers
(as the transubstantiated bread and wine). The marvelous sword, which also
harks back to Solomon, is associated with Balin's "dolorous stroke" (Book II),
with the maimed king, and with the waste land. R. S. Loomis allegorically
interprets the symbolism of the whole sequence in the *Queste del Saint Grael*
as the Old Testament (the ship, with spindles), which is replaced by the
New Testament and the cross, which was made from the same wood as the
spindles.[29] In this section of Malory's *Morte Darthur* the world appears as
a vast moral landscape where everything depends upon virtuous thought and
conduct. It is no longer sufficient, as Launcelot learns to his sorrow, to be the
best knight of arms. Now the race goes to two virgins and a chaste knight
(cf. XVII. 2).

The actions of the three triumphant knights in Malory's grail books occur
in a broad context of history and of the world grown old.[30] Malory omits an
explanatory passage from the *Queste* that associates the much-traveled tree
with the world's aging after the flood. But the omitted passage offers a
perspective on the theory of history in the *Queste*, a theory which also stands
behind Malory's grail narrative. The *Queste* reads:

> De cel Arbre vit len encore une autre merveille avenir. Car quant Nostre
> Sires ot envoié en terre le deluge, par quoi li mondes, qui tant estoit mauvés,
> fu periz, et li fruit de terre et les forez et li gaaignaige l'orent si chierement
> comparé que puis ne porent avoir si bone savor come il avoient devant, ainz
> furent adont toutes choses tornees en amertume; mes de cels arbres qui de
> celui de Vie estoient descendu ne pot len veoir nul signe qu'il fussent empirié
> de savor ne de fruit ne changié de la color qu'il avoient devant.[31]

> (Concerning this tree yet another miracle occurred. For when Our
> Lord had sent the flood in order to destroy the world, which was so
> evil, the earth's fruits, the forests, and the pasturelands paid for it
> dearly in that they no longer have the same good savor they had
> before, but all things were thus turned to bitterness. Yet the trees
> that descended from the tree of Life gave no indication that they
> were spoiled in savor or fruit or altered in the color that they possessed
> before.)

It was a doctrinal commonplace, here transmitted, that after the deluge the
earth never regained its pre-flood robustness, with the result that man,

originally a vegetarian, became a carnivore. The "twilight" of the first world age, the age of Adam, Cain, Seth, and Noah, terminated with an act of God that, except for God's initial curse on the earth (Gen. 3:17–19), aged the world to more devastating effect than ever afterward.[32]

The spindles have witnessed much in their long existence, including the fall, the first sexual union of Adam and Eve, the slaying of Abel by Cain, the construction of the ship of Faith, and the search for the sangreal. Those events span the six ages. Cain's fratricide is especially significant here since Cain, patriarch of the city of man in medieval historiography, set the pattern of sibling rivalry and fratricide for all of human history.[33] In Malory's Arthurian chronicle Cain provides the archetype for treachery and familial strife that runs its course through the *Morte Darthur*, from Balin, who kills and is killed by his brother Balin, to Launcelot, who finally slays Gareth and Gaheris, sworn brothers of the Round Table and brothers of the man whom Launcelot loves best.

The most egregious treachery in the *Morte*, however, and the treachery that best illustrates the world grown old, is Launcelot's betrayal of Arthur in his love affair with Guinevere. His failure to confess this sinful, long-lived affair prevents Launcelot from achieving the sangreal. And the issue of Launcelot's fidelity to his king and queen ultimately splits apart the fellowship of the Round Table (cf. XX. 17). We understand Galahad's perfection in part through his father's imperfection. Hence, when Galahad views the spindles on the bed's canopy, he beholds vestiges of paradise that at once affirm his own innocence and indict his father's treachery and lust. This is not Galahad's knowledge, of course; it is ours. It is knowledge achieved by readers of Malory's narrative, who interpret the story of Solomon and the spindles in context of Cain, Galahad, and Launcelot.

Corroboration of this reading occurs at the opening of Book XVIII when Launcelot, despite warnings in the grail section and despite his vows, returns to Guinevere. Indeed, the affair's sinful intensity seems to deepen:

Than, as the booke seyth, sir Launcelot began to resorte unto quene Gwenivere agayne and forgate the promyse and the perfeccion that he made in the queste; for, as the book seyth, had nat sir Launcelot bene in his prevy thoughtes and in hys myndis so sette inwardly to the quene as he was in semynge outewarde to God, there had no knyght passed hym in the queste of the Sankgreall. But ever his thoughtis prevyly were on the quene, and so they loved togydirs more hotter than they ded toforehonde. [XVIII. 1]

From the perspective of the grail quest, Launcelot is an emblem of moral and ethical failure—morally culpable in his adultery, ethically blameworthy in his treachery to king and Round Table bretheren. In his weakness, especially in his defective loving, can be seen the world's old age. Malory is explicit about this at the close of Book XVIII in the famous chapter entitled, in Caxton, "How true love is likened to summer." Love in earlier days, according to Malory (and other *romanciers,* such as Chrétien and Gottfried), was true and virtuous. Mankind in general was more patient than in later ages; that is, he subsisted in "vertuous suffraunce" and accepted his lot ungrudgingly. Now the winter of sexual discontent and newfangleness overwhelms the trothful summer of stability: "But nowadayes men cannat love sevennyght but they muste have all their desyres. That love may nat endure by reson, for where they bethe sone accorded and hasty, heete sone keelyth. And ryght so faryth the love nowadayes, sone hote sone colde. Thys ys no stabylyte. But the olde love was nat so" (XVIII.25).

If Launcelot and the events surrounding him suggest the story of Cain and Abel, though not systematically, Galahad and the events surrounding him recall the Seth legend. In Malory, and even more in Malory's source, the *Queste,* Galahad's search for the grail recapitulates, and fulfills, Seth's quest for the oil of mercy in the first world age. Both questers seek objects that at first seem to be physical—oil and grail—but that turn out to be metaphysical. The "oil" is in fact the redemption, while the "grail" is, in the *Queste* and Malory, Christ's blood or the transubstantiated communion wafer (*sang + real*). Each quest involves a journey back to a sacred time with its holy places and objects. Both Seth and Galahad are abstract, spiritual figures whom we come to know but dimly in their respective stories. They are aloof and singleminded in their quests. Individual pathos does not intrude upon their legends so that we may the better focus on the meaning of their journeys.[34]

Malory's story of the three spindles and the tree of knowledge, as I hope this analysis has demonstrated, is not a digression as much as it is an explanation. The ship of Faith, with its numinous cargo of the sword with strange girdles and the bed with spindles, mysteriously appears to clarify the path to the sangreal. The tale of the spindles reaches back to the world's earliest times. Yet the implications of that tale remain fresh for the grail pilgrims Galahad, Percival, and Bors. For those vestiges at once guarantee the significance of their quest and provide signs or emblems of mankind's failure, alluding as they do to the fall, the original fratricide, and the power of women to deflect knights from the true way. (The chivalric way and its chief spokesman, Launcelot, ultimately prove to be inadequate in the *Morte.*)[35]

From spindles to tree of several colors to pippins to withered footsteps and finally to the green gate itself: that is one route, an imaginative, literary path, back to the terrestrial paradise. The vestiges we have examined in this essay serve a double function in their settings. They indicate where mankind began his earthly voyage, a happy function. They also show the estate to which man has fallen. For the vestiges of paradise by their nature and by the portrayals of them in medieval literature offer testimony as to what man has forfeited and how this experience in the world differs from Adam's once-blessed condition. Along with foreshadowing the redemption, the point of the Seth legend is that man will never return to paradise by physical, earthly means. In late medieval literature, especially English historical and chronicle narratives, curiosity about the world and its primitive history existed side by side with a renewed sense that the world had grown old, that it had diverged to the uttermost from garden innocence. But nowadays, according to these writings, in this wretched world, in the sixth world age, we are left with only the withered imprints and carved spindles as tokens of a better time, a more fortunate place.

NOTES

1. See the terse summary of the Seth legend and the development of the tree of knowledge into the cross by the thirteenth-century Paris theologian Jean Beleth in *Rationale divinorum officiorum*, 152, in J.-P. Migne, ed., *Patrologia latina* (hereafter *PL*) 202:153. In a three-part article, M. M. Lascelles has demonstrated some relationships between the Alexander legend and legends of the holy rood: "Alexander and the Earthly Paradise in Mediaeval English Writings," *Medium Aevum* 5 (1936):31–47, 79–104, 173–88.

2. Howard Rollin Patch, *The Other World According to Descriptions in Medieval Literature* (Cambridge: Harvard University Press, 1950), pp. 134 ff.

3. I have studied this idea in my unpublished doctoral thesis "The World Grows Old" (Baltimore: The Johns Hopkins University, 1971), and in "The World Grown Old and Genesis in Middle English Historical Writings," *Speculum* 57 (1982):548–68. E. R. Curtius understands the idea as a rhetorical topos, the *"senectus-topos"*: see *European Literature and the Latin Middle Ages*, trans. Willard R. Trask (1948; rpt. New York: Harper, 1963), Index, s.v. "Topics," and p. 28. For the relation of this topic to the six world ages, see Roderich Schmidt, *"Aetates mundi*: Die Weltalter als Gliederungsprinzip der Geschichte," *Zeitschrift für Kirchengeschichte* 66 (1955–56):288–317; and Auguste Luneau, *L'histoire du salut chez les Pères de l'Eglise* (Paris: Beauchesne, 1964).

4. *Curiosity and Pilgrimage* (Baltimore: Johns Hopkins University Press, 1976), esp pp. 130 ff.

5. "The World of Mandeville's *Travels*," *Yearbook of English Studies* 1 (1971):15. Of the wonders and curiosities in Mandeville Howard remarks: "Anything is possible, he makes us feel." *Writers and Pilgrims* (Berkeley: University of California Press, 1980), p. 64.

6. Patch has collected medieval testimony as to the physical features of the earthly paradise. See his comments on the Venerable Bede, Rabanus Maurus, Godfrey of Viterbo, Peter Lombard, Alexander Neckham, St. Thomas Aquinas, and Ranulf Higden in *The Other World*, pp. 145, 146, 151–52.

7. References to Mandeville are to *Travels*, ed. M. C. Seymour (Oxford: Clarendon, 1967), cited by chapter number in the text.

8. Zacher notes the alleged roundness of the "apples of paradise" and links this roundness with Mandeville's concern for spherical shapes as emblems of the fallen world: *Curiosity and Pilgrimage*, pp. 134–35.

9. A story first narrated in the Babylonian Talmud. See *Tamid*, chap. 4, trans. Maurice Simon, in *The Babylonian Talmud*, Part I, ed. Isidore Epstein (London: The Socino Press, 1960), 6:28–29. The three chief later medieval versions of this story are the *Iter Alexandri Magni ad Paradisum* (twelfth century), *Voyage d'Alexandre au paradis terrestre* (thirteenth century), an interpolation in the Alexandre de Paris version of the *Roman d'Alexandre*, and an interpolated story in certain manuscripts of the *Fait des Romains* (1213 or 1214). These texts have been conveniently gathered and edited by Lawton P. G. Peckham and Milan S. La Du, in *Elliott Monographs in Romance Languages and Literature* 35 (Princeton: Princeton University Press, 1935). This legend does not appear in the English Alexander romances, except in Sir Gilbert Hay's *Buik of Kyng Alexander the Conqueror*, a Scottish poem of the sixteenth century that, to my knowledge, has yet to be printed in its entirety. See the relevant extracts of it published by Lascelles in "Alexander and the Earthly Paradise," pp. 87–95, 179. For summaries and bibliographies of the Alexander tradition, see George Cary, *The Medieval Alexander*, ed. D. J. A. Ross (Cambridge: Cambridge University Press, 1956); and R. M. Lumiansky, "Legends of Alexander the Great," in *A Manual of the Writings in Middle English 1050–1500*, ed. J. Burke Severs (New Haven: Connecticut Academy of Arts & Sciences, 1967), pp. 104–13, 268–73.

10. These fabulous elements of the Alexander legend derive from the Pseudo-Callisthenes. See Patch, *The Other World*, pp. 24–25 (flight); 157, 163 (well); 158–59 (trees). In medieval English Alexander romances, the most persistent fabulous legend is that of the oracular trees of sun and moon. See *Kyng Alisaunder*, lines 6738 ff. [B Text], ed. G. V. Smithers, EETS, OS 227 (London: Oxford University Press, 1952), pp. 359 ff., and Smithers' note to "Arbre sek," the dry tree, in Volume 2, EETS, OS 237 (London: Oxford, 1957), pp. 146–47; *Alexander and Dindimus*, ed. Walter W. Skeat, EETS, ES 31 (London: Trübner, 1878), pp. 5–6, lines 111–36; *The Prose Life of Alexander*, ed. J. S. Westlake, EETS, OS 143 (London: Kegan Paul, 1913), pp. 92 ff.; and Mandeville's *Travels*, ed. Seymour, chaps. 8, 30, 32. For Alexander's descent to the bottom of the ocean see *The Prose Life of Alexander*, ed. Westlake, p. 106; and Cary, *The Medieval Alexander*, pp. 31, 237–38, 340–41, and Plate VII.

11. The animals do not actually come from the earthly paradise, for they are captured by men. Nonetheless, their proximity to the archetypical garden make them beasts of rare value. See Gretchen Mieszkowski, "R. K. Gordon and the *Troilus and Criseyde* Story," *Chaucer Review* 15 (1980):129. Cf. the legend about elephants, paradise, and the mandragora tree in *The Bestiary*, ed. T. H. White (1954; rpt. New York, 1960), pp. 25–26.

12. For the *lignum aloes* see Mandeville's *Travels*, chap. 23. Mandeville doubtless had in mind the aromatic wood Agalloch rather than the bitter drug *lignaloes* (bitter aloes) when he speaks of *lignum aloes*. The Agalloch tree, which grows in tropical Asia, produces a fragrant resin and is mentioned in the Song of Songs as an aspect of the enclosed garden (medieval trope for the earthly paradise): see 4:14–15. Patch mentions "fragrant apples" borne down from the earthly paradise on the four streams Tigris, Geon, Phison, and Euphrates, according to the twelfth-century *Account of Elysaeus*. These apples cause mortals to lose interest in food and drink, and they have medicinal virtues (*The Other World* p. 149). For the "grauel" on the bottom of the river from paradise (identified as the Euphrates in the French version), see *Floris and Blauncheflour*, ed. A. B. Taylor (Oxford: Clarendon, 1927), p. 50.

13. In *Hymns to the Virgin & Christ*, ed. Frederick J. Furnivall, EETS, OS 24 (1868; rpt. New York: Greenwood Press, 1969), pp. 44–45, lines 97–128. I am indebted to Rossell Hope Robbins for this reference.

14. Esther Casier Quinn has investigated the relationships between the Seth legend and the episode of Solomon's ship in Malory: "The Quest of Seth, Solomon's Ship and the Grail," *Traditio* 21 (1965):185–222. Quinn is particularly interested in tracing the development of the holy rood tradition to the *Queste del Saint Graal*.

15. Patch, *The Other World*; Quinn, *The Quest of Seth for the Oil of Life* (Chicago: University of Chicago Press, 1962). I am heavily indebted to these works.

16. Citations from *Cursor Mundi* are to the Cotton Vespasian, A. iii. version edited by Richard Morris, EETS, OS 57 (London: Trübner, 1874).

17. Cf. also the version of the Seth legend in *þe Holy Rode* (Ashmolean MS 43, Bodleian Library, Oxford), lines 73–74, in *Legends of the Holy Rood*, ed. Richard Morris, EETS, OS 46 (London: Trübner, 1871), p. 24. The dry tree is a significant and widespread motif in medieval literature. See R. J. Peebles, "The Dry Tree: Symbol of Death," in *Vassar Mediaeval Studies*, ed. C. F. Fiske (New Haven: Yale University Press, 1923), pp. 57–79.

18. Citations to Malory, by Caxton's book and chapter numbers, are from *The Works of Sir Thomas Malory*, ed. Eugene Vinaver, 2nd ed. (New York: Oxford, 1967).

19. Quinn emphasizes the importance of Eve, as opposed to Seth, in the *Queste* version of the Seth legend and the prominent role accorded Abel. See "The Quest of Seth," pp. 190–92. Quinn accounts for the difference between the Seth/pippins legend versus the Eve/branch story as a difference of time and place: "The *Queste* author changed a conventional pattern into one more meaningful to a thirteenth-century Christian and more effective in terms of the design of his work" (p. 192).

20. Quinn, "The Quest of Seth," pp. 192 ff., downplays this aspect of Solomon's wife (see p. 200 note 51). Contrast Charlotte C. Morse, *The Pattern of Judgment in the Queste and Cleanness* (Columbia: University of Missouri, 1978), who characterizes Solomon's wife as "treacherous"

(p. 72); and Fredrick W. Locke, *The Quest for the Holy Grail* (Stanford: Stanford University Press, 1960), pp. 76–77.

21. For the holy rood legend see, e.g., *La pénitence d'Adam*, in *The Penitence of Adam*, ed. E. C. Quinn (University, Miss.: Romance Monographs, 1980): "et trop fu grans mervelle que li cedres et li cypres et li pins se tindrent tout ensamble" (p. 123); and *þe Holy Rode*, lines 121 ff. [Vernon MS], and *The Story of the Holy Rood*, lines 545–50, in *Legends of the Holy Rood*, ed. Morris, pp. 29 and 77, respectively. Cf. also the three trees, which appear to be one, in the dream of the King of Sarras, in *Joseph of Aramathie* [14th cent.], ed. W. W. Skeat, EETS, OS 44 (London: Trübner, 1871), p. 7, lines 181 ff.

22. Cf. Albert Pauphilet's analysis of similar difficulties in the *Queste: Études sur la Queste del Saint Graal* (Paris: Champion, 1968), pp. 148–49.

23. The phrase *spinel-healf* was the OE equivalent of "distaff side," as in a diplomatic text cited by Bosworth and Toller, *Anglo-Saxon Dictionary* (s.v. "Spinelhealf"): "Min yldra faeder haefde gecweden his land on ða sperehealfe, naes on ða spinlhealfe." Chaucer's Wife of Bath speaks of woman's birthright as spinning (see III. 401–2, Robinson's 2nd ed.). See also "Whan adam delf & eue span," in *Religious Lyrics of the XIVth Century*, ed. Carleton Brown and G. V. Smithers (Oxford: Clarendon, 1957), p. 96. For the political application of this concept, see Edith Rickert, *Chaucer's World*, ed. Clair C. Olson and Martin M. Crow (New York: Columbia University Press, 1948), p. 361; and Philip Lindsay and Reg Groves, *The Peasants' Revolt, 1381* (London: Hutchinson, 1947), frontispiece and p. 100. For iconographic portrayals of the motif, see Andrée Mazure, *Le thème d'Adam et Eve dans l'art* (Paris: Mazenod, 1967), p. 145.

24. *La Queste del Saint Graal*, ed. Albert Pauphilet (Paris: Champion, 1923), p. 224. In the holy rood tradition the three trees are identified as *verges*, rods, wands, or switches, as in *La pénitence d'Adam*, ed. Quinn, p. 86; or as in the "Life of Adam" transcribed by Pauphilet in his Appendix to *Études sur la Queste del Saint Graal*, pp. 199, 200; as *ȝerden*, as in "þe Holy Rode," lines 98 ff., in *Legends of the Holy Rood*, ed. Morris, p. 26; or as in "Canticum de creatione," lines 967, 976; and "þe lyff of Adam and Eue," in *Sammlung altenglischer Legenden*, ed. C. Horstmann (Heilbronn: Henninger, 1878), pp. 136 and 226 respectively; as *wandes*, as in "The Story of the Holy Rood," in *Legends*, ed. Morris, p. 72 lines 378 ff.; as *springes* or *braunches*, as in Herry Lonelich's fifteenth-century translation of the *Queste: The History of the Holy Grail*, ed. F. J. Furnivall, EETS, ES 24 (London: Trübner, 1875), pp. 397, 398; or as *piles*, "props," as in *Piers Plowman* (see below note 26).

25. *The Quest of the Holy Grail*, trans. P. M. Matarasso (Baltimore: Penguin Books, 1969), p. 233.

26. *Piers Plowman*, ed. W. W. Skeat (1886; rpt. Oxford: Oxford University Press, 1924), 1:478, 479.

27. Jerome F. O'Malley, "Sir Galahad: Malory's Healthy Hero," *Annuale Mediaevale* 20 (1981):33.

28. See Locke, *The Quest for the Holy Grail*: "Eve's sin turned the Garden into a Wasteland and handed over her children into the *baillie* of the Enemy" (p. 74).
29. *The Development of Arthurian Romance* (New York: Harper, 1963), p. 105.
30. Cf. Mark Lambert's comments on Malory's sense of the past: *Malory: Style and Vision in Le Morte Darthur* (New Haven: Yale University Press, 1975), pp. 125 ff., esp. pp. 130–35.
31. *La Queste del Saint Graal*, ed. Pauphilet, pp. 219–20. Translation mine.
32. See my "The World Grown Old and Genesis in Middle English Historical Writings," p. 563 and note 45.
33. Morse has emphasized similar patterns, in *The Pattern of Judgment in the Queste and Cleanness*, esp. pp. 95 ff. Though we may acknowledge the importance of the past and history in the *Queste* and the *Morte Darthur*, we need not subscribe to Morse's conclusion that the grail search is "a quest for the meaning of history" (p. 68).
34. On the other hand Eve, in the *Queste*, regards the branch or twig she carries out with her as an emblem of her former blessedness and of the promise of return (ed. Pauphilet, p. 212).
35. See Larry D. Benson, *Malory's Morte Darthur* (Cambridge: Harvard University Press, 1976), pp. 213–22.

The London Studia in the Fourteenth Century

WILLIAM J. COURTENAY

To one familiar with patterns of education on the Continent in the fourteenth century, where major centers of population such as Paris, Bologna, Naples, Cologne, Prague, and Vienna developed universities, it is surprising that higher education in England was confined to Oxford and Cambridge, and that the metropolitan area of London did not develop a similar institution. At a time in which the demographic, commercial, and political pre-eminence of London was beginning to dominate the physical and mental landscape of southern England, a time in which art and architecture as well as literary works were stimulated through royal patronage flowing from Westminster, one might expect a similar centralization or metropolitization of higher education and learning to have taken place. And yet London did not possess a university until the nineteenth century. In the high and late Middle Ages London had no corporation of masters or students, no faculties, no nations, no rector, no solemn congregation, no papal or royal letters of protection, no statutes, no seal; in fact, no features of internal organization or external recognition that characterize a *studium generale* in the proper sense. Consequently, historians of English higher education in the Middle Ages have ignored London and have concentrated their attention on Oxford and Cambridge.

Yet to define higher education in the late Middle Ages solely in terms of universities, or to treat universities in isolation from other types and centers of education, distorts the picture of learning in that age. London is a case in point. If one puts aside the legal, constitutional, and ceremonial aspects of the medieval university and looks only at the availability, character, and quality of intellectual life and teaching, then London was a major center of higher education in fourteenth-century England—one that bridged the worlds of learning and letters and exemplified the wider context of university education.

In retrospect, London was initially a good candidate for university status. Already by the twelfth century it possessed many of the characteristics that elsewhere (for instance, Paris) contributed ultimately to the emergence of a university. It had a sizable and enthusiastic body of students engaged in sophistical disputations, as Fitz-Stephen reveals.[1] It had a cathedral school in

Medievalia et Humanistica, New Series, Number 13 (Paul Maurice Clogan, ed.). Rowman & Allanheld, Totowa, NJ. 1985.

which theology was taught, with a chancellor in charge of instruction and licencing. It had vigorous monastic schools near the city (Westminster Abbey and St. Saviour in Southwark, in contrast to St. Denis and Ste.-Geneviève), and grammar schools within its walls (St. Paul's, St. Martin's-le-Grand, and St. Mary-le-Bow, the latter two independent of the authority of the cathedral chancellor).[2] Parallel to Paris, London was a major center of population, a commercial center, and a seat of royal government. And London cannot have been totally immune to town–gown clashes that played such an important role in the legal recognition of the University of Paris.

London's early promise did not mature in the thirteenth century. Paris retained and increased its lead as the desired destination, the appropriate setting for English students of arts and theology. When an Insular alternative or supplement to a Continental education was developed, students flocked to Oxford and, in smaller numbers, Cambridge. London became a crossroads, a stopping place for men of learning en route from one university to the other. The London grammar schools remained active in the thirteenth century and probably expanded in size, but there is no evidence to suggest that higher education experienced any comparable growth. In fact, it probably diminished as the new *studia generalia* assumed the major burden of instruction and certification in philosophy, theology, and canon law. We should not assume, however, that arts and sciences atrophied in the fourteenth century. On the contrary, London in that period experienced a revival of higher learning that altered the intellectual face of the city.

THE TOPOGRAPHY OF LEARNING

The center of what might be thought of as London's "Latin Quarter" was the district around the three oldest grammar schools of St. Paul's, St. Martin's-le-Grand to the south, and St. Mary-le-Bow a little to the east, all at the western end of the city. To that traditional base (a young student population in the age range of 7 to 14) there were in the fourteenth century an increasing number of students of university age (14 to 30) engaged in the study of logic, natural philosophy, and theology. If not in one of the religious orders, these older students would be found at the cathedral school of St. Paul's, which had not abandoned its commitment to provide instruction for diocesan clergy. The chancellor of the cathedral had an obligation to ensure that lectures and disputations were held, and he himself had to be a master of theology.

Moreover, numerous canon lawyers could be found in the neighborhood of St. Paul's and St. Mary-le-Bow. They were attached to or attracted by the business of the episcopal and archdiaconal courts of the London diocese or the court of appeal for the Canterbury Province, known as the Court of Arches, since it was held at St. Mary-le-Bow. Many of these men had received their training in canon law at a university, although some may have studied law at St. Paul's or through apprenticeship. Their presence provided an opportunity for contact and exchange between those practicing law and those studying law and theology in this part of City.[3]

The district around St. Paul's was also the center of book production in fourteenth-century London. More than half of the scribes, limners, parchmeners, bookbinders, and stationers (booksellers) of known address lived within the shadow of St. Paul's Cathedral.[4] That density suggests a center for the book market, one that coincides remarkably well with the location of the major schools.

West of St. Paul's, in the same neighborhood, were a number of mendicant convents that offered instruction in philosophy and theology to students within and occasionally outside the order. The Franciscan convent, Greyfriars, was located to the northwest of St. Paul's between St. Martin's-le-Grand and Newgate, in the less desirable quarter of the butchers, in Stinking Lane.[5] The Dominican Blackfriars lay to the southwest, along the wall between Ludgate and the Thames.[6] The Carmelite convent, Whitefriars, was situated farther to the west, on the other side of the Fleet Ditch between the townhouse of the bishop of Salisbury and the Temple.[7] All three convents were within walking distance of one another and the other schools. Only the Augustinian Hermits were outside this immediate district. Their convent lay at the northeastern edge of the city. Whether a function of location or not, the Austin Friars played a minor role in the intellectual life of fourteenth-century London.

The London convents of the Carmelites, Franciscans, and Dominicans, by the early fourteenth century, had begun to shoulder a large share of the burden of mendicant education in southern England. For example, the London Carmelite convent was a *studium generale* for the entire Order, while the Oxford convent was a *studium* for only the English province. This meant that London Whitefriars offered the full program of studies in logic, natural philosophy, and theology, and probably maintained a student population equal to or larger than the Oxford convent. Moreover, non-English Carmelites who were sent to England for advanced study went to the London convent, not Oxford.[8]

Greyfriars, London, had a similarly active and rich intellectual life. It was the principal school for the London custody, as the subdivisions of the Franciscan provinces were called, and it drew students from Franciscan convents south of London from Salisbury to Canterbury. There young friars received their advanced training in philosophy and theology before a smaller number were selected to study at a university, usually Oxford. Even the best students by the second quarter of the fourteenth century were expected to read the *Sentences* at such a custodial school before being allowed to read at Oxford or another university.[9] Since the Oxford and

Cambridge convents provided access to university degrees and had to serve Franciscans from all the custodies and from other provinces, space in the university convents was limited, and most Franciscans probably received the bulk of their education at a custodial school, such as London.[10]

Although the Dominican Order did not designate a set number of convents to be perpetual schools, but instead rotated the financial burden of education among a wider number of convents, a few houses were specifically equipped with study cells for students and provided instruction in philosophy and theology on a nearly regular basis.[11] London was one of these and, in the fourteenth century, was a *studium solemne* or *studium particulare theologiae* for the London visitation (or nation), as the Dominican provincial divisions were known. As with Oxford, the London convent accepted students from outside the visitation and province, and in some cases had the same quota as Oxford.[12]

At the western end of the "Latin Quarter" of London lay a district of abbatial, episcopal, and aristocratic palaces that had been established between the twelfth and fourteenth centuries to be near the seat of government.[13] The choicest sites lay in that stretch of land between the Thames and the principal thoroughfare from the city to the royal palace of Westminster, namely Fleet Street and The Strand. Beginning at the eastern end near Ludgate, the Thames embankment displayed the gardens and residences of the bishop of Salisbury, the Carmelites, the Temple, the bishops of Exeter, Bath, and Wells, Llandaff, Coventry, Worcester, the Savoy Palace of the Duke of Lancaster, and the "inns" of the bishops of Carlisle, Durham, Norwich, and York.

In several of these London episcopal residences in the early fourteenth century could be found distinguished masters within the *familia* of a bishop, especially if the latter was himself a man of learning. Scholar-patrons who held high office in royal service and/or church and who consequently were often resident in London already formed an important group in the late thirteenth and early fourteenth centuries: archbishops Kilwardby, Pecham, and Winchelsey at Lambeth Palace, Simon of Ghent at Salisbury Inn, John Dalderby at Lincoln Inn, and Ralph Baldock at St. Paul's. That situation prevailed into the mid-fourteenth century, despite the appointment of several lawyers and non-university civil servants to episcopal office. In fact, in the period from 1318 to 1345 a number of theologian-bishops favored Oxford graduates in arts and theology and brought them into households that were frequently in London. These scholar-clients were not part of the teaching resources of London, since as far as we know they never gave lectures, and we should not confuse them with those who provided instruction at the cathedral school and the mendicant convents. But they were an intellectual resource whose presence should not be ignored. They did engage in disputations and were expected to enrich the intellectual life of the episcopal household to which they were attached, even as they pursued a career in court and church. To the degree that they maintained an interest in ideas, as many of them did, we can assume they had some contact with the scholarly world to the east of Fleet Street as well as the political world to the west.

This scholarly community west of the Fleet coincided with the principal legal community of London, centered in the neighborhood of the Temple and the Chancery.[14] Much of the lawyers' work was conducted in Westminster hall, but their residences, places of study, and places of consultation were in Fleet Street near Temple Bar, where Serjeants' Inn came to be located, or in Chancery Lane, where one found the Inns of Court and Inns of Chancery. This was a district not only for the practice of law, but for legal education as well. By the early fourteenth century the structure of the legal community and of legal education was becoming set. Those seeking training in common law studied as apprentices in the Inns of Chancery, attending lectures on common law, participating in disputations or moot courts, and observing court cases. The best students were brought into the Inns of Court (Lincoln's Inn, Gray's Inn, Middle Temple, and the Inner Temple), voluntary associations whose names derive from the properties leased by the association for residence and instruction. These inns were governed by a small body of senior lawyers, known as benchers, whose status and duties somewhat resembled fellows of colleges at Oxford and Cambridge. In the absence of endowment and permanent property, the inns resembled halls of medieval universities. But the internal organization of seniority and teaching more closely resembled the colleges. Above the level of student apprentices (inner and utter barristers) were the lecturers, or readers, from whose ranks the serjeants-at-law were chosen. That elevation required their resignation from the Inns of Court and their incorporation into Serjeants' Inn.

This system of legal education more closely resembled the fourteenth-century university, particularly one primarily devoted to law, than is generally recognized. Students were enrolled in corporations that rented property and that were under the control of advanced students. Instruction took the form of lectures and disputations (the arguing of an assigned position in a case). The better students advanced through a series of academic stages, across a minimum or standard number of years, that eventually included the giving of two or more courses of lectures.[15] The ceremonies surrounding the creation of a new serjeant-at-law were comparable to and generally exceeded those connected with the inception of a new regent master. Advancement to the level of serjeant-at-law required resignation from the "student-run" inns, or corporations.[16] Differences certainly did exist. Yet Plucknett's observation that Fortescue was wrong when (ca. 1470) he "likened the serjeants to the doctors in the universities," since apprentices rather than serjeants taught in the Inns of Court, is less valid for the fourteenth century than for the thirteenth.[17] Much of the teaching at a late medieval university was done by the bachelors, and regent masters were occupied as much with administration as with teaching.

It is worth noting that while the elementary to graduate levels of education in London were centered at the west end of the city, the postgraduate theologians congregated in the Fleet and Strand, to the west of the city, in close association with the students, attorneys, barristers, and serjeants-at-law. We are becoming more aware of the degree to which theology and law interpenetrated at Oxford and Cambridge, and a similar cross-fertilization was probably present in the London setting.

If London's academic landscape did not include colleges, we should also remember that the role of colleges in early fourteenth-century Oxford was also minor in comparison to halls and rented rooms. And to the extent that intellectual life in contemporary Oxford or Paris depended on mendicant houses of study or on brilliant secular scholars, London possessed very active and notable equivalents.

LIBRARIES AND CURRICULUM

Beyond the topography of learning, a second aspect of London schools is the extent, content, and quality of education. Overall, the student community of London was much smaller than that of Oxford or even Cambridge. The number of grammar students may have been comparable and the number of mendicants may even have been larger, but over against the bulk of Oxford undergraduates and non-mendicant students in the higher faculties, London had only its cathedral school. Thus the total scholarly population of London was probably not more than 400, a quarter of the size of Oxford. Yet the London academic community did operate as a consortium of autonomous but interrelated units, and it did maintain a high level of instruction. At London one could obtain the content of an Oxford education, and at least on the level of logic, natural philosophy, and theology the schools of London provided equivalent training to that acquired at a university.

We know least about the content of the curriculum at St. Paul's. The interests of those appointed to the office of chancellor and the size and character of the library suggest, however, that it should have been strong in logic, both the *logica antiqua* and the *logica moderna*, mathematical physics, and somewhat conservative in theology. In the early fourteenth century considerable care was taken to appoint to the office of chancellor scholars of distinguished reputation, most of them from Merton College, Oxford, thanks to the patronage of Stephen Gravesend, Bishop of London from 1318 to 1338. The list of chancellors appointed by Gravesend included Thomas Wilton (1320–27, but absent in Paris the first two years), William Reynham (1327–33), Thomas Duraunt (1334–37), and Thomas Bradwardine (1337–49), who was elevated to the see of Canterbury in 1349, but whose tenure in that office was almost immediately terminated by the plague.[18] Gravesend may not himself have been a fellow of Merton College, although it is possible he could have been affiliated before going to Paris ca. 1306, presumably to study theology. His ties with Merton, however, are reflected in the patronage he provided to Mertonians and in his bequest of the largest portion of his library to Merton College.

In the fourteenth century the cathedral chancellor was obliged to give lectures himself or find a qualified substitute if illness, the other duties of his office, or absence prevented his presence in the classroom.[19] If the lectures Robert Winchelsey gave at London while he was chancellor at St. Paul's are any indication, the chancellor was expected to provide advanced lectures in theology equivalent to what would be taught at a similar level in a university.[20] We may assume, therefore, that others were teaching in addition to the chancellor and that the intellectual views of the chancellor set the quality and tone for the theological program.

Unfortunately, with the exception of Bradwardine, we are not as well informed on the ideas and intellectual ties of the chancellors in the second quarter of the century as we would wish. Wilton was a doctor of Paris and widely cited on the Continent in the fourteenth century. His famous debate with Walter Burley over the intention and remission of forms probably took place on the eve of his return to England to assume the duties of his office.[21] Although Burley at one point linked the views of Wilton and John of Jandun, and all three figures have been associated with Averroism in the literature, that label is too vague to provide much insight into Wilton's ideas. His association with Scotus seems more firmly grounded.[22] In all probability he continued his strong interests in natural philosophy while at London.

Less is known of the interests of Reynham, apart from his possession of a copy of the last book of Thomas Aquinas's commentary on the *Sentences*.[23] Duraunt borrowed the Psalms commentary of the Dominican Nicholas Gorham during his tenure in office, which he may have used in his biblical lectures or simply had copied.[24] Bradwardine is our best indication of the continuing scholarly interests of the chancellors of St. Paul's, since we know he wrote as well as taught while in London, completing there his monumental *Summa de causa Dei*.[25] Bradwardine's campaign against the Pelagians among his contemporaries certainly influenced his teaching at London and gave a strong Augustinian and biblical character to theology at St. Paul's.

The library of St. Paul's was already rich by the mid-thirteenth century and was greatly expanded in theology and canon law through the bequest of Bishop Ralph Baldock, who died in 1313.[26] Baldoch's will left 126 volumes of works written before 1290, more than adequately covering Oxford and Parisian texts and commentaries in arts and theology of the thirteenth century. More recent works entered in the course of the fourteenth century. We know only a portion of the acquisitions, since inventories have not survived and the

list of donations is incomplete. A number of books in canon law from Gravesend's library were given to St. Paul's.[27] Bradwardine's library, which was
probably rich in quality if not in size, may well have been divided between
Merton, St. Paul's, and Canterbury.[28]

The library of the almonry school, separate from that of the cathedral,
also grew in the fourteenth century through the bequests of its school-
masters. William de Tolleshunt in 1328 left various books on grammar, logic,
and natural history that were appropriate for the elementary and secondary
levels.[29] But he also left books in natural philosophy and logic that were
more appropriate for the "undergraduate" level, along with works on medicine,
civil law, canon law, and sermons that could have served the needs only of
more advanced students in the "graduate" disciplines. That is less true of the
extensive bequest of another schoolmaster at St. Paul's, William Ravenstone,
in 1358.[30] The majority of his 84 manuscripts were works in grammar, the
classics, mathematics, logic, music, and liturgy that would have served the
needs of the boys in the grammar school. Yet we also find there some works
on physics, canon law, and theology.

We are better informed on the content of teaching among the mendicant
convents. As has already been noted, *studia* of the type we encounter at
London were required to provide the basic curricula of the arts and theological
programs of the universities. This meant that there would be one or more
masters or bachelors lecturing on the logical and scientific works of Aristotle,
along with lectures in mathematics. For example, it is now reasonably certain
that the Aristotelian commentaries of William of Ockham were the product
of lectures given to students at London Greyfriars during the years 1320 and
1324.[31] One or more lecturers in theology would instruct students in the
Bible and the *Sentences*. During those same years, Walter Chatton lectured on
the *Sentences*, probably in the same London convent.[32] At the end of that
decade another Franciscan, Adam Wodeham, lectured on the *Sentences* at
London before beginning or completing his time as *Sententiarius* at Oxford.[33]

Various types of disputations were held in the London convents. Formed
bachelors might also engage in quodlibetal disputations. Most of the *Quodlibeta* of Ockham were composed and delivered at a non-university *studium*
in England before 1324, almost certainly at London.[34]

The quality of teaching was quite high. In general, whatever mendicant
talent was displayed in the lecture halls of Oxford, that same talent had
already lectured or would soon lecture at a non-university *studium* of the
order. These periods of non-university teaching would occur just before
reading the *Sentences* at a university, after completing requirements for
regency and awaiting an opportunity to incept, or after becoming master
of theology. In this system London was probably assigned the largest share
of talent, as the above illustrations of Ockham, Chatton, and Wodeham would
suggest.

Some of the educational character and administration of the London convents was in the hands of the provincial minister or prior, who was often resident in the London convent of the order. The orders usually elected men of distinguished learning, most of whom had already held the office of regent master at a university. John Baconthorpe, perhaps the most noted Carmelite theologian in the first half of the fourteenth century, was their Provincial in the years 1326 to 1333.[35] At roughly the same time, Simon Boraston was the Dominican Prior Provincial (1327–36), followed soon after by Richard de Winkley (1336–39).[36] Both men were noted theologians, had been regent masters at Oxford, and continued a life of active scholarship after their regencies. In 1339, toward the end of his term in office, Winkley prepared an inventory of the Dominican library at London, which must have contained several hundred volumes by then.[37] Unfortunately, that document has not survived. The list of Franciscan Provincial Ministers is even more distinguished.[38] During a particularly productive period for the Franciscan school in the fourteenth century, that office was held by Richard Connington (ca. 1310–16), William of Nottingham (1316–30), John of Rodington (ca. 1336–40), and John Went (ca. 1340–48). All had been lectors at Oxford, and their opinions were frequently cited by other masters.

We know only a fraction of the books that once existed in the mendicant libraries of London, which were among the richest in England. All were dispersed at the time of the Reformation, and very little remains today. Moreover, the items mentioned by Leland and Bale are only those that attracted their notice, and some of those certainly entered those collections in the fifteenth century.[39] But what evidence we have is worth a reexamination. The libraries were shelved according to subject categories: scriptural commentaries, sermons, patristic literature, logic, natural philosophy, and theological works such as *Sentences*, commentaries, quodlibets and disputed questions, and various theological treatises. The Dominican library possessed most of the works of Fishacre and Kilwardby, some writings of Grosseteste, and numerous commentaries of English Dominican authors.[40] They must also have had all or most of the works of Thomas Aquinas, although none was noted by either Leland or Bale. The Carmelite library held, in addition to the basic collection, works of Carmelite authors, such as Baconthorpe, Brome, Beston, Benningham, and Walsingham. Perhaps more unusual, they also had several works of Fitzralph and Ockham's commentary on the *Physics*.[41] It is less surprising that the Franciscan library had almost all the philosophical and theological works of Ockham as well as scriptural commentaries and theological works of more recent Franciscan authors: Adam Wodeham on the Song of Songs, Henry Costesey on Psalms, Robert Cowton on the *Sentences*.[42] What is remarkable is that there is no mention of the obvious: works by Bonaventure or Scotus, and the surprising inclusion of several works of Holcot, Fishacre, and Bradwardine.[43]

The picture of London's intellectual life should be augmented by including the non-teaching but active scholars resident for a time in London, specifically those masters attached to the household of a bishop whose governmental responsibilities required his presence in London as much as in his own diocese. John Grandisson, bishop of Exeter (1327–69) and a conscientious churchman, was resident from time to time at Exeter Inn. His door and table would have been open to the scholars who benefited from his patronage, among them Richard Fitzralph, the Dominican Richard Winkley, and Thomas Buckingham.[44] The same holds true for the important and oft-mentioned circle of scholars who surrounded Richard de Bury, Bishop of Durham.[45] Before his appointment to the see of Durham, Bury was already attended by a large household staff that included a number of clerks and masters, and his patronage of Oxford bachelors and doctors of theology increased after his consecration as bishop. Between 1334 and his death in 1345 Bury's household included at various times such distinguished Oxford masters as Thomas Bradwardine, Walter Burley, Richard Bentworth, Richard Fitzralph, Robert Holcot, Richard Kilvington, Walter Seagrave, John Maudith, and John Acton. While they were part of the episcopal *familia*, these "scholar-clients" were expected to travel and reside with the bishop. Before 1340 (i.e., when at one time or another most of the above-mentioned scholars were attached to his household), Bury's principal residence was Durham Inn in London, not in the north of England, as is sometimes imagined.

WORKSHOPS OF LEARNING

A third aspect of the intellectual life of London in the early fourteenth century is the surprisingly large number of scholastic works that were written or revised there. It was probably in London that Ockham wrote his commentaries on Aristotle's logic and physics, revised the first book of his *Sentences* commentary (the *Ordinatio*), wrote his monumental *Summa logicae*, and engaged in the majority of his quodlibetic disputes.[46] It was also in London that Walter Chatton apparently gave his *Reportatio*, the only full commentary on the *Sentences* left by that important Franciscan author.[47] Adam Wodeham lectured on the *Sentences* at London, portions of which were later incorporated into his *Lectura secunda*.[48] It was in his London lectures that Wodeham gave his most extensive and perceptive treatment to problems of epistemology.[49] All copies of Robert Holcot's *Sentences* commentary are products of a later revision which, in view of the number of times London is used in the text as an example, may have been completed in that setting.[50] Walter Burley remained active during the period in which he was associated with Bury in London. The works he composed, revised, or completed during that period are his commentary on the *Liber de sex principiis*, the *Expositio super artem veterem*, the last section of his commentary on Aristotle's *Physics*, his commentary on the *Ethics*, and his commentary on Aristotle's *Politics*.[51] Finally, one of the most widely read and influential works of the period, Thomas Bradwardine's *Summa de causa Dei*, was completed in London in the years before 1344.[52]

CONCLUSION

London was not a medieval university, a *studium generale*. It was rather a composite of many *studia generalia*. Its schools fed and were fed from universities, especially Oxford. It was a less structured academic environment, where those who might never attend a formal university could come into contact with the books, ideas, and personalities on which Oxford's reputation was based. Once Oxford's premier position was firmly established in the thirteenth century, no political, ecclesiastical, or cultural exigencies arose that would have permitted London to crystalize those *studia* into a real university. Such a development would have gone against royal and papal policy. But the quality of intellectual life did not thereby suffer. Being the political, demographic, and commercial capital of England, London ultimately acquired the best of Oxford, brought there by the educational structure of the mendicant orders and the career ambitions of secular postgraduates. Through them the schools of London sustained a quality of intellectual life in the first half of the fourteenth century that made it in the unacknowledged third center of learning in England.

NOTES

1. William Fitz-Stephen, *Description of the Most Noble City of London*, in E. K. Kendall, ed., *Source Book of English History* (New York, 1900), pp. 65–71.
2. On the schools of London, see John Stow, *A Survey of London* (1603), with introduction and notes by C. L. Kingsford, Vol. I (Oxford, 1908; 1971), pp. 71–73; Nicholas Orme, *English Schools of the Middle Ages* (London, 1973), pp. 168–70, 210–11.
3. A. T. Carter, *A History of the English Courts*, 5th ed. (London, 1927), pp. 143–49; B. L. Woodcock, *Medieval Ecclesiastical Courts in the Diocese of Canterbury* (London, 1952), pp. 6–8.
4. Paul Christianson, "Books and Their Makers in Medieval London," *Wooster* 96, no. 3 (Spring, 1982):10–15. Although the evidence assembled by Christianson begins in the late fourteenth century, the development of craft neighborhoods in London, such as the one connected with book production, is earlier. I would like to thank Linda Voigts of the University of Missouri at Kansas City for bringing this article to my attention.
5. *The Victoria History of the Counties of England, A History of London*, vol. I (London, 1909), pp. 502–7; C. S. Kingsford, *The Grey Friars of London* (Manchester, 1915).

6. *The Victoria History*, pp. 498–502.

7. Ibid., pp. 507–10.

8. Margaret Poskitt, "The English Carmelites," *The Aylesford Review* 5 (1963):226–37; "The English Carmelite Province," *The Aylesford Review* 1 (1956):98–102; Franz-Bernard Lickteig, "The German Carmelites at the Medieval Universities" (Ph.D., dissertation, Catholic University of America, 1975).

9. This practice seems to have become common among the Franciscans by the 1320s, first on the Continent and then in England. The Austin Friars pursued a similar policy. The papal legislation for the Franciscan Order in 1336 made this practice officially binding; "Ordinationes Benedicti XII," *Archivum Franciscanum Historicum* 30 (1937):349; M. Brlek, *De evolutione iuridica studiorum in ordine minorum* (Dubrovnik, 1942). On Augustinian practice see E. Ypma, *La formation des professeurs chez les Ermites de Saint-Augustine de 1256 à 1354* (Paris, 1956); Ypma, "Les 'Cursores' chez les Augustins," *Recherches de Théologie ancienne et médiévale* 26 (1959):137–44; Ypma, "La promotion au lectorat chez les Augustins et le 'De lectorie gradu' d'Ambroise de Cora," *Augustiniana* 13 (1963):391–417.

10. On the Franciscan educational system, see A. G. Little, "Educational Organization of the Mendicant Friars in England (Dominicans and Franciscans)," *Transactions of the Royal Historical Society*, n.s. 8 (1894):49–70; Brlek, *De evolutione iuridica studiorum*; A. G. Little, "The Franciscan School at Oxford in the Thirteenth Century," *Archivum Franciscanum Historicum* 19 (1926):803–74; W. J. Courtenay, *Adam Wodeham* (Leiden, 1978), pp. 45–53.

11. Outside the convents of Oxford and Cambridge which, from their origin, functioned as houses of study, there were other convents that regularly functioned as *studia artium, studia naturalium* and *studia theologiae*. These were, in order of importance, London, York, and Northampton. King's Langley (Langley Regis) near St. Albans was a regular *studium artium* and *studium naturalium* for all visitations in preparation for Oxford.

12. At the Chapter of 1314 it was affirmed that the Irish convents were permitted to send the same quota of students to London and Oxford, namely two. *The Victoria History*, p. 500 n. 44.

13. On the abbatial and episcopal residences on the west end of London, see Marjorie B. Honeybourne, "The Fleet and Its Neighbourhood in Early and Medieval Times," *London Topographical Record* 19 (1947), esp. pp. 68–73; M. B. Honeybourne, *A Sketch Map of London Under Richard II* (London: London Topographical Society, 1960); C. L. Kingsford, "Historical Notes on Medieval London Houses," *London Topographical Record* 10 (1916):44–144; Timothy Baker, *Medieval London* (London, 1970). Help in locating some of this material was provided by John Clark of the London Museum.

14. T. F. T. Plucknett, *A Concise History of the Common Law*, 3rd ed. (London, 1940), pp. 195–202.

15. John Fortescue, *De Laudibus Legum Anglie*, ed. & trans. S. B. Chrimes (Cambridge, 1942), pp. 116-25.

16. Plucknett, *Concise History*, p. 201 n. 4.

17. Ibid., pp. 201-2; Fortescue, *De Laudibus*, pp. 120-21.

18. For the biographies of Gravesend, Wilton, Reynham, Duraunt, and Bradwardine, see A. B. Emden, *A Biographical Register of the University of Oxford*, 3 vols. (Oxford, 1957-59). For mention of the appointment or tenure of Reynham, Duraunt, and Bradwardine as chancellors at St. Paul's, see the *Register* of Stephen Gravesend in *Registrum Radulphi Baldock, Gilberti Segrave, Ricardi Newport, et Stephani Gravesend, episcoporum Londoniensium*, ed. R. C. Fowler, Canterbury and York Series (London, 1911), pp. 253, 280, 302, 309, 312, 313.

19. W. A. Pantin, *The English Church in the Fourteenth Century* (Cambridge, 1955; Notre Dame, 1963), p. 111.

20. Ibid. Winchelsey's *Quaestiones disputatae apud London* are found in Oxford, Magdalen College, MS. 217.

21. Emden, *Biographical Register*, vol. 3, pp. 2054-55; J. Weisheipl, "Ockham and Some Mertonians," *Mediaeval Studies* 30 (1968):184-87; "Repertorium Meronense," *Mediaeval Studies* 31 (1969):222-24.

22. P. Glorieux, "Duns Scot et les 'Notabilia Cancellarii,'" *Archivum Franciscanum Historicum* 24 (1931):3-14.

23. Emden, *Biographical Register*, vol. 3, p. 1571.

24. Ibid., vol. 1, pp. 611-12.

25. Ibid., vol. 1, pp. 244-46; G. Leff, *Bradwardine and the Pelagians* (Cambridge, 1957), pp. 2, 266; H. A. Oberman, *Archbishop Thomas Bradwardine: A Fourteenth Century Augustinian* (Utrecht, 1958), pp. 17-18; Weisheipl, "Repertorium," pp. 177-83; Weisheipl, "Ockham," pp. 189-93.

26. On the library of St. Paul's, see W. Dugdale, *History of St. Paul's* (London edition, 1818), pp. 313, 324-38, 392-401; J. W. Clark, "The Libraries at Lincoln, Westminster and St. Paul's," *Cambridge Antiquarian Society, Proceedings* 9 (1896-98):37; Emden, *Biographical Register* vol. 3, pp. 2147-48; N. R. Ker, *Medieval Libraries of Great Britain*, 2nd ed. (Oxford, 1964), pp. 120-21.

27. Emden, *Biographical Register*, vol. 2, pp. 805-7. Among his bequests Gravesend left a *Liber concordantiarum* to Duraunt.

28. Nothing is known of the content or fate of Bradwardine's personal library, but he certainly would have had a number of books on contemporary logic, natural philosophy, and theology in addition to copies of his own works.

29. E. Rickert, *Chaucer's World* (New York, 1948), pp. 121-22.

30. Ibid., pp. 122-26.

31. See introductions to Ockham's *Summa logicae*, ed. Ph. Boehner, G. Gal, and St. Brown (St. Bonaventure, N.Y., 1974), 47*-56*; and *Quodlibeta septem*, ed. J. Wey (St. Bonaventure, N.Y., 1980), 26*-41*.

32. See introduction to Ockham's *Summa logicae*, 47*-56*.

33. Courtenay, *Adam Wodeham*, pp. 31-32, 123-31, 166-71.

34. Ockham, *Quodlibeta*, 26*-41*.
35. Emden, *Biographical Register*, vol. 1, pp. 88–89; B. M. Xiberta, *De scriptoribus scholasticis saeculi XIV ex ordine Carmelitarum* (Louvain, 1931), pp. 167–240, 499.
36. W. Gumbley, "Provincial Priors and Vicars of the English Dominicans," *English Historical Review* 33 (1918):243–51; A. G. Little, "Provincial Priors and Vicars of the English Dominicans," *EHR* 33 (1918):496–97; Emden, *Biographical Register*, vol. 1, pp. 221; vol. 3, p. 2060.
37. J. Bale, *Index Britanniae Scriptorum*, ed. R. L. Poole and M. Bateson (Oxford, 1902), p. 513, noted that he derived his information "ex inventario Bibliothecae Fratrum Praedicatorum Londini per provincialem eorum Ricardum de Winkele, A.D.1339."
38. A. G. Little, *Franciscan Papers, Lists, and Documents* (Manchester, 1943), pp. 189–207.
39. Many of the manuscripts in the libraries of the religious orders had probably already been dispersed through loan or theft by 1536 when John Leland began his inventory tour of English antiquities on behalf of Henry VIII. The subject groupings in Leland's lists suggest that he went through the libraries, section by section, noting what remained or at least what had value to him and possibly the king. John Leland, *De rebus Britannicis collectanea*, vol. 4 (London, 1770), pp. 49–54.
40. On the contents of the Dominican library in London, see Leland, pp. 51–52; Bale, p. 513; N. R. Ker, *Medieval Libraries of Great Britain*, 2nd ed. (London, 1964), p. 124.
41. On the Carmelite library, see Leland, pp. 52–54; Ker, pp. 124–25.
42. On the Franciscan library, see Leland, pp. 49–51; Ker, pp. 123.
43. Specifically, Fishacre's commentary on the *Sentences*, Holcot's Sapiential commentary and his commentary on the *Sentences*, and Bradwardine's *De causa Dei*.
44. Emden, *Biographical Register*, vol. 2, pp. 800–801 on Grandisson; vol. 2, pp. 692–94 on Fitzralph; vol. 3, p. 2060 on Winkley; and vol. 1, pp. 298–99 on Buckingham; K. Walsch, *A Fourteenth-century Scholar and Prelate: Richard Fitzralph in Oxford, Avignon, and Armagh* (Oxford, 1981), pp. 47–50.
45. On the Bury circle, see J. de Ghellinck, "Une bibliophile au XIV siècle: Richard d'Aungerville," *Revue d'histoire ecclésiastique* 18 (1920):271–312, 482–502; 19 (1923):157–200; N. Denholm Young, "Richard de Bury (1287–1345)," *Royal Historical Society Transactions*, 4th ser., 20 (1937):135–68; Neal Ward Gilbert, "Richard de Bury and the 'Quires of Yesterday's Sophisms,' " in *Philosophy and Humanism: Renaissance Essays in Honor of Paul Oskar Kristeller*, ed. E. P. Mahoney (New York, 1976), pp. 229–57. Katherine Walsh has also noted that the Bury circle was primarily in London; see Walsh, p. 20.
46. See above, note 31.
47. See above, note 32.
48. See above, note 33.
49. Courtenay, *Adam Wodeham*, pp. 210–14; G. Gal, "Adam Wodeham's

Question on the 'Complexe Significabile' as the Immediate Object of Scientific Knowledge," *Franciscan Studies* 37 (1977):66-102; K. Tachau, "The Problem of the *Species in medio* at Oxford in the Generation after Ockham," *Mediaeval Studies* 44 (1982):394-443; "The Response to Ockham's and Aureol's Epistemology: 1320-1340," in *English Logic in Italy in the 14th and 15th Centuries*, ed. A. Maierù (Naples, 1982), pp. 185-217.

50. R. Holcot, *In quatuor libros sententiarum quaestiones*, IV, q. 3: "Similiter tu qui es Londonie, haberes dubitare an aliquis homo sit Rome conversus in te." Most manuscripts have London, e.g., London, Brit. Lib., Royal 10.C.6, fol. 115vb, Oxford, Oriel 15, fol. 196[rb], Cambridge, Pembroke 236, fol. 95(93)[rb], Oxford, Corpus Christi 138, fol. 88[r], Oxford, Balliol 71, fol. 127[vb], Oxford, Merton 113, fol. 63[ra], Troyes, Bibl. de la Ville 634, fol. 59[vb], Paris, B. N. lat. 14576, fol. 95[ra]; Paris, B. N. lat. 15884, fol. 59[va]; while Florence, Bibl. Naz. J VI 20, fol. 58[va], and Heiligenkreutz 185, fol. 70[vb] have Paris as the example.

51. Weisheipl, "Ockham and Some Mertonians," pp. 174-88; "Repertorium Mertonense," pp. 185-208; A. U. Juarez, *La filosofia del siglo XIV. Contexto cultural de Walter Burley* (El Escorial, 1978).

52. Courtenay, *Adam Wodeham*, pp. 117-18; "Augustinianism at Oxford in the Fourteenth Century," *Augustiniana* 30 (1980):58-70.

The Probable Date and Purpose of Chaucer's Troilus

D. W. ROBERTSON, JR.

I.

Although it has long been customary to assign a date for Chaucer's *Troilus* during the period 1380-86, preferably toward its close, most Chaucerians have devoted little attention to events in England during that time. Since the poem was probably read before a court audience, some of whom, as Derek Pearsall has indicated, were men who were not only deeply interested but directly involved in those events,[1] we can hardly dismiss the historical situation as being irrelevant.

Generally speaking, it is safe to say that English prestige declined steadily after about 1370, that fears of invasion from abroad reached a kind of climax in 1385 and 1386, and that this situation was widely held to be the consequence of moral decline that led providentially to adversities,[2] an understandable attitude among men who were, like Chaucer himself, deeply moved by attitudes found in *The Consolation of Philosophy* of Boethius. The interests and attitudes of the time undoubtedly had much to do with the shaping of Chaucer's great poem, and unless we can share them, at least in imagination, we shall deprive ourselves of an opportunity to appreciate it. Unless we understand, if only in a general way, the purpose for which it was devised and very carefully crafted, we can hardly appreciate the literary stratagems designed to fulfill it. In the following pages I shall discuss the relevant historical events, some basic attitudes, a few literary stratagems, and finally and very briefly the poem itself.

Concerning the probable character of the audience, Pearsall, in the article referred to above, argues that it included "household knights, career diplomats, and civil servants." Chaucer's own diplomatic missions were carried out under the auspices of the Chamber, which also came to serve eventually as the center of social activity at court, and may have been at least in part responsible for such activity at the time the poem was written.[3] Although the Chamber after 1356 no longer served as an administrative office for royal lands, it became increasingly important for its services on "the king's secret business," so that instead of the three Chamber knights in 1377, there were eleven by

143

Medievalia et Humanistica, New Series, Number 13 (Paul Maurice Clogan, ed.). Rowman & Allanheld, Totowa, NJ. 1985.

1385, and seventeen in 1388. Richard often employed these men on his Council and rewarded them with lands and offices.[4] They included old followers of Prince Edward and friends of Princess Joan, who gathered about her a group of men interested in reform, and who for this reason have become known as "Lollard Knights," although their sympathies were probably more closely allied with the ideals of Philippe de Mézières than with those of John Wyclif.

It will suffice to mention a few of them and to supply some relevant facts about them, concentrating on the years before 1387. First, Sir Lewis Clifford, perhaps the godfather of Chaucer's son Lewis but in any event a close friend, had been both a squire and knight under Prince Edward, was a Garter Knight in 1377 and became a royal knight in 1381. He was among those appointed to remain with Princess Joan during Richard's foray into Scotland in 1385; and he, his son-in-law Philip la Vache, a Chamber Knight from 1378, Sir John Clanvowe, William Beauchamp, and many others were given livery of mourning for her after her death in August 1385. Clifford was one of her executors. He is said to have joined Philippe de Mézières's Order of the Passion, whose aim was to establish an international crusading movement based on peace between France and England and governed by a strict moral discipline, either in 1385 or shortly thereafter. Clifford was abroad on diplomatic missions in late 1385 and early in 1386, bringing home with him on his return Deschamps's poem in praise of Chaucer.[5] The French poet had attended a peace conference in 1384.[6] Clifford's second mission was probably made in connection with John of Gaunt's forthcoming crusade, to which we shall return in a moment.

William Beauchamp, the younger brother of Thomas Beauchamp, Earl of Warwick (1339–1401), is said to have had a university education. He was Chamberlain between 1378 and 1381, and in May 1380 he, Sir John Clanvowe, Sir William Neville, and two prominent London merchants went with Chaucer before Bishop Sudbury, the Chancellor, to witness Cecily Champain's release of Chaucer from charges of rape or other trespasses.[7] His interest in the estate of his deceased friend John Hastings, Earl of Pembroke, led to a famous legal dispute, but it was not discreditable to him.[8] Chaucer probably accompanied him on a mission to Calais in 1387. Sir John Clanvowe, a Chamber Knight since 1382, was to write a transparently Chaucerian poem inspired partly by *The Parliament of Fowls*, and partly by the Knight's Tale, as well as a moral treatise, *The Two Ways*, possibly for the child of a friend or an ecclesiastic engaged in elementary teaching.[9] He was, like Clifford, busy abroad in connection with arrangements for Gaunt's crusade in the early part of 1386. Also like Clifford, he was one of Joan of Kent's executors. His friend William Neville, a very close companion, had been a knight of King Edward's household and a Chamber Knight after 1381. Toward the close of their careers they participated together in Louis of Bourbon's unsuccessful crusade.

Among the knights closely associated with Princess Joan was Sir Richard Stury, who was ransomed along with another royal squire, Geoffrey Chaucer, after Edward's campaign of 1359. Whereas Chaucer brought only £16 to his captors, Stury, who was praised for his bravery by Froissart, was worth £50. He became a Chamber Knight some time around 1371 and thereafter served frequently on diplomatic missions. Unfortunately, at the "Good Parliament" of 1376, where he served as *prolocutor*, he reported to the king that the Commons were seeking to depose him, and for this indiscreet exaggeration he was banished from the court and lost the friendship of Prince Edward, who was sympathetic with the reformers. The court and Princess Joan soon forgave him, however, and in 1377 he was engaged in peace negotiations with the French, seeking a marriage between young Richard and a French princess, in company with Guichard d'Angle (d. 1380), who was one of Richard's tutors and a friend of both Oton de Granson and Deschamps. With them was Geoffrey Chaucer, probably in a clerical capacity.[10] Stury, who headed a commission of walls and ditches of which Chaucer was a member in 1390, was an active diplomat and member of the Council until his death in 1395. His literary interests are attested by the fact that he owned a copy of the *Roman de la rose* (BL MS Royal 19 B XIII), one of Chaucer's favorite books. Sir John Montagu, a royal knight after 1383 and heir to the earldom of Salisbury through his uncle, was closely associated with these men and was a poet in his own right, admired for his work by Christine de Pisan, a lady of ready if not always astute moral sensibilities.

It is fairly safe to assume that one or more of these men formed a part of the audience who assembled to hear Chaucer read his poem. We should also include John Gower and Ralph Strode, the Oxford logician who had become Common Pleader for the City of London, since both are mentioned at the close of the poem. And if the date about to be suggested is credible it would not be rash to include John of Gaunt and some of those planning to accompany him in Spain, including Chaucer's son Thomas. We should also expect some ecclesiastics like Thomas Rushook, Richard's confessor, who was transferred from Llandaff to Chichester in 1385; clerks of both the royal and Lancastrian households; and ladies, including Philippa Chaucer, with their handmaidens. (The apology to the ladies toward the close of the poem implies their presence.) We have no means of knowing how large the audience was, but we can be fairly certain that it was requested for a specific social occasion, attended by persons of some prominence, that might involve at least five days of festivities. It is unlikely that Chaucer wrote anything very extensive without considering the possibility of an occasion for its public delivery; and it seems very likely that a friend, or group of friends, seeking to help him increase his prestige, asked him to prepare what he had written for presentation at a specific time and place.

II.

Before speculating about the occasion and the individual or individuals responsible for Chaucer's appearance, I shall review briefly certain aspects of events in England that contributed to a loss of national prestige. As George Holmes has well described them, English fortunes had been gloomy before the Good Parliament of 1376.[11] King Edward had not kept a firm hand on his government during the last years of his reign, and with the transition to the new reign matters were not much improved, especially from a military point of view. The Aquitaine won by Edward in the Treaty of Bretigny was drastically reduced by French forces under du Guescelin in 1372, and in the early summer of 1373 he retook much of Brittany. The English response, a naval expedition led by the king, lasted only a few weeks, although a force led by Sir John Neville of Raby took and held Brest, which was besieged. In March 1373 Sir William Montagu, Earl of Salisbury, failed to relieve the siege. In July Gaunt undertook his famous march from Calais to Bordeaux but did not relieve Brittany, perhaps because he thought Aquitaine more important. During 1374 and 1375 the French outmaneuvered the English both diplomatically and militarily, so that when the Good Parliament met the lords had no successes to proclaim, there was a very real threat of attack on the coasts by Castilian naval forces, and Charles V was readying his own naval forces to be used on the expiration of a truce. Indeed, in 1377 the French captured Rye, burned Lewes, overran the Isle of Wight, and burned Hastings.[12] The Scots massacred a gathering at a fair at Roxburgh, and the Duke of Anjou successfully invaded Gascony. In that year Peter de la Mare, a protegé of Edmund de Mortimer, Earl of March, who was once more speaker for the Commons in Parliament, complained that English chivalry had once been "most energetic, ardently desirous of great enterprises, each man eager to perform great deeds of arms, one above the other," but, he lamented, it is now "together with all other virtues placed behind; vice is praised, advanced, honored, and not at all chastised" (*RP*, 3:24). We should notice that "chivalry" is here regarded, as it is in Chaucer's description of his Knight, as a virtue, not as a form of outmoded and empty panoply. Memories still lingered of King Edward's cultivation of chivalric virtue in the Order of the Garter and in tournaments to stimulate the courage and dedication of his followers that had produced such obvious success abroad.[13] The new reign with its child king had nothing to compare with it.

In the following year Gaunt besieged St. Malo, but probably because of the negligence of the Earl of Arundel in preparing a mine the siege had to be abandoned, a fact that sullied Gaunt's reputation. Castilian galleys attacked Cornwall and burnt the town of Fowey, and it became evident that the government was in serious financial difficulties. In 1379 Sir John Arundel, the Marshall, after the south coast had been ravaged by his own troops, set out for Brittany (according to Walsingham's gossip taking with him nuns seized as companions for his men), only to have his fleet, his troops, and himself, not to mention the alleged nuns, destroyed in a storm. The Scots attacked in the north in 1380. Thomas of Woodstock conducted a great raid from Calais to Brittany, encouraging the disheartened Commons to levy the now-famous poll tax. It was well intentioned enough, designed as a substitute for the old levies of a tenth and a fifteenth that had demanded a fixed sum from each locality and had now become inequitable; but it was so poorly administered that it precipitated the Great Revolt of 1381, which had clearly been brewing before the allegations in Parliament in 1377 concerning "counsellors, abettors, and maintainers in the country," who for their own profit had used "exemplifications out of the Book of Domesday" to cause villeins to refuse their customary services, to menace ministers of their lords, and to gather in "great routs" threatening force (1 R II 7, *SR*, 2:3; cf. *RP*, 3:21).

In his remarkable address to Parliament in 1381 (*RP*, 3:100–101) Sir Richard Waldgrave, the Speaker, painted a depressing picture of the state of the kingdom, urging that "if the government of the realm is not within a short time amended, the realm itself will be completely lost." He spoke of the "outrageous number of familiars" in the household and of corruption in the courts, including the Chancery, the King's Bench, and in the Exchequer. There were, he said, outrageous numbers of quarrels and maintainers (probably referring in part to those who were profitably encouraging villeins to abandon their services) who were like kings in the country so that right and loyalty were made to hardly anyone.[14] In language reminiscent of Archbishop Mepham,[15] he complained of "the purveyors for the said household of the king and of others," referring to the higher nobility, who "pillage and destroy the people,"[16] and of the "subsidies and tallages" levied to their great distress. The ministers of the king and of others, he said, commit "grievous and outrageous oppressions"; great treasure was levied for the defense of the realm, but the people were nevertheless "burned, robbed, and pillaged" by their enemies from abroad, and no remedy was provided.[17] These things and others, he said, had moved the "lesser commons" to riot and make mischief, and he warned that greater mischiefs might ensue. This was a thoroughly reputable analysis.[18] Running through it is the theme that greed and self-interest were corrupting the administration of justice at home and, at the same time, weakening the defense of the realm against its enemies abroad.

Jealousies and factions began to make themselves apparent at court, while the situation abroad deteriorated. When the Revolt shook the kingdom, Gaunt, whose magnificent house in London, the Savoy, was destroyed, had been negotiating with the Scots, who treated him with respectful deference and even offered to assist him when Henry Percy sought to prevent his return to England. A bitter quarrel resulted, resolved only when Percy made a formal apology in Parliament. In 1382 Philip van Artevelde acknowledged Richard to be king of France, but the forces he assembled against the French were annihilated and he was himself killed. In October Bishop John Gilbert told Parliament that England had never been in greater danger of invasion. Brigandage was rife in the country, and many ships were destroyed off the northern coast. The disastrous crusade of Bishop Despenser of Norwich in 1383 and Richard's failure to assist him after his initial success hardly improved matters, and in 1384 Philip of Burgundy took control of the Netherlands but left Ghent its municipal freedom. England was fast losing its Continental allies and with them the protection of its trade.

At home factionalism grew at court, and morale was shaken by the quick temper of the young king and by his clear tendency to place his personal interests above the common profit of the realm. He was preoccupied with his favorites, the most prominent of whom was the youthful Robert de Vere, Earl of Oxford, who was spoiled by the king and easily moved to jealousy. He was undoubtedly responsible for suborning a Carmelite friar to accuse John of Gaunt before the king of seeking to kill him and seize the kingdom. This incident occurred at the Salisbury Parliament, where Richard told the Earl of Arundel to "go to the Devil" when he criticized the government of the realm. De Vere probably hoped that Richard's quick temper would move him to precipitous action against Gaunt. Indeed, the king is said to have gone into a tantrum and to have thrown his hat and shoes out the window, and Thomas of Woodstock, betraying an equal lack of self-control, is said to have drawn his sword and threatened to kill anyone who called his brother a traitor.[19] Gaunt was able to calm the king. But de Vere tried again early in 1385, this time by arranging a meeting of the Council at Waltham, where he hoped to have Gaunt accused, tried, and executed for treason by suborned justices. But the Duke heard of the plot and refused to attend; instead, he confronted Richard at Sheen with an appropriate military following. The two were finally reconciled by Princess Joan, who brought them together at Westminster, Richard having meanwhile drawn his sword before Archbishop Courtenay when he, together with some members of the Council, sought to reprimand him, as they met on barges on the Thames, for plots like that against Gaunt.

III.

Since *Troilus* is usually assigned to the latter part of the period 1380–86, it will repay us to examine the last two years in some detail, including events in the lives of Chaucer and his family. In France Charles VI assembled a great fleet for the invasion of England and sent 1,600 men under Jean de Vienne to aid the Scots, planning a simultaneous attack on England from the south and the north. These actions produced widespread consternation in England, leading to preparations to defend the coast, to the requisition of convoys for the wine fleet, and to a depression in the rising cloth trade that lasted until 1388.[20] The Chancellor, Michael de la Pole, realizing that the realm lacked financial resources for aggressive action, had been pursuing a determined peace policy toward France since 1383.[21] He now saw that policy collapsing before his eyes, while the "war party" at court, led by the Earls of Buckingham and Arundel, became more and more restive. Pole now resorted to an unsuccessful effort to raise scutage, which had not been levied for fifty years, to finance a campaign led by the king in Scotland. Richard summoned Gaunt, who led the largest force, to meet him at Newcastle on March 24.

Near York the king's half-brother, John Holland, killed young Richard Stafford, the son of the earl, in a quarrel. Richard was a royal favorite, and the king angrily avowed that he would treat Holland like any other felon, much to the distress of Princess Joan; but Holland fled into sanctuary at Beverley. As the army of almost 12,000 men crossed the border,[22] Richard, in a somewhat feeble imitation of Edward III, created two new dukes (his uncle the Earl of Cambridge became Duke of York, and his uncle the Earl of Buckingham, Thomas of Woodstock, the Duke of Gloucester) and knighted various other persons. The Scots and their French allies, confronted by much larger forces than their own, prudently retreated northward without a confrontation. Although Richard's articles of war had forbidden attacks on religious,[23] he burned two monasteries and would have burned a third had not Gaunt intervened. The army reached Edinburgh without a battle, and de Vere urged the king to return home, which he did. It is not surprising that Walsingham, echoing a charge at least as old as the *Aeneid*, said that the court circle was made up of "knights of Venus rather then of Bellona."[24] (Walsingham is a good source for popular gossip, or for propaganda spread by interested magnates,[25] and this probably represents fairly widespread opinion in the countryside.) In November de Vere was made Marquis of Ireland, and the Chancellor hoped to collect sufficient funds from a ransom for John of Blois, the claimant to Brittany, to finance his projected campaign in that country.

The French fleet was prevented from sailing by an action taken by the town of Ghent, which distracted the forces drawn up along the coast. Meanwhile, the news of the Portuguese victory at Aljubarotta, assisted by English archers, had reached England before Parliament met in October. The Commons, dissatisfied with Pole's management of the royal revenues and alarmed by invasion threats, was now prepared to listen favorably to Gaunt's proposals for a crusade in Spain, rejected earlier in favor of Despenser's crusade. A few days before the opening of Parliament Chaucer was appointed to a commission of the peace from Kent. Among his fellow justices was Sir Arnold Savage, who once accompanied Gaunt on a peace mission. He had been a member of the royal household since Richard's accession, his mother having acted as nurse to the young king. He had been knighted in Scotland. To anticipate a little, he was sheriff of Kent at the time of Chaucer's election to Parliament in 1386. Such elections were not "democratic" in the modern sense, and the sheriff himself, often dominated by any interested magnates, determined the outcome. There is no evidence that Chaucer was a prominent Kentish freeholder, and it is a fair assumption that his election resulted from favorable action on the part of someone of higher rank. Sir Arnold, who probably had some literary interests since he was later to act as executor for John Gower,[26] probably found such action congenial. He is said to have later joined Gaunt's crusade.

When Parliament met in October 1385, the government was heavily in debt, the people were not in the mood for heavy taxation, the successes of Edward III on the Continent were now nostalgic memories, clouded by the realization that the advantages he had gained had somehow faded away, and the country seemed hardly capable of defending itself. It was fairly easy to conclude that through "evil counsellors," or household extravagance and corruption, Richard, abetted by his favorites and the chancellor, had frittered away both the moral and the financial resources of his kingdom. Among his "extravagances" was a grant made to Chaucer under the signet (endorsed by de Vere) allowing him to appoint a permanent deputy at the wool wharf.[27] A bill introduced by the Commons demanded, among other things, that controllers and other customs officials perform their duties in person and not by deputy, and the entire bill was endorsed by the king. Michael de la Pole did nothing about it and, in fact, was probably responsible for having it removed from the rolls of Parliament. His action, or inaction, was largely responsible for his impeachment in 1386.[28] Chaucer and his friends probably knew that this bill was pending some time before Parliament met, and that it would eventually be implemented. The appointment to the peace commission probably resulted from their desire to increase his prominence in anticipation of an eventual loss of his position. In any event, Parliament granted a modest subsidy on the basis of the concessions represented in the bill, and approved Gaunt's crusade in Spain. Neither Richard nor his chancellor wanted a direct confrontation with France, and it is likely that for Gloucester and Arundel, Gaunt's venture represented positive and potentially fruitful action. It is possible also that Richard and his favorites were happy to have Gaunt out of the country, although in 1389, when de Vere was out of the way, Richard was anxious to have him back, and even assumed his livery when he returned. Meanwhile, those actively seeking peace with France may have thought that a diversion in Spain might help negotiations with the French, as indeed Gaunt's initial success in Asturias seemed to do. Meanwhile, however, the situation on the Continent was not improving, for Ghent capitulated to the French in December, assuring French control of the Low Countries.

Some indication of the possible source of influence in assisting Chaucer is provided by the fact that on February 19, 1386, John of Gaunt personally supervised the admission of Philippa Chaucer, along with his son Henry of Derby (the future Henry IV) and certain other members of his family, including two sons of Philippa's sister Katherine Swynford, into the fraternity of Lincoln Cathedral. (Gaunt was lord of the castle at Lincoln and a patron of the cathedral, protecting its rights in the town.) Henry Percy, perhaps as a gesture of friendship, joined in the same year, and King Richard and Queen Anne joined in 1387 during their ramblings.[29] By the time of Philippa's admission to the Lincoln fraternity it had probably already been decided that Chaucer's son Thomas would accompany Gaunt on his crusade, where he evidently performed well, for the Duke granted him an annuity for life dated at Bayonne in 1389. During February John Holland agreed to furnish three chaplains for his victim Richard Stafford and was restored to favor. He allowed himself to be overcome by the charms of Gaunt's daughter Elizabeth, however, seduced her, quickly married her, and as a new member of the Lancastrian family, so to speak, was made Constable of the expeditionary force.[30] Meanwhile, Gaunt had obtained a papal bull endorsing his crusade and providing plenary pardons for all those who sided with him. The crusade was proclaimed publicly at St. Paul's on February 18, 1386, and the new bishop of Llandaff, William of Bottlesham, and John Gilbert, bishop of Hereford, roamed through the country preaching it, assisted by Carmelite friars. On Saturday March 25 at an elaborate ceremony of farewell, Richard presented gold crowns to King John of Spain, as Gaunt styled himself, and Queen Constance, who set off soon afterward toward Plymouth with their two remaining unmarried daughters and, probably, with an impressive entourage of household ministers, participants, and well-wishers.

Meanwhile, diplomatic negotiations with the French continued. In February Richard lavishly entertained Leo of Armenia, who was seeking to establish peace between England and France so they could unite in a crusade against the Turks, whose threat to Christian territory was becoming steadily more alarming. The negotiations led to an agreement whereby Richard would meet King Charles and Philip of Burgundy on the Continent in March, and Richard granted Leo an annuity of £1,000.[31] Charles and Philip proceeded to Bologne, but Richard failed to arrive at Calais, since Michael de la Pole could not convince the French that Gaunt should be allowed to pursue his aims in Spain. Fears of invasion were by no means over in England, and in the spring, commissioners of array were sent to the southern counties, and the ports and the town of Calais were fortified. Military activity lapsed for a time in France, probably because of the illness of the Duke of Burgundy. A truce with Scotland, which had been deserted by Jean of Vienne, who did not like living conditions there, was signed on June 27, removing at least for a time the military threat from the north. But shortly after the departure of John of Gaunt in early July the French buildup on the coast resumed, and by September there was assembled the largest invasion fleet ever seen in Europe, with some 30,000 men and elaborate equipment for establishing footholds on the English coast. It was compared by one writer with the fleet that attacked Troy,[32] a comparison, as we shall see, that was not inappropriate. At some time during this period Clanvowe and his friend Neville were sent to help organize the defense of the south coast, where unpaid soldiers were being troublesome. The king, meanwhile, was rather ostentatiously disregarding the French and devoting his attention to de Vere's preparations for departure for Ireland, showering privileges and benefits on his favorite, who did not in fact depart.

Chaucer was elected to Parliament in September. By the time it met he had probably made arrangements to give up his residence at Aldgate, and on October 15, during the session, he gave his testimony at the Scrope–Grosvenor trial, an event that has led to a great deal of discussion about his assertion that he was "del age xl ans et plus armez par xxvii ans," which affords evidence of his approximate date of birth. The trial actually allowed him to appear before a prominent gathering and, in addition, to make a favorable impression on the Scropes, one of the most prominent families in England.[34] John of Gaunt and his followers had given their testimony (in favor of the Scropes) at Plymouth before their departure for Spain, and it is quite possible that the Duke arranged for Chaucer to testify. At Parliament the Commons was ready to join the "war party" at court, demanding the dismissal of Michael de la Pole, whose diplomacy had clearly failed and who had prevented the reforms passed in 1385 from being implemented. After being threatened with deposition at Eltham, where he had retired from Parliament, Richard returned and acceded to the new demands. Pole was replaced by Bishop Thomas Arundel, the brother of the earl,[35] and the new treasurer was Gaunt's friend Bishop John Gilbert. Gloucester and the Earl of Arundel were now in effective control of the government. Petitions were introduced in Parliament complaining about the behavior of Richard's friend the London merchant Nicholas Brembre. The Commons also asked that the statute concerning fees and robes for justices be reissued,[36] a subject recalled by Chaucer in his description of the Sergeant of the Law, who had often been a justice of assize:[37] "Of fees and robes hadde he many oon."

The Commons complained also that lands seized by escheators were regranted before the injured parties could bring their cases to court, and that when they sought a remedy they found that those to whom their lands had been regranted had letters of protection (*RP*, 3:222–23). Richard replied, rather ineffectively, that such persons should seek a remedy from the chancellor, although the practice was in violation of Edward's statute on the subject of escheators (*SR*, 1:367–68). (Richard had a deplorable habit of regranting newly escheated lands to his favorites.) The Commons further asked, again echoing Edward's statute against fees and robes, that no prorogations be granted in cases involving land, causing justice to be delayed. It is clear that while the lords were thinking nostalgically of Edward's conquests abroad, the Commons was thinking nostalgically about his justice. In December Chaucer was deprived of his position at the Customs House, an eventuality he had probably been anticipating for some time. Considering Richard's obvious extravagance in the use of the signet or secret seal for grants made to his household favorites,[38] it seems unlikely that Chaucer would have regarded his own dismissal from what had become a merely nominal office with much resentment.

To extend our glance, very briefly, into the following year, we find that Richard spent some ten months in his "gyrations," during which he obtained legal opinions concerning the legality of the acts of the October Parliament and returned to London only to precipitate what amounted to a civil uprising and the "Merciless Parliament" of 1388, which succeeded, by very crude means indeed, in removing what many regarded as his "evil counsellors" and establishing a short-lived government by Council. Chaucer was not to obtain another lucrative office until after Richard declared himself of age and resumed power on May 3, 1389. In July, this time under the Privy Seal, a warrant was issued naming him Clerk of the Works, an office more eminent than any he had held before.

Chaucer's personal reaction to the October Parliament of 1386 has aroused some discussion. It has, for example, been plausibly argued that his account of the Trojan Parliament in which Antenor is ransomed for Criseyde (*Troilus,* ed. Robinson, 4:141–217) is a reflection of his discouragement at the decisions affecting him.[39] But the analogy between the two parliaments is not very convincing. There was no Hector in the English Parliament to oppose the proceedings, which under the circumstances were understandable enough. And in the Trojan parliament Hector is just as blind as anyone else to the behavior of Antenor; he simply objects that Trojans do not sell women, chivalrously fulfilling his obligation to protect Criseyde incurred immediately after her father's defection (*Troilus,* 1:117–23). There is no evidence that King Priam is being either recalcitrant or threatened by his own noblemen, and it can not be seriously argued that Criseyde is promoting the chivalry of Troy, as, for example, Blanche of Lancaster had once done in England. The frequent assertion that the comparison between the spread of the "noise of people" and the spread of fire in straw is an allusion to Jack Straw is not very convincing either, since the "lesser commons" did not attend parliament in England and were not well represented there. The implication seems to be rather that if Troy lacked wise leadership its people were likely to act unwisely, just as the senses are likely to rebel if a man is not governed by reason. The unwise leadership began when the Trojan court welcomed Helen, in effect abandoning Pallas for the sake of Venus. Troilus has done exactly the same thing, and at this point has been "burning" for some time. The action of the Trojan parliament is in effect suicidal, and is parallel with the immediate reaction of Troilus, who, having been misled by his senses, calls on Death to destroy him, foolishly cursing Fortune, whom he says, again foolishly, he has always worshipped above all other gods. Readers of *The Consolation of Philosophy* or, for that matter, of Chaucer's poem "Fortune," should be fully aware of the dangers of this kind of blind devotion, and it is quite likely that many in Chaucer's audience found Troilus ridiculous, if not laughable. It would be difficult to think of Chaucer reacting to his dismissal in a manner in any way resembling the reaction of Troilus.

Again, it is not easy to think of an appropriate date in 1387 to which we could assign the probable delivery of Chaucer's poem, unless we make the unlikely assumption that Richard asked for it while engaged on his travels or during the turbulent period after his return to London. Troy is under siege as Chaucer describes it, and a similar situation existed in England almost at any time between 1377 and the close of 1386. The French, for reasons not well understood, abandoned their invasion plans in December of that year. It is true that in the same month the Council at Amiens determined to renew the effort in 1387, but as it turned out King Charles had only the resources to send some forces into Spain to oppose Gaunt. The Scots attacked in 1388, enjoying a victory at Chevy Chase, but that seems a very late date for the poem. The year 1386 seems more promising than either 1385 or 1387. Gaunt's preparations for departure and the festivities connected with it would have provided a suitable occasion. Specifically, the days before and including that of the "coronation" ceremony arranged by Richard suggest a likely date, although a later date at Plymouth while the expedition was waiting to set forth is another possibility. John of Gaunt, clearly concerned about Chaucer's family, was most probably involved in arrangements for presenting the poet in a favorable light before persons of eminence so that he might find something ro replace his income at the Customs House, and in this effort he probably found Chaucer's friends at court ready to cooperate. I do not mean to suggest that Chaucer suddenly composed a long poem for a specific occasion, but that he put the finishing touches on a poem he had been working on for some time at the request of someone who knew about it.

IV.

Before turning to the poem itself I shall discuss its general relevance to England, the kind of ideals we may safely assume to have been held by Chaucer's friends at court and, very briefly, some points concerning literary technique. First, the English, influenced by traditions stemming from Geoffrey of Monmouth's *History of the Kings of Britain*, regarded themselves as inheritors of the traditions of ancient Troy. "Britain" was the realm established by "Brutus," the great-grandson of Aeneas, or as Chaucer called it in his poem addressed to Henry IV, "Brutes Albion," and London was often called "New Troy." The fall of Troy thus served as a kind of perpetual warning, especially against following the example of Paris, the young Trojan prince who chose Venus over the busy life of Juno or the wise contemplation of Pallas.[40] Paris is made to say with unwitting irony in Ovid's amusing Epistle (*Heroides*, 16:48–49), "One of the seers said that Ilion would burn with the fire of Paris." Chaucer, in effect, makes Troy burn with the fire of Troilus. Gower, who uses the commonplace association of England with Troy in *Vox clamantis*, complains, near the close of his poem attacking the evils of his time in England, that his country "who was once holy is becoming the goddess Venus herself."[41]

That idleness and lecherous self-indulgence were inimical to chivalric endeavor, reflected in Walsingham's remark about Richard's court quoted above, appealed strongly to the medieval mind, and indeed, had antecedents in both Virgil and Ovid. Thus, in a sermon preached at St. Paul's in May 1375, Bishop Brinton of Rochester, having explained that those who wish others to be subject to them should be ruled by reason themselves, said further that the honor of a king depends on military power, sane counsel, clerical wisdom, and the just rule of the people, quoting, with reference to the first, John of Salisbury on the oath of a soldier. He went on to say that the English under Edward were once victorious in war, but because of their sins, God, who "was once an Englishman," had receded from them. (The sins he had in mind were those of idleness and lechery.)[42] And in the following year, in a sermon praising the recently deceased Prince Edward, he said, "What is surprising, therefore, if the English are unfortunate in war, when in England everywhere reign lechery, adultery, and incest, so that few, and especially lords, are content with their wives."[43] In 1346 Bishop Bradwardine, in a famous sermon celebrating English victories, vigorously castigated the French for being soldiers of Cupid and Venus, attributing their defeat at least partly to this fact. The fruit of their lechery, he said, was "a stinking and intense burning."[44] Chaucer's repeated references to the "fire" that burns Troilus are singularly appropriate. In short, the virtue of chivalry and devotion to Venus were traditionally regarded as being incompatible.[45]

John of Salisbury insists repeatedly throughout the *Policraticus*, a book that Chaucer knew, that self-indulgence and the pursuit of Venus undermine not only military valor but the general efficacy of a prince, using the Terentian braggart soldier as an exemplar for ridiculing the weaknesses of his own contemporaries in England. And in the popular commentary on the *Aeneid* attributed to Bernard Silvestris, the Trojan horse is used as a figure for *luxuria* that brings with it all the other vices.[46] Troy burned because its leaders led it to desert Pallas for Venus, and it seemed possible that New Troy might burn in the same way for what were thought of as essentially the same reasons. Since the days of Marcabru, moreover, venereal preoccupation had been thought of as one of the worst deterrents to crusading zeal. Hence the attention accorded it by Philippe de Mézières in *Le songe du vieil pelerin* (1:52–56), where Luxure describes her baleful influence under her mistress Venus.

Chaucer was able to add depth and authority to his poem by suggesting various kinds of what might be called "analogies" or, to use a medieval term, "similitudes," many of which are implied rather than stated. Eugene Vinaver has called our attention to the use of anology in romances, where one episode may be made to recall and comment upon a much earlier episode in the interwoven fabric of the narrative.[47] Chaucer's shorter narrative made this technique impractical. But he could and did suggest a number of analogies simultaneously, appealing to the memories of a reasonably literate and sophisticated audience well grounded in the classics and the Scriptures.

First, there is an obvious analogy within the poem itself between the macrocosm represented by Troy and the microcosm represented by Troilus. The fall of Troy and the fall of Troilus take place simultaneously, and the carefully traced fall of the man offers an explanation and a paradigm for the fall of the city. A similar device had been used in the commentary on the *Aeneid* just mentioned, where Troy is made through "moralization" a figure for the human body in order to emphasize the moral causes of its destruction. John of Salisbury had used the analogy between a man and the commonwealth the other way around, to emphasize the interdependence of all of society's "members" or groups and the necessity for reason and wisdom on the part of the ruler, and the further necessity for an interest in the welfare of the whole on the part of the individuals making up the "members." This is a fruitful similitude rather than an "organic theory of the state."[48] The same kind of analogy is adduced by Gower in the Prologue to his *Confessio Amantis* (945–62), begun at a time roughly contemporary with *Troilus*. In Chaucer's poem, while Pandarus, who protected Paris from Menelaus while Pallas was still guiding Troy,[49] is busily encouraging Troilus in his self-destructive passion, his brother Calchas is assisting the Greeks in their efforts to destroy the city. And while Antenor, presumably, is seeking the same end, his sister Trojan Antigone helps to bring about the aid of Criseyde in the destruction of Troilus.

A concentration on the microcosm facilitated the development of further analogies from a variety of sources, of which I shall here mention only a few. For example, frequent allusions to ideas and doctrines from *The Consolation of Philosophy*, which Chaucer had probably been translating at about the time he was fashioning his poem, suggest that Pandarus is in part an inverted Lady Philosophy, whose part Stoic and part Epicurean teachings represent, as Philosophy says (1:pr. 3), "cloutes . . . out of my clothes," used to induce Troilus to embrace worldly joys rather than to forego them for the sake of his people.[50] Again, his assiduousness in urging Troilus on recalls the Terentian parasite who affixes himself to Epicureans in the pages of the *Policraticus* (especially Bk. 3). Chaucer can also evoke such analogies for a single episode. For example, the ruse Pandarus arranges to bring Troilus and Criseyde together in Deiphebus's house (2:1513-26) is reminiscent of that employed by Jonadab, "a very wise man," to bring together the ill-fated Amnon and Thamar (Douay, 2 Kings, 13). There are, of course, analogies in fourteenth-century life, and these are in some ways the most important of all, since the "background" analogies simply reinforce them by calling forth implications arising from associations in the minds of the audience, made pleasurable by recognition. Thus Pandarus is a counselor to a prince, in fact the only member of Troilus's retinue we meet in the poem. His destructive aid recalls the "false counsellors" who urge princes to follow their own inclinations rather than the dictates of wisdom, vigorously condemned in Chaucer's Melibeus and often said to be busy about the English court. Again, Pandarus leads Troilus in prayer and causes him to beat his breast in contrition for his sons against the God of Love (1:932-38) as though he were a priest. (Bishop Brinton had complained bitterly about confessors who failed to correct the sins of magnates guilty of adultery or other similar transgressions.)[51] Pandarus actually offers to help Troilus if he wants his brother's wife (1:676-79) and, after progress has been made with his own niece, acts to "quike alwey the fir" that burns him (3:484).

Troilus is in some ways another Paris, or a transformation of Paris into a similitude of Troy itself. Although less aggressive than either his brother or his rival Diomede, he repeats his brother's unfortunate choice; and just as Helen betrayed Paris for Deiphebus, whom she in turn betrayed to the Greeks, so Criseyde betrays Troilus for Diomede. As Mary-Jo Arn has indicated,[52] the theme of betrayal is introduced early in the poem when Pandarus refers to Oenone's Epistle to Paris in the *Heroides* (1:652 ff.), hardly tempered by his observation that even if he, like Oenone, cannot cure his own frustrated love, he can advise Troilus and will not restrain him even if he wants Helen, with whose character he seems to have been familiar. This action suggests that in a sense he is once more "assisting" Paris in a new guise.

An ominous background to the poem is afforded by both direct and indirect allusions to Theban history and legend, most explicitly in the story of Niobe, which Pandarus characteristically misapplies; in Criseyde's "Romance of Thebes" (2:106), with its story of Amphiarus whose implications (WB Prol. 740-46, "Mars," 245 ff.) Pandarus does not wish to face; and in Cassandra's interpretation of Troilus's dream. The Theban material in the poem, suggestive of the ill consequences of civil or fraternal strife, not, as we have seen, unknown in the English court, has been ably examined by David Anderson,[53] and a few details will suffice here. In the Knight's Tale Chaucer shows Palamon complaining about Juno, whom Boccaccio calls the "dea de' matrimonii," angry at Thebes "per gli adulterii da Giove, suo marito, commessi con le donne tebano," because she "hath destroyed wel ny al the blood / Of Thebes." Juno was also said to be inimical to Troy after the judgment of

Paris, as well she might be, and the behavior of Troilus and Criseyde can hardly have pleased her.[55] Nevertheless, Pandarus, after having suggested "That in the dees right as their fallen chaunces, / Right so in love ther come and gon plesaunces," hardly an idea pleasing to Juno, continues ineptly to console Troilus by saying, in connection with Criseyde (4:1116–18),

> blisful Juno, thorugh hir grete myght,
> Shal, as I hope, hir grace unto us sende.
> Myn herte seth, "certayn, she shal nat wende."

And Criseyde later (4:1538) amusingly invokes Juno in connection with her sworn intention to return to Troy. It may be that Chaucer thought of Hecuba as the daughter of King Dymas of Thebes. Ovid, immediately after his account of Ceyx and Alcyone, calls her a child of Dymas (*Met.* 11:761), identified by one mythographer as a king of Thebes.[56] But whether or not Troilus shares the "blood of Thebes," he does share with the Thebans a neglect of Juno, and is hardly kind to Pallas, Apollo, or Diana. Criseyde and Diomede both have connections with the ill-fated "Seven against Thebes." She, the daughter of Argia (Chaucer's "Argyve"), is the fruit of a Chaucerian union between Calchas and the wife of Polynices, who corrupted the wife of Amphiorus with the "Brooch of Thebes." This also makes her first cousin to Diomede, the son of Argia's sister Deiphyle. Finally, if Trojan Antigone is Criseyde's niece, her deceased husband must have been a Chaucerian younger brother of Laomedon, the father of Priam, Anchises, Antenor, and Antigone. (Antigone, as we shall see, also had her difficulties with Juno.) It is difficult to escape Anderson's conclusion that "Chaucer added the specter of Thebes to the background of *Troilus* to underscore an implicit theme of the poem, namely that one fallen city may serve as a warning to another not yet fallen. As Thebes should have been to Troy, so Troy should be to England."

Vinaver makes a further point about the romances of Chrétien de Troyes that may be valid for *Troilus* as well, as Ida Gordon has suggested.[57] He tells us that the French poet "lets the characters enact a line of argument that happens to interest him, no matter what kind of characterisation, real or unreal, may emerge as a result."[58] Since the analogies to which we have called attention determine the patterns of action to be followed by the characters, Gordon is probably correct, although Chaucer does maintain a reasonable verisimilitude in contemporary terms. Criseyde is widely hailed as a "complex" character, and the motivations of Pandarus have been difficult to explain. But the problems are not so grave as they at first seem. Troilus is a prince distracted from his obligations by a self-indulgent passion, and such princes were not unknown in the fourteenth century. Criseyde, who has a very good opinion of herself (2:746–49) and is rather vain, is easily impressed by a man obviously above her in station who wishes to take advantage of her.

She can, moreover, readily cite salubrious doctrines in all sincerity without understanding their relevance to her own conduct, a not uncommon trait. And Pandarus is not unlike familiar gnathonic persons who attach themselves to their betters, as he does both in his defense of Paris and in his eagerness to satisfy the appetites of his prince.

One further point about Chaucer's technique is, I think, often misunderstood because of a change in taste. In spite of his ultimate seriousness of purpose, Chaucer, again like Chrétien, delights in teasing his audience; and he very seldom writes at any length without a smile. He had undoubtedly read and thoroughly digested John of Salisbury's elaboration of an Horatian maxim (*Satires*, 1:1.23–24) in the *Policraticus* (8:11): "Nothing prevents one from speaking the truth with a smile and from illustrating in fabulous narratives that which may be detrimental to good morals." John is about to relate the story of the widow of Ephesus, and the point is illustrated once more in his obvious admiration for the *Eunuch* of Terence, skilfully used in the argument of *Policraticus* 8 to show that tyrants are actually Epicureans. The basic principle was known even to Harry Bailly, who says in the Prologue to the Cook's Tale (4355), "A man may seye ful sooth in game and pley," although he is himself, being something of an Epicurean, slow to grasp the "sooth" of what he hears.

To return to John of Salisbury, we find him innocent of the idea that a tragedy should be solemn. He had read Boethius, rather than Aristotle, who told him that tragedies portray the downfall of men of high estate who foolishly, and hence from a medieval point of view amusingly, subject themselves to Fortune and suffer the Providential consequences. Thus John was able to write of those who abandon the obligatory "warfare" of "the life of man upon earth" (Job 7:1; 2 Cor. 10:4) as mere players subject to the whims of Fortune as they act out "the comedy or tragedy of this world" (*Pol.* 3:8). Such players are "comic" because their actions are ludicrous, even though the consequences may be providentially "tragic" or disastrous. Even Shakespeare, later, often made his tragic protagonists ridiculous and introduced comic scenes into his tragedies, not as "relief" but as witty thematic reinforcements. The change in taste exemplified in Joseph Wharton's attack on wit and his assertion that the sublime and the pathetic, which are solemn matters, are the true subjects of poetry had not yet taken place. In Chaucer's day wit still reigned.

V.

As we have seen, *Troilus* was most probably written at a time when England was in danger from invasion from abroad, and quite possibly at a time when hopes were raised for a remedy in the crusade of the Duke of Lancaster. Meanwhile the king and his ministers, not to mention ordinary merchants and peasants, seem to have been guided more by immediate self-interest than by consideration for the welfare of the realm. Chaucer set out to show how "invisible foes," as he calls them at Troy, make possible the destruction of a commonwealth by "visible foes" without, using a negative example to make the positive appeal at the close of his poem more poignant. The example is the story of Troilus, and it will repay us to glance briefly at his behavior as a prince and as a chivalric leader.

When we first meet Troilus he is attending the festival of the Palladium, the sacred image of Pallas, who was regarded in the Middle Ages as the goddess of wisdom, a virtue recognized as being of special importance in a prince or knight, who should be, as Chaucer puts it elsewhere, worthy and wise. Pallas is said to have protected Troy until the Palladium was stolen by Diomede.[59] This brings us a further analogy, since it was Diomede who in effect stole Troilus's image of Venus, Criseyde, plunging the young prince into self-destructive wrath under the inspiration of the "Herynes," who lead him to the "angry Parcas," ministers of destiny. Instead of dutifully paying homage to Pallas, whose festival was traditionally celebrated at Athens, by holding philosophical conversations,[60] Troilus and his young followers are idly, and I use this word advisedly,[61] "beholding ay the ladies of the Town." Thus Troilus, foolishly defying Venus when, as Chaucer says, "Th'eschewing is only the remedye,"[62] is practically inviting the arrow of Cupid. As he makes fun of lovers for their labor in winning, their uneasiness in keeping, and their woes and pains at losing, at the same time he is indicating his own condition and his own fate.[63]

An analogy for this action is a bit of wisdom from Ecclesiasticus (9:7-9): "Look not around thee in the ways of the city, nor wander up and down into the streets thereof. Turn away thy face from a woman dressed up, and gaze not upon another's beauty. For many have perished by the beauty of a woman, and hereby lust is enkindled as a fire." He sees Criseyde, her image (Cupid's arrow) sticks to his "hertes botme" bypassing his reason as it usually does, so that he abandons his companions, not to mention Pallas, and retreats to his chamber, where, having defied Ovid's precept (*Rem. am.*, 579) "beware of solitary places!" he begins to burn. He soon resigns his "estaat royale" to her, repeating in effect the Judgment of Paris, so that he ceases to worry about either the siege or his own salvation. He actually decides that death is the only solution to his problem, and he prays to Criseyde, whom he has seen only once and that briefly, and concerning whose character he is completely ignorant, to have mercy on him and save him from "the death." This is silly enough, but when Pandarus comes and offers assistance, Troilus first tells him to go away, for he will die. Love, he says, has overcome him, and his burning desire is so great

> That to be slayn it were a gretter joye
> To me than kyng of Grece ben and Troye.

These are truly deplorable sentiments in a prince whose nation is under attack, and we can well imagine how Chaucer's audience would have regarded their own companions substituting "France" and "England" for "Grece" and "Troye." We can rest assured, moreover, that this commonplace analogy did occur to them, and that they recognized in Troilus an extreme exemplification of what some of them, in one way or another, had been doing. Since Troilus has no wish to marry, he is reduced to either inaction or subterfuge.

Pandarus is ready to supply the subterfuge, in spite of his own amorous difficulties. He can help, he says, even if Troilus loves Helen, and he advises Troilus not to weep like Theban Niobe. Niobe's seven sons and seven daughters were shot down by Apollo (wisdom or truth) and Diana (chastity) after she defied their mother, Latona, a goddess of wisdom. If anything, this reference emphasizes the foolishness of angering any of these deities, or disregarding the virtues they represent, a point emphasized once more, and again inadvertently and hence amusingly, when Pandarus says that although Troilus may suffer pains as sharp as those suffered by "Ticius in helle," he can still be of assistance. Tityus became a common figure for insatiable libido, for which naturally there is no cure, for he attempted to rape Latona, was shot down by Apollo and Diana, and sent to hell where he suffers the eternal torment of having his liver (Pandarus's "stomak" was thought to be the seat of libido in women) gnawed by "volturis." Having explained that Fortune's wheel always turns and Troilus may yet rise upon it, but omitting the obvious consequence that he will also fall if he rises upon it, Pandarus generously offers in true gnathonic fashion, to get his own sister for him if he wants her. Having discovered that it is his niece, Criseyde, rather than his sister, for whom Troilus burns, he leads him in prayer to Cupid and asserts that if Criseyde does not love in accordance with "natural" love, by which he means what would have been regarded as "natural" after the Fall when human nature was corrupted, rather than "celestial" love, he will hold it a vice in her.

Having grown hotter through encouragement, Troilus prays to Venus for help, although, amusingly, it is the business of Venus to make the fire hot (a fact abundantly evident in the *Roman de la rose*), and, falling upon his knees before his parasite, entrusts his life and death to him, saying, "fy on the Grekes alle!" as though the attack on the city did not matter. He becomes like a lion on the battlefield and friendly and gentle to everyone at home, not to save or encourage his countrymen, but to make an impression on Criseyde. This is almost an echo of Bradwardine's accusation, in the sermon referred to above, that the French, subjecting themselves to Cupid and Venus, seek "a name upon earth" so that "they may be loved by foolish women." The witty satire of this book has been generally neglected in favor of more sentimental and serious concerns.

In the second book, an amusing reflection of contemporary court manners somewhat exaggerated for effect, Pandarus and Criseyde seek to maneuver themselves into a situation where Troilus can have his will and Criseyde can preserve her "honor," which would suffer if a secret and illicit affair became known. Pandarus paints for her little pictures of Troilus discussing military strategy in "the paleis garden, by a welle," playing idly at darts, and mournfully confessing his sins to the God of Love; or in his bedchamber groaning for love. The military strategy was obviously not the subject uppermost in his mind, although Criseyde, who is flattered, disregards this obvious implication. When she sees him from a window with his battered helm and shield she is impressed by his prowess, his high estate, his reputation, but more than anything else by the fact that his distress is all for her. She argues with herself about the most profitable course she could take, but determines not to take another husband who might be dominating or unfaithful, and is clearly impressed both by her own attractiveness and by the exalted station of her lover. She hears the song of Antigone, who, the mythographers tell us, thought herself to be more beautiful than Juno, so irritating that deity that she turned her hair into serpents, a punishment later mitigated by having her transformed into a stork.[64] But Criseyde is impressed by the song praising love rather than Junonian marriage, and the later picture of her tearing her "ownded" hair may be reminiscent of this suggested analogy as well as being, along with the hand-wringing, a signal of *tristitia*, or worldly sorrow. When she grants Troilus "love of friendship" the young prince is gladder than if someone had given him "a thousand Troys," again an indication of his lack of any sense of chivalric or princely obligation, what we today might describe as "social conscience." The fire "of which he brente" becomes even hotter. Pandarus develops his plot to bring the two together, invovling lies to Deiphebus, to Helen, to Criseyde, and a feigned illness on the part of Troilus. I need not print out that none of the actions in this book has much to do with "chivalrie, trouthe, honour, fredom, and curtesie," although they do illustrate false virtues that resemble these virtues on the surface. Our word for simulated virtue is hypocrisy.

Book III is a comic account of the activities of Venus, "plesaunce of love," who is invoked at the outset, along with a brief account of the activities of Jove that so offended Juno and some veiled hints of divine love. As Troilus lies in bed at Deiphebus's house, Criseyde and Pandarus appear, and she, quite properly, asks him for "lordshipe," which is the last thing he has in mind. He asks to be under her "yerde" or dominion, and in fact he plays, from a medieval point of view, a curiously feminine role in the subsequent narrative, consistent with the commonplace idea that passion makes men effeminate. Criseyde says that if he will keep her "honor" (meaning her reputation) she will receive him into her service, providing he will have no sovereignty in love, thus reversing her original proper request. When Pandarus offers to bring the couple together to "speke of love," as he laughingly puts it, Troilus is overjoyed, but he groans to deceive Helen and Deiphebus entering from the garden, to which Pandarus has cleverly led them. Improper aims lead to worldly stratagems, or, as they are now called, "cover-ups," and under the guidance of Pandarus Troilus becomes adept at them.

When he and Pandarus are alone, the latter seeks to excuse his pandaring, asking that Troilus keep everything secret, since if anyone knew what he had done it would be considered "the werste trecherie." Chaucer's audience knew, of course, and could hardly have escaped making that judgment themselves and the further observation that the "treachery" was not only condoned but encouraged by Troilus. Pandarus also warns against boasting and lying, although it is clear that he is himself a skilled liar. Troilus swears secrecy and promises to serve Pandarus as a slave forever, calling his action "nobility, compassion, fellowship, and trust," and offering to get Pandarus his sister Polyxena, his sister Cassandra, or Helen, or "any of the frape" if he wants one of them.[65]

Thus our prince offers to become an unscrupulous pander himself, as well as a parasite to a man beneath him in status. He devises the stratagem of pretending to be preoccupied with the problem of the siege, in which he has no real interest, at the temple of Apollo when he is actually with Criseyde. The virtues of wisdom and truth, represented by Apollo, are once more carelessly defied. For by lying to Criseyde Pandarus gets her to his house, although she, a kindred spirit, is clearly aware of the lie. Pandarus, however, needs still another lie to bring the lovers together. Troilus, after lurking in a "stewe," feels compelled to say a prayer to Venus, whom he promises to serve until he dies. This self-dedication to idleness and lust is hardly propitious either for himself, for Criseyde, or for the people of Troy, whose "Hector the Second" is thus abandoning them. The amusing ineptitude of the prayer constitutes a kind of witty comment on the speaker, for it is hardly propitious for what he has in mind. He mentions Venus's unsuccessful love for Adonis, the love of Jove for Europa, which had disastrous consequences, the love of Mars for Venus, which led to his great embarrassment, the frustrated love of Phebus for Daphne, and the love of Mercury for Herse, which provoked the wrath of Pallas. He even calls on Diana, who is unlikely to find his enterprise agreeable, and he finally addresses the Fates, ministers of destiny, who shape the ends of all those who lose their free will through passion, including, of course, Troilus himself (5:1-7). There can be little doubt that this ridiculous performance produced laughter in the fourteenth century.

Criseyde, always full of good doctrine, lectures Pandarus at length on the fleeting character of worldly joys and her lover on the evils of jealousy. The young prince faints in confusion and is thrown in bed by Pandarus, actions that further detract from his princely dignity. Even more conversation is necessary before the two lovers subside into the uneasy heaven of Venereal bliss where, unfortunately, both feel that their delights may be mere dreams or in any event transitory. Criseyde has just pointed out that they are transitory by nature, although it is amusing that neither she nor her lover shows any sign of recognizing this fact. Next morning Troilus thanks Pandarus for having rescued him from "Flegetoun, the fiery flood of helle," a river, as a popular mythographer says, "signifying the fires of wrath and cupidity with which human hearts are inflamed,"[66] passions later to be elaborated by Chaucer in his portraits of Arcite and Palamon in the Knight's Tale. But Troilus immediately finds himself back in this river, urging Pandarus to arrange a new assignation because, as he says, "I had it never half so hote an nowe." This constitutes a witty comment on the "rescue."

The unquenchable fire was thought to be one of the disadvantages of lust, not a plaintive comment on the human condition. Thus the plight of Tityrus was thought to illustrate the fact that "when the action is once performed it is not enough for lust, for it always breaks out again."[67] The idea had been elaborated by John of Salisbury, who said, echoing Terence (*Eunuch*, 2:3),

> The touch of the bodies of others, and the more ardent appetite for women is next to insanity. Whatever any of the senses attempt is game and play compared with those things brought about by this frenzy. From it we desire, we are wrathful, we are passionate, we are worried, and after our pleasure has been fulfilled we inflame ourselves again through a certain dissatisfaction, seeking to do that, when we repeat it, leaves us once more dissatisfied. [*Pol.* 8:6].

These points are well illustrated in the remainder of the poem. Although we may feel compassion for those who suffer from spiritual maladies of this kind, as Chaucer says he does at the outset (1:47–51) and as Boethius urges us to do (*Cons.* 4:pr. 4), they are especially dangerous in persons of responsibility and trust, upon whose integrity the welfare of others depends. Chaucer observes, "And thus Fortune a tyme led in joie / Criseyde and eek this kinges son of Troye."

Troilus has abandoned his reason, a fact driven home by his ridiculous corruption of one of the meters of *The Consolation of Philosophy* (2:m. 8; *Troilus*, 3:1744–71), in the course of which he substitutes his own list for the divine love of the original, so that he and his beloved are "Fortune's fools." Hence, as Chaucer assures us in the Proem of Book IV, Fortune blinds fools who listen to her song. Troilus has cursed the day, and the Muses are now the Furies, daughters of Night, together with Mars, the god of wrath and war. The season places the sun in Leo, so that the malignant "dog days" afford a background to the events described.

Parliament makes the exchange we have already discussed, and Troilus like a wild bull butts his head against the wall of his chamber, wishing that Fortune had killed his father, or his brothers, or even himself rather than depriving him of Criseyde's solaces. This reaction is not only ignoble but treasonable. He can neither support Hector nor carry Criseyde away by force for fear of ruining her reputation and of adding to the ignominy brought upon Troy by Paris, in whose footsteps he has been surreptitiously treading. Soon he is meditating in a temple where, in despair, he confuses simple and conditional necessity in such a way as to defend the proposition that "al that comth, comth by necessitee." This conclusion eliminates moral responsibility along with free choice. Finding Criseyde in a swoon and thinking her dead, he draws his sword to kill himself, thinking thus to defy the gods and Fortune in particular and demonstrating little princely fortitude.

Criseyde recovers in time to prevent this act, thanks Venus for their narrow escape, and suggests they go to bed, where the relief from their difficulties is only temporary. She promises to return to Troy within ten days, calling attention to her father's covetousness and the possibility of peace, concerning which there had been almost continuous negotiations (as there had been between the English and the French). She convinces her lover that they should not "steal away," for such an action would dishonor them, and people would accuse him of "lust voluptuous and coward drede," as though Troilus had not already demonstrated these qualities. They should, she says, "make a virtue of necessity," quoting Boethius, and remember that Fortune overcomes only wretches. As for herself, Criseyde says, rather amusingly, that she loved Troilus only for his "moral vertu, grounded upon trouthe," and because his reason always bridled his delight.

The Fates, ministers of destiny, rule over the last book. Diomede wins Criseyde's "friendship" by the time the two have reached the Greek camp. Chaucer devoted considerable time to the torments of Troilus, to his bitterness, his frustration, his isolation from his fellows, and to his gradual realization of Criseyde's unfaithfulness. Having scorned Pandarus's Ovidian advice in Book IV (400–27) to find another love, Troilus now disregards the further Ovidian advice to destroy old letters (*Rem. am.*, 718–22) and to avoid places where he has enjoyed Criseyde (*Rem. am.*, 725–26). Toward the close Chaucer remarks that Fortune "Can pull awey the fetheres brighte of Troye / Fro day to day, til they ben bare of joye."

The city suffers the fate of Troilus. After the treacherous slaying of Hector by Achilles, Troilus becomes convinced of Criseyde's defection to Diomede, and goes out to fight not to protect the town, but to seek vengeance on Diomede and his own death. When he has achieved the latter and his spirit has ascended above the mutable realm of the elements, he looks down, laughs at those who wept for his death, and damns all "oure wil that folweth so / The blynde lust, the which that may nat laste." This, Chaucer assures us, is the end of Troilus's worthiness, of his royal estate, of his lust, and of his nobility. He urges the "yonge fresshe folkes" in his audience not to love the transitory attractions of the world, but to love Christ, who will not betray them, and concludes with a prayer to the Trinity to defend himself and his countrymen from visible and invisible foes.[69] The visible enemies were at the time threatening to strike, and unless the invisible enemies within were conquered, they might well succeed. The prayer closes with a plea to Jesus to make "us," meaning the English, worthy of His mercy for the love of Mary, who was not only a source of compassion because of her humanity but the traditional sponsor of English chivalry and an appropriate mentor for a crusade.[70]

Chaucer's *Troilus* offers a vivid example of the degrading and ultimately disastrous consequences when a man of noble estate and great physical valor, but little fortitude, places his own private will, misled by the attractiveness of ephemeral satisfactions, above what was traditionally called "the honor of God and the common profit of the realm." When Chaucer enjoins the youth of the realm to abandon "worldly vanyte," he generalizes his lesson, for Venus is a goddess of *luxuria* as well as of *concupiscentia carnis*, in its narrower sense, and the idolatrous lust for a woman had long been a figure typifying any concupiscent passion. Chaucer hints strongly at this principle in his ironic praise of love as being something far better than avarice (3:1373–93) immediately after Criseyde has given Troilus the Brooch of Thebes, and the idea was strongly suggested earlier in Troilus's formulaic criticism of lovers before he saw Criseyde. The fate of Crassus (3:1373–93) and, presumably, all of his imitators forced to drink molten gold, is actually similar to the fate of Troilus and of Troy. Chaucer undoubtedly had in mind the extortionate abuses that King Edward had vainly sought to remedy and that Sir Richard Waldgrave and his successors among the Commons in Parliament had later sought to remedy,[71] as well as the sexual behavior of the chivalrous. He was seeking a renewed dedication on the part of his audience, couched in terms then most likely to be appealing, however they may strike us now, stressing the obligation of the English to set their love where it would lead neither themselves nor their countrymen to the burning destruction that had devastated old Troy, and to behave, as reason then demanded, with due reverence for wisdom and its restraints, now represented by *Sapientia Dei Patris*, or Christ, rather than by Pallas.

In the atmosphere of England in the mid-1380s it is not unlikely that many in his audience were inspired by what he had to say and renewed their own dedication. He had, after all, neither castigated them directly as a preacher might have done, nor cast any aspersions on particular individuals. He had simply urged them, with a great deal of wit and learning, to love as they should not only for their own welfare, but for the welfare of England. A new dedication would have been especially appropriate, in just these terms, for those about to set out for Spain with the Duke of Lancaster.

NOTES

1. See Derek Pearsall's perceptive and cogent article "The *Troilus* Frontispiece and Chaucer's Audience," *YES* 7 (1977), esp. pp. 73–74.

2. See, e.g., John Barnie, *War in Medieval English Society* (Ithaca, 1974), pp. 28, 103, and the sermons cited below.

3. The social importance of the Chamber at a somewhat later date has been discussed by Richard Firth Green, *Poets and Princepleasers* (Toronto, 1980), chap. 2.

4. See the discussion by J. H. Tuck, *Richard II and the English Nobility* (London, 1973), pp. 62–85.

5. Information about some of the Chamber knights is available in W. T. Waugh, "The Lollard Knights," *Scottish Historical Review* 11 (1914): 55–92; and in Kenneth McFarlane, *Lancastrian Kings and Lollard Knights* (Oxford, 1972). McFarlane is, I think, too quick to attribute "Lollard" views to these men. Cf. F. R. H. Du Boulay, "The Historical Chaucer," in Derek Brewer, ed., *Geoffrey Chaucer* (London, 1974), pp. 45–46; D. W. Robertson, Jr., "Simple Signs from Everyday Life in Chaucer," in John P. Hermann and John J. Burke, Jr., eds., *Signs and Symbols in Chaucer's Poetry* (University, Alabama, 1981), pp. 18–19; and Paul Strohm, "Chaucer's Fifteenth-Century Audience and the Narrowing of the Chaucer Tradition," in Roy J. Pearcy, ed., *Studies in the Age of Chaucer* 4 (1982):9–13.

6. J. J. N. Palmer, *England, France and Christendom* (London, 1972), pp. 33, 37, 228. The subject of Chaucer's connections with French poets is now being explored by James I. Wimsatt.

7. See Martin M. Crow and Clair C. Olson, *Chaucer Life-Records* (Oxford, 1966), pp. 343, 347.

8. R. Ian Jack, "Entail and Descent: The Hastings Inheritance," *BIHR* 38 (1965):1–11.

9. These have been edited with an introduction by V. J. Scattergood, *The Works of Sir John Clanvowe* (Totowa, N.J., 1975). The conjecture about the purpose of the treatise is my own.

10. *Life-Records*, pp. 49–53.

11. *The Good Parliament* (Oxford, 1975), pp. 21–62.

12. See C. F. Richmond, "The War at Sea," in Kenneth Fowler, ed. *The Hundred Years War* (London, 1971), pp. 115–16.

13. The connotations of the word *chivalry* were still very much like those associated with the good knight by John of Salisbury, *Policraticus*, 6:2–19. Attitudes toward it varied, however. See Barnie's discussion, *War in Medieval English Society*, chap. 3.

14. For the general situation, see J. R. Madicott, *Law and Lordship*, Past and Present Supplement 4 (1978). Edward and his Council had ordained in 1346 (*SR*, 1:303–6) that justices "do equal law and execution of right to rich and poor without having regard to any person," that justices disregard royal letters or other letters contrary to right and justice, that they take fees and robes from no one except the king, that they should counsel great and poor alike, and that they should take no gifts "except meat and drink, and that of small value." The justices of assize were to inquire of "sheriffs, escheators, bailiffs of franchises, and their under ministers, and also of ministers, common embracers, and jurors in

the county, of the gifts, rewards, and other profits which the said ministers do take of the people to execute their office, and for making array of panels, putting in the same suspect jurors and of evil fame, and of maintainers, embracers, and jurors that do take rewards against the parties, whereby losses and damages do come daily to the people, in subversion of the law." Justices were required to take an elaborate oath to fulfill the terms of the ordinance. As Madicott shows, however, the ordinance was not well observed.

15. *Speculo regis Edwardii III*, ed. J. Moisant (Paris, 1891), who attributed the two "recensions" he published to Simon Islip, although they are now usually attributed to Mepham and dated ca. 1330. On the traditional character of the complaints in this work, see G. L. Harriss, *King, Parliament, and Public Finance in Medieval England* (Oxford, 1975), chap. 5.

16. Edward had issued what has been called "the principal statute of the Middle Ages on the subject" of purveyance in 1362. See Harriss, *King, Parliament*, p. 376. This provided that purveyors for the household now be called buyers, that the prices paid be those of nearby markets, that indentures be used instead of wooden tallies on which the persons, quantitites, and prices should be clearly recorded, that no menace be used, no bribes taken, and that a commission be appointed in every county to inquire into abuses. Similar rules applied to the purveyors for the households of magnates. The statute was unfortunately not well observed. Waldgrave's complaint in some ways resembles the petition of the clergy in 1377. See Dorothy Bruce Weske, *Convocation of the Clergy* (London, 1937), pp. 72–73.

17. Cf. Eleanor Searle, *Lordship and Community: Battle Abbey and Its Banlieu* (Toronto, 1974), p. 345.

18. We might add that lesser ecclesiastics were increasingly suffering excommunication for failure to pay subsidies. See J. Donald Logan, *Excommunication and the Secular Arm in Medieval England* (Toronto, 1968), pp. 54–57, and the table on p. 68. As the peace rolls reveal, impoverished chaplains were turning to crime. There was, meanwhile, a growing tendency toward oligarchical government in the towns, causing discontent among lesser tradesmen. As R. B. Dobson has observed, *The Peasants' Revolt of 1381* (London, 1970), p. 13, the "traditional description of the 1381 rising as a 'Peasants' Revolt' . . . is in itself deceptive."

19. A vivid account of these events is given by Sydney Armitage-Smith, *John of Gaunt* (London, 1904; repr. N.Y., 1964), pp. 382–87.

20. On the cloth trade, see E. M. Carus-Wilson, "Trends in the Export of English Woolens in the Fourteenth Century," *EcHR* 2 Ser. 3 (1950–51): 174. As she puts it, "These were years of panic and confusion in England."

21. See Palmer, *England, France and Christendom*, chap. 3.

22. Armitage-Smith, *John of Gaunt*, pp. 295, 437–9. For the numbers, however, see Palmer, p. 60.

23. *Black Book of the Admiralty*, ed. Sir Travers Twiss (Rolls Series, 1871), 2:453.

24. Quoted by May McKisack, *The Fourteenth Century* (Oxford, 1959),

p. 438. On the *miles amoris*, see D. W. Robertson, Jr., *A Preface to Chaucer* (Princeton, 1962), pp. 408–10.

25. Cf. Anthony Goodman, "Sir Thomas Hoo and the Parliament of 1376," *BIHR* 41 (1968):145.

26. On Sir Arnold Savage, see J. S. Roskell, *The Commons and Their Speakers* (Manchester, 1965), pp. 139, 362. His famous address to the commons is recorded *RP*, 3:456.

27. *Life-Records*, pp. 168–69. Although de Vere endorsed the petition, he may have been urged to do so by someone else.

28. For the ordinance of 1385, omitted from the rolls of Parliament for that year, and for the Chancellor's neglect of it, see J. J. N. Palmer, "The Impeachment of Michael de la Pole," *BIHR* 42 (1969), esp. pp. 96–97, 100.

29. J. W. F. Hill, *Medieval Lincoln* (Cambridge, 1948), p. 258 and note 4.

30. He was lavishly rewarded on his return to England and subsequently treated with great generosity by the king, who made him Duke of Exeter in 1397. He participated in a rebellion to restore Richard after his deposition and was beheaded on orders from the Countess of Hereford in 1400.

31. See Palmer, *England, France and Christendom*, pp. 68–69. The material following relies heavily on this study, which sheds new light on the events of 1386 and on the motivation of Richard and his uncles.

32. Ibid., p. 74.

33. *Life-Records*, p. 370.

34. Sir Richard had fought at Crécy in 1346 and in other campaigns under Edward. He accompanied Gaunt on his march to Bordeaux in 1373 and was appointed Steward of the Household on Richard's accession. He served as Chancellor in 1378–80 and again in 1381–82. During 1385–88 he was a trier of petitions in Parliament. His son William, who was to serve as Gaunt's Seneschal in Aquitaine and who became the first Earl of Wiltshire in 1397, and his son Stephen were also prominent. Richard was in Gaunt's retinue in Scotland, and William was one of Gaunt's executors.

35. Bishop Arundel's connections and his political career between 1386 and 1397 are discussed by Margaret Aston, *Thomas Arundel* (Oxford, 1967), chap. 12.

36. See note 14, above.

37. Cf. Richard W. Kaeuper, "Law and Order in Fourteenth-Century England," *Speculum* 54 (1979):734–84.

38. This provoked a complaint in Parliament in 1387 (*RP*, 3:247). Cf. Tuck, as cited in note 4, above.

39. See John P. McCall and George Rudisill, "The Parliament of 1386 and Chaucer's Trojan Parliament," *JEGP* 58 (1959):276–88.

40. Cf. ibid. and D. W. Robertson, Jr., "The Concept of Courtly Love as an Impediment to the Understanding of Medieval Texts," in F. X. Newman, ed., *The Meaning of Courtly Love* (Albany, N.Y., 1968), p. 11; *Chaucer's London* (New York, 1968), pp. 2–4, 150, 167, 178, 221–22; "Simple Signs from Everyday Life in Chaucer," p. 212 n. 27; and David Anderson,

"Theban History in Chaucer's *Troilus*," in *Studies in the Age of Chaucer* 4:133.

41. For the context of this observation, see *Major Latin Works of John Gower*, trans. Eric W. Stockton (Seattle, 1962), pp. 284–86.

42. *The Sermons of Thomas Brinton, Bishop of Rochester*, ed. Sister Mary Aquinas Devlin, O. P., Camden Third Series 85 (1954), pp. 46–48.

43. Ibid., pp. 346–7; cf. pp. 338–39. For the underlying philosophical principle, see Boethius, *Cons.* 3:m. 5.

44. The passage is quoted in English in "The Concept of Courtly Love," p. 6.

45. Cf. the account and the references in *A Preface to Chaucer*, pp. 108–10. The account of *Troilus* in the pages below draws on the discussion in this work and is not inconsistent with it.

46. *The Commentary on the First Six Books of the Aeneid of Vergil*, ed. J. W. and E. F. Jones (Lincoln, Neb., 1977) pp. 102–3.

47. Eugene Vinaver, *The Rise of Romance* (Oxford, 1971), chap. 6.

48. A similar device was employed by Bishop Brinton in his sermon "On Unity," *Sermons*, pp. 109–17.

49. Cf. Boccaccio, *Genealogie deorum gentilium libri*, ed. V. Romano (Bari, 1951), 1:304.

50. Cf. Alan Gaylord, "Uncle Pandarus as Lady Philosophy," *PMASAL* 46 (1961):571–95; and John P. McCall, "Five-Book Structure in Chaucer's *Troilus*," *MLQ* 23 (1962):279–308.

51. Brinton, *Sermons*, Sermon 51, p. 245.

52. "Three Ovidian Women in Chaucer's *Troilus*: Medea, Helen, and Oenone," *ChauR* 15 (1980):6–9. The citations of Classical story by Pandarus are almost uniformly inept, commenting humorously on what he is trying to say.

53. See note 40, above.

54. *Teseida*, ed. A. Roncaglia (Bari, 1941), pp. 446, 383. Cf. Boccaccio, *Genealogie*, p. 438; and the Third Vatican Mythographer in G. H. Bode, *Scriptores rerum mythicarum Latini tres Romae nuper reperti* (repr. Hildesheim, 1968), 1:166.

55. Second Vatican Mythographer in Bode, 1:143; cf. Anderson, "Theban History in Chaucer's *Troilus*," p. 131.

56. First Vatican Mythographer in Bode, 1:63. The same source, p. 64, affords authority for Apollo's courtship of Nisa, daughter of Admetus, mentioned in Pandarus's account of Oenone's letter. Nisa may have appeared in a gloss on the Epistle, in an Italian translation, or even in the text itself, which is problematical. Cf. Boccaccio in Roncaglia, *Teseida*, p. 390.

57. "Characterisation in Chaucer's *Troilus and Criseyde*," in W. Rothwell et al., *Studies in Medieval Literatures and Languages in Memory of Frederick Whitehead* (New York, 1973), pp. 118–19.

58. Vinaver, *Rise of Romance*, p. 30.

59. *Remigii Autissiodorensis commentum in Martianum Capellam*, ed. Cora E. Lutz (Leiden, 1962), 1:183; Boccaccio, *Genealogie*, p. 465; Thomas Walsingham, *Archana deorum*, ed. R. A. van Kluyve (Durham, 1968), p. 189.

60. See Guillaume de Conches, *Glosae super Platonem*, ed. E. Jeauneau (Paris, 1965), p. 71; and Jeauneau's "*Lectio philosophorum*," (Amsterdam, 1973), p. 239.

61. On idleness and Venus, see Ovid, *Rem. am.*, 135–68; and for a discussion, Robertson, *Preface*, p. 92 and note 69.

62. See B. F. Huppé and D. W. Robertson, Jr., *Fruyt and Chaf* (Princeton, 1963), p. 112 and note 16. The basic idea is Pauline.

63. Troilus's reference to the labor in winning, fear in keeping, and sorrow in losing reflect the *De miseria humanae conditionis* of Innocent III (1:15). The first part of this chapter is paraphrased by the Man of Law in the prologue to his Tale (99–119), although that worthy fatuously goes on to describe the joys of the wealthy, abandoning Innocent's characterization of their miseries of which the predicament Troilus describes is paramount. Its application to lovers by Troilus associates them with the avaricious, treated at length in Innocent's Second Book, which contains chapters on avaricious princes and justices (3–5). Troilus's blindness is discussed at length in a forthcoming study by Chauncey Wood. On lust and avarice, see the closing remarks below.

64. Bode, 1:55, 63, 98.

65. The "frape" are by no means uniform in character. Polyxena's moving death, in the course of which she seeks to preserve her virgin modesty, is described by Ovid, *Met.*, 13:441–80.

66. Third Vatican Mythographer, Bode, 1:176.

67. Ibid., 1:177.

68. See R. E. Kaske, "The Aube in Chaucer's *Troilus*," in R. J. Schoeck and Jerome Taylor, eds., *Chaucer Criticism*, Vol. II: *Troilus and Criseyde and the Minor Poems* (Notre Dame, 1961), 2:167–79.

69. Chaucer's contrast between the love of worldly vanity, typified by lust, and the love of Christ may have reminded many in his audience of a widely used school text, the *Cartula* (*PL*, 184:1307–14), which elaborates this theme. On its use in schools, see Nicholas Orme, *English Schools in the Middle Ages* (London, 1973), pp. 104–5. If and when this boyhood reminiscence occurred, it was probably pleasant.

70. Geoffrey of Monmouth's Arthur, widely emulated in England during the fourteenth century, carried an image of the Virgin on his shield. Garter knights wore her image on their shoulders during ceremonials. For the Wilton Diptych as a work commissioned in anticipation of a joint French and English crusade, see *England, France and Christendom*, pp. 205, 242–44.

71. For a more detailed account of later parliamentary complaints, see my forthcoming "Chaucer and the Economic and Social Consequences of Plague," to appear in the Papers of the Fifteenth Annual Conference of CMRS, SUNY Binghamton.

Fools and Schools: Scholastic Dialectic, Humanist Rhetoric; from Anselm to Erasmus

MARJORIE O'ROURKE BOYLE

Scholastic dialectic rebuked the fool, who said in his heart there was no God; humanist rhetoric conceived a fonder fool, who said in his heart that *he* was God.

When Erasmus composed ΜΩΡΙΑΣ ΕΓΚΩΜΙΟΝ, id est, *Stultitiae laus*[1] (1509→1511) to amuse and so to edify, he enrolled all dunces in the school of "foolosophy." No mere convention, its lampoon of scholasticism spewed the gall of his own experience at the Collège de Montaigu, whose austere halls he had unwittingly entered fourteen years earlier. He went there, he said, not daring "to import my barbarous Muses, with their uncouth foreign accent, into this famous university of Paris."[2] His aim, "God willing," was "to seek my doctorate in theology."[3] Erasmus's penury as a student there was equalled by the parsimony of mind and spirit instituted by Jan Standonck, its reforming principal.[4]

Decades later Erasmus would satirize Montaigu, punning on *mons acutus*, as "Vinegar College" itself. For the meager board was indeed sour, the bedding so stiff as to ensure that sleepless nights would succeed already restless days. Youthful bodies were further broken by floggings, a discipline meant to "tame spirits," especially those wild with talent, such as he. The cubicles of rotting plaster to which the students were consigned promised disease, or death, from the stinking latrines nearby, and Erasmus, whose delicate constitution had already forced him to abandon the monastery at Steyn, fell ill after only a few months under this quasi-monastic regimen.[5] After fitful attempts to resume formal studies, he soon abandoned the project altogether.

For the four to five thousand tyros who matriculated in the faculty of arts at Paris, the first two years of the curriculum were devoted to the learning of logic, the third to mastering the physics, metaphysics, and ethics of Aristotle. The study of logic was divided into two distinct endeavors: the first year dedicated to the textbook of Peter of Spain and to topics such as exponibles, consequences, and insolubles; the second to Porphyry's *Isagoge*, then the logic of Aristotle, with various metaphysical questions also broached in these

173

Medievalia et Humanistica, New Series, Number 13 (Paul Maurice Clogan, ed.). Rowman
* Allanheld, Totowa, NJ. 1985.

lessons.[6] Subjected to a rigorous schedule from the first class at four A.M. to the last interrogation at 7 P.M., students sought their diversions. Erasmus's earliest record was not a brilliant examination, but an exchange of jocular notes with another bored student, who recommended in conclusion: "As for those prattlers, let us take no more notice of them than an Indian elephant does of a gnat."[7] The sophistication of his private studies only exacerbated his impatience with the thin airs to which the achievements of formal logic under the masters of the thirteenth and fourteenth centuries, from Peter of Spain (d. 1277) to Paul of Venice (d. 1429), had evidently dwindled.

The Parisian purveyors of learning, boasting of a theological acumen exceeding all other schools,[8] are the special butt of Moria. In mocking mortal folly she groups the sophists and dialecticians with the lawyers, who smugly roll the Sisyphean rock while they pile opinion on opinion, gloss on gloss, to exaggerate the difficulty of their labors.[9] Logicians match lawyers in garrulity, rattling on like "Dodonean bronze." This phrase, a metonym for cymbal or bell, was proverbially applied to a person of excessively reprobate and unseasonably rude speech. One tradition related in the *Adagia* (1508), which Erasmus had just published, reported that in Dodona there were two lofty columns, on the one positioned a bronze basin, on the other a hanging figure of a boy with a bronze whip in hand. As often and as gustily as the wind would blow, the lash would repeatedly strike the vessel, which would then reverberate incessantly. Another tradition related that its oracle of Jove was himself girded all about with bronze cymbals, which having once touched his body would resound successively in full circle, clanging perpetually. Thus was Dodonean bronze proverbial, Erasmus wrote, for "a glibly garrulous person, whom if you but ping with one verbal particle continuously resounds with such a volley of words that there is no end to his chattering."[10] This verbal battery of which Moria accuses the sophists recalls the mock panegyric by an earlier humanist, Lorenzo Valla, who asigned that exemplary scholastic, Thomas Aquinas, to play the cymbals in the heavenly choir.[11]

Moria rues such querulous gab. Armed with three syllogisms, the logicians wrangle fiercely over goat's wool, shouting down Stentor in their altercations.[12] Insisting that they personify wisdom, the philosophers strut like "asses in lions' skins."[13] But then, as Moria observes, "the philosophers are all agreed that theirs is a profession for asses."[14] Mocking the logical convention of using "ass" as a syllogistic term—as in *quod homo sit asinus*[15]—she divulges that "these asses can settle matters large and small if they give the word, and their estates multiply, while the theologian who has combed through his book-case in order to master the whole of divinity nibbles at a dry bean and carries on a non-stop war with bugs and lice."[16] Such a theologian was Erasmus, subsisting on rotten eggs and heels of bread at Montaigu, within halls so infested that the new statutes of the college in 1503 would prescribe measures for the control of pests. Meanwhile, Erasmus had departed in disgust with "a body plagued by the worst humors, plus a most generous supply of lice."[17]

Reflecting the alliance of nominalist logic with natural philosophy at Montaigu, which was renowned as a center for dynamics and kinematics,[18] Moria ridicules those who pretend access to the secrets of Nature. These cosmologists are touched by "a pleasant form of madness, which sets them building countless universes and measuring the sun, moon, stars and planets by rule of thumb or a bit of string, and producing reasons for thunderbolts, winds, eclipses and other inexplicable phenomena." Although they are too purblind to notice the plainest manifestations of Nature—a stone in the path, a ditch in the road—they claim to see such insubstantial forms as ideas, universals, quiddities, even Prime Matter itself. To dazzle the common crowd they superimpose and intertwine geometrical diagrams. They marshal in line and deploy here and there the letters of the alphabet,[19] as Moria scornfully refers to their use in supposition theory.[20]

The barbarous employment of letters she particularly ridicules in a reincarnation of Scotus, who attempted to prove how the mystery of Jesus is concealed in the actual letters of his name. The fact that "Jesus" is declinable in three distinct cases, she reports, symbolizes the triune nature of God; the ending of these cases in s (nominative), m (accusative), and u (ablative) indicates that he is the sum, middle, and ultimate. Subjecting these letters next to mathematical analysis, the speaker bisected the holy name equally. The letter s standing in the middle was thus revealed to be the Hebrew 𝒲, pronounced *syn*. "And *syn*," says Moria, "sounds like the word I believe the Scots use for the Latin *peccatum*, that is, sin. Here there is clear proof that it is Jesus who takes away the sins of the world."[21]

Such fantastic extrapolations, popular since patristic numerology, Erasmus would replace with sound grammar in a humanist resort to usage as the consensus of erudite and upright men. Despite the creative incursions of Rodolphus Agricola and Lorenzo Valla into scholastic logic, modeling a humanist counterpart which was responsive and responsible to an audience, and therefore allied with rhetorical invention and judgment,[22] speech at Paris was scarcely humane. Erasmus's own "barbarous Muses," conjured by talent and shaped by his encounters with Agricola and Valla, were elegant in comparison with the coarse talk of his masters, refined only in its subtleties. As he cartooned himself in the lecture-hall: "If only you could see your Erasmus sitting agape among those glorified Scotists, while 'Gryllard' lectures from a lofty throne. If you could but observe his furrowed brow, his uncomprehending look and worried expression, you would say it was another man. They say the secrets of this branch of learning cannot be grasped by a person who has anything at all to do with the Muses or the Graces; for this, you must unlearn any literary lore you have put your hands on, and vomit up any draught you may have drunk from Helicon. So I am trying with might and main to say nothing good in Latin, or elegantly, or wittily; and I seem to be making progress," he reports. "So there is some hope that, eventually, they will acknowledge me."[23]

Caricature? Thi self-portrait climaxes a letter to a former pupil, Thomas Grey, in which he playfully explains the excuse for a lapse in their correspondence. "Why, something I will tell you about, extraordinary, but true. I, yes I, that former theologian, have lately turned Scotist!" So absorbed was he in the lecturer's fancies that he could scarcely be roused, he tells. Erasmus assures his confidant that, nevertheless, he is not now writing in his sleep, although the sleep of the divines at Paris is indeed wondrous. "*We* not only write in our sleep; we wench, and tipple, and spread gossip in our sleep."[24] Erasmus then tells a tale on which the interpretation of the *Moria* hangs.

"There once was a certain Epimenides, he who wrote that all Cretans are liars, being a Cretan himself and at the same time speaking quite truthfully." One day he entered a deep cave to meditate where, while he was nibbling his nails in thought over instances and quiddities, sleep overtook him. Forty-seven years later he awoke in a world so changed that he doubted his own existence. Now, centuries later, his skin is preserved as a relic in that holiest of holies of Scotist theology, the Sorbonne, where those theologians who have attained to the title *magister noster* consult it as an oracle when syllogisms fail. While Epimenides was fortunate in regaining his senses, however belatedly, Erasmus observes that "most of our present-day theologians never wake up at all, and believe themselves quite wide-awake when in fact they are drugged with mandrake." Then addressing his correspondent he asks, "But tell me, dear Thomas, what do you think Epimenides' dreams were of, all those years? Why, of course those very super-subtle subtleties that today are the boast of the sons of Scotus; for I should be prepared to swear that Epimenides was reincarnated in Scotus." Erasmus denies, however, that he scorns the discipline of theology itself. "I merely wished to make a joke," he explains, "at the expense of a few quasi-theologians of our own day, whose brains are the most addled, tongues the most uncultured, wits the dullest, teachings the thorniest, characters the least attractive, lives the most hypocritical, talk the most slanderous, and hearts the blackest on earth."[25]

Although the "Gryllardus" who so wearied Erasmus has been likened to the porcine "Gryllus" of a Plutarchan dialogue,[26] his actual identity cannot have escaped the students who dumbly thronged his lecture-hall. Was this barbarous lecturer not indeed as fabled as the Epimenides whose paradox he wrestled to resolve, John Major himself?

When Erasmus attended lectures at Paris, nominalism was again in the ascendancy, a royal reprieve for its instruction having been granted in 1481 against a realist monopoly on the truth. A hub and a haven of logic until the humanist critique of "logomachy" defeated that method by 1520, Paris hosted the best dialecticians of the day.[27] The two masters most audited during Erasmus's residence there were Thomas Bricot (d. 1516), who edited John Buridan's version of Aristotle, which he established together with Buridan's own *Summulae logicales* and the *Tractatus* of Peter of Spain as the foundation of nominalist teaching; and Jean Raulin (1443–1514), another leading nominalist, who commented on the logic of Aristotle.[28] With the turn of the century, however, a Scotsman born in the same year as Erasmus, Johannes Major Scotus, or John Major or Mair (1469–1550), assumed importance. Already master of arts upon Erasmus's arrival, Major became regent of arts in 1495, teaching logic at Montaigu while pursuing the advanced degrees in theology. By 1506, when he received the doctorate in sacred studies, he was the most prominent master for arts in all of Paris.[29] Judging from the frequency of his name on the certificates of study issued to arts undergraduates, his courses seem to have been the most popular at the university.[30] To the discipline of Montaigu, Major attracted a clever and willing company of colleagues and students.[31] "Never again," it has since been judged, "was scholastic logic to be the focus of attention from such an able group of men."[32] Major proved as prolific in his writing as in his lecturing: re-editing texts of his nominalist predecessors William of Ockham, Robert Holkot, and Gregory of Rimini; commenting on Aristotle, Buridan, Peter of Spain, and Peter Lombard; and issuing his own ruminations on predicables, predicaments, syllogisms, terms, topics, consequences, exponibles, insolubles, obligations, sophisms and, at length, the infinite.[33] In this press of work he exhibited no care for style. His books have been evaluated as displaying "all the nefarious abuses common to this last stage of terminist logic: prolix and digressive, burdened by an endless disarray of examples and counter-examples, excessively subtle and obscure in their staccato of distinctions and sub-distinctions, obdurate in their analysis of logical minutiae. . . . The ungainly homeliness and total lack of concern for beauty which these books betray was not an accidental shortcoming, but rather the conscious result of a frame of mind perfectly formulated by Mair himself."[34] When reproached for this barbarism, he notoriously replied, "Science has no need for fine language."[35]

During Erasmus's co-residence with him at Montaigu, Major already must have evidenced the qualities that would soon propel him to renown. "More than anyone else," it has been stated, "Mair was responsible for the excessive attention and time given to dialectic at Montaigu College, and by so doing he clearly drew the line of confrontation between medieval learning—of which he was called 'the depository'—and the fresh, new approaches of Renaissance Humanism. The decisive experiences of men like Erasmus, Vives, Rabelais and Vitoria, during their studies at Paris, cannot be fully appreciated without the sharp contrast between their restless projection into the future and Mair's medievalism."[36] Erasmus can hardly have been impressed with Major's burgeoning attitude that "science has no need for fine language." Although Major might conclude a barbarous text with a verse from Virgil, and later would acquire some Greek from Girolamo Aleandro and some sympathy for Jacques Lefèvre d'Etaples, he was definitely no humanist.[37] He deprecated "the Bible and the easier parts of theology."[38] In his obligatory commentary on the first book of the *Sentences*, his *Dialogus de materia theologica* (1510), he averred that the theologian owed a debt not only to the Greeks, but also to the barbarians. Rebuking humanist methods, he pronounced in defense of scholastic inquiry that "these questions, which they [humanists] think futile, are like a ladder for the intelligence to rise towards the Bible. . . . This method has been in use for 300 years. If you think it is against reason, common error creates, to quote the proverb, the law."[39]

This obscurantism would thrust him into public conflict with Erasmus by 1527 when Major was commissioned by the faculty of theology at Paris to examine the *Paraphrases in Novum Testamentum*. He himself had published an exposition of Matthew's gospel, which he stated in the very title as "literal."[40] Major was, however, already the covert target of Erasmus's pen in the letter to Grey, but especially in the *Moria*. Certain characterizations of "Gryllardus," the tedious lecturer of whom Erasmus complained, seem not to square factually, for he was identified as a Scotist, an Englishmen, and elderly. Instead Peter Tartaretus, licensed in theology in 1496, was then the single Scotist of note at Paris.[41] The designation *Scotista* referred, however, to the shared nationality and name of John Duns Scotus and John Major Scotus. Erasmus wrote to Grey, who was English, describing the eponymous Scotus as "one of your countrymen (for though Scotus, like Homer of old, has been claimed as a son by rival parts of the world, the English lay special claim to him)."[42] Just prior to matriculating at Paris, Major had resided in 1493 at Cambridge,[43] as Erasmus may have known. The indication of old age probably repeated the humanist commonplace about scholastics as senescent in their dialectic.[44] A contemporaneous student in arts at Paris described Major: "The sweat of his academic labor was making him old before his time."[45] One salient fact, however, identifies Major as the model for Gryllardus and as the prototype of the masters at Paris who have succumbed to the sleep of Epimenides. In 1497, the very year of Erasmus's satiric letter to Grey penned from Montaigu, Major's promising career there was marred by a serious illness. He was afflicted with a complaint, one he thought congenital, whose principle symptom was an extreme sleepiness. Severely troubled by dreaming, although he had rarely recalled dreams before the onset of this condition, as he himself attests, Major's somnolence was so profound that once asleep he was exceedingly difficult to awaken.[46]

This drowsy dialectician, pratting like Epimenides the Cretan in the obscure cave of quiddities, nodding off to dreams between the major and the minor of a syllogism (no doubt to the delight of the undergraduates and to his own fame), figures importantly for interpreting the *Moria*. His shadow lurks in the Scot who barbarously carves up the name of Jesus to prove the truth of redemption. Yet more devastatingly does Moria censure him in deprecating herself, for while *Moriae encomium* is the praise of folly, and by compliment the praise of More, it is by detriment the praise of Major. His surname is but a latinization of the Scottish Mair which, in a pun on comparative forms (more), corresponds to the English More. While the better part of folly lauds the evangelical humanism of More,[47] the baser part trumpets the uninspired barbarism of Major. Laughingly Moria agrees with that logician's deprecation of himself as "Major only in name."[48] Moria demurs to explain herself by the usual practices of definition or division. A definition can only sketch her shadow; real presence is the guarantee of true perception. A division would betray her universal substance, she explains.[49] Yet she does indeed split her identity into the antithetical More and Major, who bear the same name, hers. She thus evokes the very questions of signification which embroiled realists and nominalists at Paris in controversy. Is there verily a "universal" *folly*? Or are there only individual *follies*? Can one and the same term signify, moreover, not only many realities, but two distinctly opposite ones? Moria enters this debate not by logical definitions or division, as she avows, but by the rhetorical technique of description.

A procedure Cicero recommended to be frequently appropriate when conflicting opinions rendered formal definition too difficult was description (*descriptio*). In considering the thesis as a type of question, he judged that, if it concerned a matter of learning rather than action, it required attention to its reality, its definition, and its quality. Three inquiries were appropriate: Does it exist or not? What is it? What are its qualities? The second question Cicero further divided according to definition and description. Either the issue debated was a matter of difference or identity, such as whether pertinacity is the same thing as perseverence, and thus required definition; or alternatively, "the description and so to say the pattern of a particular class has to be expressed, e.g., what sort of person is a miser, or what is pride?"[50] Description, which corresponded to the Greek χαρακτήρ (character or hallmark) illustrated, in sum, the character and behavior of a type, such as a flatterer.[51] Erasmus himself had advised as a method of enriching style ἐνάργεια or *evidentia*, that "vividness" which "consists mainly in the description of things, times, places, and persons. We employ this whenever, for the sake of amplifying or decorating a passage, or giving pleasure to our readers, instead of setting out the subject in bare simplicity, we fill in the colours and set it up like a picture to look at, so that we seem to have painted the scene rather than described it, and the reader seems to have seen rather than read."[52] The categories of virtues and vices that provided the stock of the classical description readily suggested all manner of "folly," fond and vile, human and divine. In her persona Moria reconciled their antinomies, as manifested basely in Major's barbarism and mystically in More's humanism.

Moria's unitive transcendence of the categorical opposition of virtue and vice was highlighted, like the artistic technique of *chiaroscuro*, by the shadow on her text of another scholastic fool, who late in the eleventh century intruded upon the meditations of Anselm in the monastery at Bec. The figure of the fool in the *Proslogion* and in the *Moria* can provide a heuristic for the divergent modes of religious discourse, the scholastic and the humanist. Expressing a "faith seeking understanding," Anselm famously formulated in his *Proslogion* the ontological argument for the existence of God. Addressing the request of his Benedictine brethren for necessary reasons against unbelief, he constructed an argument based on the assent of faith to God as "something-than-which-nothing-greater-can-be-thought." The dialectical device for this was the objection posed by Ps. 13:1 (Vg): "The fool says in his heart, 'There is no God' " (RSV). How can this be, he inquired, since even the fool intellectually understands the premise? What is understood intellectually can be conceived really, for the latter is the greater. "Therefore," he concluded, "there is absolutely no doubt that something-than-which-a-greater-cannot-be-thought exists both in the mind and in reality." Indeed, he continued, it cannot be conceived of as not existing. Anselm then identified this highest reality as the Creator, above whom no creature can ascend to judge. "Why, then," he pondered, "did the Fool say in his heart, 'there is no God' when it is so evident to any rational mind that You of all things exist to the highest degree? Why indeed, unless because he was stupid and a fool."[53]

The role of the fool in the *Proslogion* has been interpreted as an intervention necessitated by "the 'revealability' of the creation" and as signifying "the apostolic purpose of true Christian reflection." The meditation of Anselm proceeded from a theological charity which embraced the unbeliever, who sought, in common humanity with the believer, for a reason for faith. The collaboration of the fool was necessary for monastic contemplation, the vocation of which enveloped universally the Adam for whom Christ died. In arguing with the fool rather than with the rational man, the Christian intellectual thus re-established, re-created man from precisely his fallen nature. He participated, therefore, in the redemptive work of Christ himself, so "that God may be everything to everyone" (1 Cor. 15:28 RSV), to the fool as surely as to the monk.[54]

This inspirational interpretation, although perhaps romanticized, was corroborated historically by the particularly missionary impulse that animated theology in the generation of Anselm and after. While the prior of Bec was unlikely to have encountered an atheist, he was, nevertheless, forced by dissenters into polemic. Heretics and sects were again multiplying within Latin Christianity, as they once had in the patristic era. Trade, diplomacy, war, and daily social commerce also brought the "infidels"—Jews, Moslems, and Greek schismatics—within the ken of even the cloistered. Apologetic became imperative. This exigency profoundly affected intellectual life in the twelfth century, and the ensuing keen arguments of scholastics with unbelievers, real and imaginary, significantly altered the development of speculative theology, both in doctrine and method.[55]

Anselm's concluding tautology—the fool is foolish—reflected the identification of folly and stupidity, folly and sin, and stupidity with sin which was prevalent in medieval moralizing,[56] as in the biblical Wisdom literature that it glossed. The fool's role in the *Proslogion*, it has been stated, was to establish and justify the monastic vocation as a contemplative imitation of the Redeemer.[57] In himself, however, this fool was, like Anselm's concept of evil, nothing.[58] He must be nothing, moreover, because he was the very definition of nescience. If the thought of the monk affirmed being, in an intellectual ascent from his own cogitation to the existence of God, then the vacuity of the fool must signify non-being. This thin character of philosophical invention was not a subject, but a foil to a subject. He spoke no dialogue, which might have proved his existence, except through the single utterance of his antithesis, the psalmist as sage who invented his imaginary interior sentence: " 'There is no God.' " Nor did this fool respond to Anselm's argument with him, except through the mediation of another monk, Gaunilo, who composed on his behalf a formal reply.[59] As Anselm in turn commented: "Since it is not the Fool, against whom I spoke in my tract, who takes me up, but one who, though speaking on the Fool's behalf, is an orthodox Christian and no fool, it will suffice if I reply to the Christian."[60] The figure of the monk, rather than that of the fool, was enhanced by this scholastic argumentation. This will not prove so in the humanist creation of Erasmus, whose fool will elevate herself above monks, censuring them as creatures who belie in reality what their name signifies.[61]

Anselm, it has been proposed, was a "secure technician" who intellectually mastered and pleasurably exploited the varieties of paradox. In his devotional writings he employed "rhetorical paradoxes," such as the oxymoron "mater admirabilis virginitas, virgo amabilis foecunditas," to inspire the wonder of faith. In his technical expositions he resolved logical antinomies, such as free will and determinism, to deepen the understanding of faith.[62] While the prior of Bec could turn an elegant phrase, his figurative language seems rather to repeat the stock of biblical and patristic antitheses.[63] Indeed, his particular mental habit has otherwise been described as eschewing paradox in favor of clear statement, optimistically and closely examining the components of contradiction so as to determine the opposition as merely apparent.[64] That the cast of Anselm's mind was *not* characteristically paradoxical is arguable from the very nature of the scholasticism he is claimed to have fathered. As a dialectician, Anselm required a technical language, free of the anomaly and of the regress that paradox would contain. It was precisely the self-conscious artificialization of the Latin language to express truths involving semantic categories not distinguished by ordinary grammar that was the hallmark of scholastic thought. Its barbarism in the judgment of humanists such as Erasmus, who defined propriety by grammar as conveyed in usage, was its very violation of natural language to elucidate definitional problems.[65] The fool of Anselm's *Proslogion*, therefore, was necessarily a straightforward character.

The challenge of unbelievers, which Anselm addressed, also provoked his successors to question providence when the infidels proved by their mastery, even hegemony, of the arts to be neither as stupid nor as foolish as the monk had supposed.[66] *Follis*, from which the word "fool" derives, is a windbag, suggestive of puffed cheeks and the hot air of nonsense. But the wind is an archaic symbol of spirit,[67] and "the wind," as Christ acknowledged to the rabbi Nicodemus, "blows where it wills" (John 3:8). So it was that while medieval piety moralistically booked passage for every type of fool aboard the ark of damnation, in that climactic construction the *Narrenschiff*,[68] humanist piety conceived of fools who might be saved. In Anselm's *Proslogion* the fool was merely typical: the liar. He failed to speak the truth, even in the privacy of his own heart, because he was definitionally pure nescience. In medieval society and culture, however, there were fools who were truth-sayers. Natural fools owed the veracity that blurted through their babble to an uninhibited perception of reality. And out of the mouths of such fools, as of babes, oft came wisdom. In folk belief these fools were "touched in the head" by the finger of God, and thus inspired in their speech. Artificial fools owed their veracity to the artifice of their author, who capitalized on the tolerance allowed natural fools to voice common sense or venture severe judgment. Such real and literary variations on the dumb, depraved fool deviated from Anselm's tautology—the fool is foolish—to intimate Erasmus's oxymoron: the fool is wise.

The assumption of Anselm's ontological argument was that human rationality is analogous, in kind although not in degree, to divine rationality. Whereas Anselm in the *Proslogion* had demonstrated to the fool that his native intelligence signified the truth of divine existence, Erasmus in the *Moria* proved God differently. He argued for the fool, speaking on her own behalf, as not merely signifying divinity but as coinciding with it. This ontological coincidence, the fool as God, he predicated, moreover, not in the order of intellect, but of passion. "All the emotions," Moria explained, "belong to Folly, and this is what marks the wise man off from the fool; he is ruled by reason, the fool by his emotions." In self-defense she argued that "these emotions not only act as guides to those hastening towards the haven of wisdom, but also wherever virtue is put into practice they are always present to act like spurs and goads as incentives toward success." Moria countered the Stoic denial of passion that fabricated as its wise man a marmoreal statue devoid of human sense or sensibility. Such a sage, if he indeed were wise or human, was fit only for the realm of ideas, she judged. For in his self-sufficiency and self-satisfaction he avoided nothing, erred not, ignored nothing but perceived everything, and weighed all precisely. In sum, she decided, "the wise man's a bore. Anybody would prefer someone from the ordinary run of fools."[69]

It was an extraordinary fool, however, who embodied the passion to ignite in man the divine furor. Shifting from the theocentric perspective of scholasticism to the Christocentric focus of his evangelical humanism, Erasmus's fool identified herself with God inhominized. The death of Christ was not a reasonable act, she argued, and so by definition it was unwise. If folly means being swayed by the will of the passions, then in its consummate Passion the death of Christ crucified was the death of a fool.[70] This voluntaristic conception of Christ as subject to emotion countered the ontological argument of Anselm. God as known scholastically in the exercise of reason was displaced by Christ as appreciated humanistically in the experience of passion. The norm for this was incarnational: God's descent to man by assuming the figure of a fool, rather than man's ascent to God by assuming the posture of a sage. Conversely, only through the imitation of Christ, only by donning his motley of flesh, would man ever ascend to God. This was the mystery prefigured in the prophets and manifested in the saints, as Moria herself disclosed.[71] The divine sanction that Christ conferred on folly transformed the contemptible and lowly fool of Anselm's logic into the "affectionate" and "adorable" one of Erasmus's rhetoric.[72]

Their differing paradigms of the divine, the one theocentric and cognitive, the other Christocentric and affective, determined the divergent theological methods of the *Proslogion* and the *Moria*, as dialectical and rhetorical respectively. Dialectic seeks an act of the intellect (judgment) through compulsion of reason, and it secures its religious end in contemplation. Rhetoric seeks an act of the will (assent) through persuasion of feeling, and it secures its religious end in conversion. The singular focus of the theologian, Erasmus believed, is to speak so eloquently as to transfigure humanity. "This is your first and only sighting; perform this vow, this one thing," he urged him in his methodological treatise *Ratio verae theologiae* (1518), "that you be changed, that you be seized, that you weep at and be transformed into those truths which you learn." Instructing the transmutation of oratory into act, speech into flesh, in imitation of the divine Logos, he wrote: "The special sighting of theologians is to expound Scripture wisely; to render its doctrine according to faith, not frivolous questions; to discourse about piety gravely and efficaciously; to wring out tears, to inflame spirits to heavenly things."[73]

As rhetorical theology, the *Moria* was intended to inspire such a conversion by Platonic ascent from the visible and carnal appearance of folly to its invisible and spiritual reality. Erasmus's pastoral concern for the conversion of the heart faithfully reflected the sense of Psalm 13:1, whereas Anselm's *Proslogion* did not, for the biblical fool (*nabhal*) was not he who denied the existence, but rather the providence, of God. His "atheism" was practical, not intellectual. It derived from the observation that the wicked often prosper while the just fail, so that God proves ineffectual. Discounting God as a factor in human affairs, the fool therefore indulged in corrupt living. The appropriate ministry for this fool, consequently, was not intellectual argumentation, but a summons to repentance. Erasmus endeavored to issue this call in the *Moria* by persuading the fool to perceive himself as he is—foolish. He then sought to elevate this fallen human nature to its redemptive exemplar in the folly of the pefect man, Christ. Since eternal verity was the measure of temporal life, the fool was urged to consider the last things in this *memento mori* occasioned by the remembrance of More.[74]

The *Moria* was also provoked, however, by the remembrance of Major, and the vacuous speculation at Paris to which the intelligent and ardent inquiry of Anselm had depreciated, propelled by the momentum of reason itself and abandoning in its course any intention of dialogue, be it with friend or fool. Rhetoric requires an audience, and Moria meant to entertain, enlighten, and edify hers. Unlike the fool of Anselm's *Proslogion*, who could not even speak on his own behalf, Moria indulged herself on hers. "Now I don't think much," she confided, "of those wiseacres who maintain it's the height of folly and conceit if anyone speaks in his own praise; or rather, it can be as foolish as they like, as long as they admit it's in character. What could be more fitting than for Folly to trumpet her own merits abroad and 'sing her own praises'? Who could portray me better than I can myself?"[75] Pressing on her listeners her every wit and whim, she avowed that "for my part, I've always liked best to say 'whatever was on the tip of my tongue.' "[76] This rhetorical effusiveness shattered the silence to which Anselm's fool was reduced by logical cogency. And Moria will never shut up. She is irrepressible because the mystery she utters is inexhaustible.

In the opposition of rhetoric to dialectic, the fool as described rather than defined in Moria personified a humanist ideal of religious discourse. Erasmus achieved this not by employing rhetoric generally, but particularly, in the epideictic genre. Such a style, Cicero had advised, was the proper field for sophists, a schoolish exercise.[77] Had Erasmus wished to debate the concept of folly or to indict the crime of folly he would have selected the deliberative or juridical genres. His highly original choice of the epideictic mode for treating folly, and his even more unconventional choice of praise rather than blame for it, upset morality and law alike. Moreover, his device by which folly spoke in her own praise involved a paradox, for the titular Greek, ΜΩΡΙΑΣ ΕΓΚΩΜΙΟΝ, is syntactically ambiguous. It allows for either an objective or an auctorial genitive; that is, praise about folly or praise by folly. For this reason the *Moria* has been termed "paradoxical rhetoric" in the example of such classical versions as Gorgias's praise of Helen, Isocrates' praise of Thersites, Synesius's of baldness, Lucian's of the fly, Ovid's of the nut, and pseudo-Virgil's of the gnat. A rhetorical paradox has been defined as "the formal defense, organized along the lines of traditional *encomia*, of an unexpected, unworthy, or undefensible subject." This was "an ancient form designed as *epideixis*, to show off the skill of an orator and to arouse the admiration of an audience, both at the outlandishness of the subject and the technical brilliance of the rhetorician."[78]

Unless the term "paradox" be altered from its historical designation as developed in Stoic logic, however, these examples are not paradoxes, rhetorical or otherwise.[79] They are rather ironies, surprising violations of the rhetorical canon of decorum in which something commonly supposed unpraisable is indeed praised. In his dedicatory epistle of the *Moria* to More, Erasmus justified "the triviality and the humour of the theme" by referring to the encomiums of Virgil on the gnat and the *moretum*, of Ovid on the walnut, Polycrates and Isocrates on Busiris, Glaucon on injustice, Favorinus on Thersites and the quartan fever, Synesius on baldness, Lucian on the fly and on the parasite.[80] Had Erasmus composed the *Moria* simply in praise of folly, in analogy with these examples, it too would be merely ironic. It is, however, authentically paradoxical. What distinguished his encomium is that, unlike the classical examples that ironically praised the unpraiseworthy, it was not third-person but first-person discourse. Virgil praised the walnut, and Lucian lauded the fly, but Erasmus did not praise folly. Folly praised herself. This is the precise technique that made the *Moria* paradoxical. Why? Because the logical problem of semantic self-reference was thereby involved.

The exemplar of this type of paradox was The Liar. The subject of at least six books of deliberation by Chrysippus and one by Theophrastus, all lost, the antimony of The Liar was preserved classically in various forms by such authors as Cicero, Alexander, Gellius, and Sextus Empiricus. This most celebrated of paradoxes posed the problem: If you say that you are lying and you speak the truth, then you are lying. A variant, the Epimenides, was cited by St. Paul: "Epimenides the Cretan said all Cretans are liars" (Titus 1:12-13). How logicians of antiquity attempted to solve the problem is unknown, but the effort allegedly caused a fatality. As his epitaph intoned, "Philetas of Cos am I / 'Twas The Liar that made me die, / And the bad nights caused thereby."[81] With the demand of modern science for the empirical validation of truth, Galileo Galilei would scoff at this paradox as arbitrary and unverifiable sophistry. As his own Simplicio would report it: "This is one of those forked arguments called 'sorites,' like that of the Cretans who said that all Cretans were liars. It follows therefore that the Cretans were not liars, and consequently that he, being a Cretan, had spoken the truth. And since saying that Cretans were liars he had spoken truly, including himself as a Cretan, he must consequently be a liar. And thus, in such sophisms, a man may go round and round forever and never come to any conclusion."[82] In the intervening centuries between antiquity and modernity, however, the paradox was debated zestfully.

Its revival from obscurity coincided with discussions originating early in the thirteenth century of the Aristotelian fallacy *secundum quid et simpliciter*. The source was likely a commentary on the *Sophistici elenchi* at 25. 180a27–b7, although one also reflecting other influences, perhaps Stoic.[83] Such paradoxes and also sophisms, which medieval logicians termed *insolubilia*, were scrutinized with increasing interest.[84] Complicated variants were invented such as, "Socrates says, 'What Plato says is false,' and Plato says, 'What Socrates says is true,' and neither says anything else. Is what Socrates says true or false?" Logicians identified the difficulty as owing to the attempt at a certain sort of self-reference. Such an insoluble was defined as "a proposition having with respect to itself a reference of its own falsity, or else one that is not true, being totally or partially illative." No consensus was achieved on the epistemological import or the resolution of such paradoxes, however, and by the beginning of the fifteenth century Paul of Venice could report fifteen differing opinions.[85] The increasing availability of ancient texts in humanist editions prompted some commentary on paradoxes which, replacing the medieval term *insolubile* with the Ciceronian *inexplicabile*, seems to have been exclusively classical in inspiration. Whereas medieval logicians discussed paradoxes in works specifically devoted in whole or in part to insolubles, or in commentaries on Aristotle's *Sophistici elenchi*, these authors usually referred to them under miscellaneous and sometimes unexpected headings. While solutions were rarely ventured, the novel view was proposed that insoluble sentences were not propositions at all, and therefore were not susceptible to assessment as true or false.[86]

Among those who offered in the fifteenth and early sixteenth centuries a more scholastic, and more sophisticated, treatment of semantic paradoxes, the problem of self-reference continued to be the starting-point for analysis. These logicians disagreed principally concerning the legitimacy of self-reference itself. Arguing against the weighty William of Ockham, who had maintained that a proposition in which the term "true" appeared could not be included within that term's range of reference, several types of solution were advanced to argue that insolubles were authentic propositions. These were the claim that a proposition implied its own truth, whether logically or virtually; the claim that it asserted its own falsity; the distinction between two kinds of signification, direct and indirect; and the distinction between the conditions for affirmative and negative propositions. At Paris in Erasmus's day, Tartaretus, Bricot, and Major himself were energetic and egregious in these debates. The publication of Major's *Insolubilia* marked the turn of the century. Other contemporaries of Erasmus, who would eventually become his controversialists, were also entangled in the solution of the insoluble, notably Lefèvre d'Etaples (d. 1536), Josse Clichtove (1472–1543), and Johann Maier von Eck (1486–1543), as was young Luther's teacher of logic, Jodocus Trutvetter (d. 1519).[87]

Erasmus braved the scene with Moria's initial words: "Stulticia loquitur."[88]

Save for this avowal, "Folly speaks," and her ensuing oration in first-person discourse, there would be no self-reference, hence no semantic paradox, in the *Moria*. The modern logical term, "semantic paradox," is somewhat confusing in this historical context, since the paradox of the *Moria* depends on a grammatical, syntactic ambiguity (the objective versus subjective genitive of the title), rather than on a lexical, semantic ambiguity in the classical sense. Moreover, the titular Greek does contain semantic ambiguity, again in the classical sense, in that *Moria* may mean either "folly" or "More," and again either "More" or "Major." Nevertheless, the paradox of the *Moria* plainly belongs to the class arising from the problem of self-reference, for if folly speaks the praise of folly there is no means of verification internal or external to that statement. This lack of a logical criterion—Moria's "insolubility"—is the primary source of the frustration interpreters have commonly experienced in attempting to sort out her mystery.

Erasmus exploited paradox to confound logic itself. By the device of the paradoxical fool he sought to render dialectic itself ridiculous. Moria argues that she, "folly," is alone the universal term, comprising the divine and human orders and every particular within them, however varied or antithetical. She proves this by an equivocation of the meaning of folly, which usually ranges from the pejorative to the permissive. Moria, however, extends "folly" to include even its antonym "wisdom," so that sinners and saints alike are legitimately predicated of her. The rationale for this license with language is Moria herself in her highest theophany, Christ as wisdom made foolish, and folly, wise, who as the Logos, the paradigm of speech, ultimately determines and interprets all meaning.[89] Sophistically undertaking sophistry to the ruin of dialectic, Moria fancies "to play the Sophist before you, and I don't mean by that one of the tribe today who cram tiresome trivialities into the heads of schoolboys and teach them a more than feminine obstinacy in disputation." She rather follows the ancient preference for the name *sophist* to that of *philosopher*, for she is, she says, no lover of wisdom. The sophists of old eulogized the gods, and as she intends to do the same, both for herself and for Christ, the name fits.[90] Having defined herself, *Stulticia* in Latin, MΩPIA in Greek, as "the true bestower of 'good things,' "[91] she claims that she can prove her own truth from top to bottom. She'll demonstrate it, she states, not by recourse to "the crocodile," "the heap," or "the horned," referring to voguish classical paradoxes. "No, with what is called sound common sense I can put my finger on the spot."[92] Again, eschewing Stoic enthymemes, she seeks to prove her point, namely herself, "by means of a simple illustration,"[93] a rhetorical method.

She does, nevertheless, steal one method from the logicians to justify her self-praise: the distinction. There is folly, and there is folly. If the masters of dialectic wish to appear sane, she observes, they too should distinguish insanity from insanity.[94] This distinction of follies is embodied in the persons of More and Major, who bear the same name but signify its common reality, Moria, in contrary ways. The rhetorical recourse of the encomium is to demonstrate the resolution of the paradox of self-reference as not in logic, but in life. Thomas More in person is the resolution of The Liar, as revealed in Moria's pun on the verse "I speak as a fool, but I am more / I speak as a fool, but I am More" (2 Cor. 11:23).[95] In being More, Moria transcends Major—*plus ego*—to deserve the praise of folly, and hence, to solve the paradox. This moral argues for the nominalist rather than the realist theory in the controversy over universals. It derives, however, less from epistemological speculation than from empirical observation. What matters to Erasmus as a rhetorical theologian is not the universal stuff, but the individual act.

In the end, if dialecticians will not concede that More solves the paradox in person, perhaps they will yield, Moria hopes, to the humanist resolution of laughter. As she observes, "Often what can't be refuted by argument can be parried by laughter."[96] Among the crowd of modern logicians intrigued by The Liar,[97] Marvin Minsky echoes Moria's comic resort. Considering the attitude of children to logical paradoxes, he relates that "I have often discussed Zeno's paradox with little kids. I ask a kid to try to walk halfway to a wall, and the kid does it. Then I say, 'Now walk halfway from where you are now to the wall,' and then I ask him what would happen if he kept that up. 'Would you ever get to the wall?' If the child appreciates the problem at all, what happens is that he says, 'That is a very funny joke,' and he begins to laugh. This seems to me to be very significant." Minsky is reminded of the Freudian theory of humor in which what is funny represents a forbidden thought escaping the censor. "These logical paradoxes are cognitively traumatic experiences. They set up mental oscillations that are almost painful—like trying to see both sides of the liar paradox: 'The sentence that you are now reading is false.' These intellectual jokes represent the same sort of threat to the intellect that sexy or sadistic jokes do to the emotions. The fact that we can laugh at them is valuable. It enables us to get by with an inconsistent logic."[98]

While inconsistent logic presents no threat to Minsky as a modern mathematician, it proved to Erasmus the fault of the *scientia sermocinalis* being touted at Paris by "moderns" of another era. Convinced of its failure to treat of mysteries transcending reason, as manifest in the divine folly that transcended logic, he sought as an evangelical humanist to promote the substitution of rhetoric for dialectic. Its figurative language and alluring argument he considered truer indices of the truth than the blunt language and coercive argument of logic. Moria argued that there is "nothing less sensible than misplaced sense." Man needed to acknowledge his foolish condition and to adapt himself to it.[99] To the protests of the philosophers that it is wretched to live in folly, with its attendant illusion, deception, and ignorance, she retorted: "It isn't—it's human. I don't see why they call it a misery when you're all born, formed, and fashioned in this pattern, and it's the common lot of mankind. There's no misery in remaining true to type." To the argument that the sciences allowed man to compensate by wit for what nature had denied him, she responded that these daemonic inventions were useless to happiness and even an obstacle to knowledge. The native instinct by which men in the Golden Age thrived without such sacriligeous and mad inquiry into the beyond was the ideal.[100] "It's a true sign of prudence," she argued, "not to want wisdom which extends beyond your share as an ordinary mortal, to be willing to overlook things along with the rest of the world and wear your illusions with a good grace. People say that this is really a sign of folly, and I'm not setting out to deny it—so long as they'll admit on their side that this is the way to play the comedy of life."[101]

Since "man's mind is so formed that it is far more susceptible to falsehood than to truth," Moria recommended a Skepticism in the manner of the true Academics.[102] Surveying the Parisian theologians, she deplored those dialectical " 'maxims' of theirs which are so 'paradoxical' that in comparison the pronouncements of the Stoics which were actually known as paradoxes seem positively commonplace and banal."[103] Rejecting her wisdom, those masters refused to acknowledge with any good grace the comedy of life in which they strutted in their illusory parts. For this intellectual conceit, their paragon John Major, expounding The Liar to the sophomores, merited his end: he slept the sleep of Epimenides, the Cretan liar himself. Erasmus thus confidently declared to Thomas More the superior profit of his own nonsense over gathering the goat's wool: "For, as there is nothing more frivolous than to handle serious topics in a trifling manner, so also there is nothing more agreeable than to handle trifling matters in such a way that what you have done seems anything but ridiculous. Others will judge me; but unless my vanity altogether deceives me, I have written a Praise of Folly without being altogether foolish."[104]

NOTES

1. Ed. Clarence H. Miller, in *Opera omnia* (Amsterdam, 1979), IV-3, hereafter abbreviated as *ASD*.
2. To Hector Boece, in *Erasmi Epistolae*, ed. P. S. Allen et al., 12 vols. (Oxford, 1906-58), I, p. 155, ll. 7-9 (Ep. 47, 8 November 1495), hereafter abbreviated *EE*; trans. R. A. B. Mynors and D. F. S. Thomson, *The Collected Works of Erasmus* (Toronto, 1974), I, p. 94, hereafter abbreviated as *CWE*.
3. To Nicolaas Werner, *EE* I, p. 160, ll. 23-24 (Ep. 48, 13 September 1496); *CWE* I, p. 98.
4. For Montaigu, see Marcel Godet, *La Congrégation de Montaigu (1490-1580)* (Paris, 1912); Augustin Renaudet, *Préréforme et humanisme à*

Paris pendant les premières guerres d'Italie (1498-1517) (Paris, 1916), especially pp. 267-73.

5. "Ἰχθυοφαγία," in *Colloquia*, ed. Leon-E. Halkin et al., *ASD* I-3, pp. 531-32, ll. 1318-78; trans. Craig R. Thompson, *The Colloquies of Erasmus* (Chicago and London, 1965), pp. 351-53.

6. E. J. Ashworth, *Language and Logic in the Post-Medieval Period* (Dordrecht and Boston, 1974), pp. 5-6.

7. To and From Publio Fausto Andrelini, *EE* I, pp. 235-36 (Ep. 96-100); Ep. 100, p. 236, ll. 2-3 (?May 1499); *CWE* I, p. 190.

8. *Moria, ASD* IV-3, p. 128, ll. 63-64.

9. Ibid., p. 142, ll. 348-55.

10. *Adagia*, 1. 1. 7, in *Opera omnia*, ed. J. Clericus, 11 vols. (Leiden, 1703-06), II, 28B-D; hereafter abbreviated as *LB*. See also *Lingua, sive de usu et abusu* (1526), ed. F. Schalk, *ASD* IV-1, p. 245 l. 240-p. 261 l. 802.

11. Lorenzo Valla, *Encomium sancti Thomae Aquinatis*, in *Opera omnia*, ed. Eugenio Garin (Basel, 1540; rpt. 2 vols.; Turin, 1962), II, pp. 390-96; and see Salvatore I. Camporeale, "Lorenzo Valla tra Medioevo e Rinascimento: Encomion s. Thomae—1457," *Memorie Domenicane*, VII (1976). See also J.-P. Massaut, "Erasme et Saint Thomas," in *Colloquia Erasmiana Turonensia: 12e Stage internationale d'étude humanistes, Tours, 1969*, ed. Jean-Claude Margolin, 2 vols. (Paris, 1972), II, pp. 581-611.

12. *Moria, ASD* IV-3, p. 142, l. 356-p. 144, l. 360.

13. Compare ibid., p. 144, ll. 361-63, p. 74, ll. 70-71; trans. Betty Radice, *Praise of Folly and Letter to Martin Dorp 1515* (Harmondsworth, 1971), p. 67.

14. Ibid., p. 112, ll. 750-51; trans., Radice, p. 114.

15. Johannes Buridanus, *Sophismata* 6. 4, ed. T. K. Scott (Stuttgart, 1977), pp. 108-9.

16. *Moria, ASD* IV-3, p. 112, ll. 751-54; trans. Radice, p. 114.

17. "Ἰχθυοφαγία," in *Colloquia, ASD* I-3, p. 531, ll. 1323-24; trans. Thompson, p. 351.

18. Especially under the aegis of John Dullaert of Ghent, for whom see Hubert Elie, "Quelques maîtres de l'Université de Paris vers l'an 1500," *Archives d'histoire doctrinale et littéraire du Moyen Age*, 18-19 (1950-51):222-24.

19. *Moria, ASD* IV-3, p. 144, ll. 361-78; trans. Radice, p. 151.

20. See Ashworth, "Multiple Quantification and the Use of Special Quantifiers in Early Sixteenth Century Logic," *Notre Dame Journal of Formal Logic*, 19 (1978):599-613.

21. *Moria, ASD* IV-3, p. 164, ll. 611-21; trans. Radice, p. 170. Similarities between the general structure of the *Moria*, identified as a mock encomium with the exterior form of a university oration, and the satire on schooling within it are suggested in Sander L. Gilman, *The Parodic Sermon in European Literature: Aspects of Liturgical Parody from the Middle Ages to the Twentieth Century* (Wiesbaden, 1974), pp. 28-29.

22. Lisa Jardine, "Lorenzo Valla and the Intellectual Origins of Humanist Dialectic," *Journal of the History of Philosophy* 15 (1977):143-64; Cesare Vasoli, "Le *dialecticae disputationes* de Lorenzo Valla .e la critica umanistica della logica aristotelica," *Rivista critica di storia della filosofia* 12 (1957):412-34; 13 (1958):27-46; idem, "Dialettica e Retorica in Rodolfo Agricola," *Atti dell' Accademia toscana di scienze e lettere 'La Colombaria'* 22 (n.s. 8) (1957-58):307-55.

23. To Thomas Grey, *EE* I, p. 192, ll. 74-82 (Ep. 64, August 1497); trans. *CWE* I, pp. 137-38.

24. Ibid., p. 190, ll. 5-14; trans. p. 135.

25. Ibid., p. 190, l. 15-p. 193, l. 92; trans. pp. 135-37.

26. Allen, ibid., p. 192 n. 75.

27. Ashworth, *Language and Logic*, p. 6.

28. Elie, "Quelques maîtres de l'Université de Paris vers l'an 1500," pp. 196-200.

29. Ibid., pp. 205-12.

30. James K. Farge, *Biographical Register of Paris Doctors of Theology 1500-1536* (Toronto, 1980), p. 305.

31. See Elie, "Quelques maîtres," pp. 212-28; John Durkan, "The School of John Major: Bibliography," *The Innes Review* 1 (1950):140-57.

32. Ashworth, *Language and Logic*, p. 7.

33. For his bibliography, see Farge, *Biographical Register*, pp. 308-11.

34. Carlos G. Noreña, "Spanish Logicians of Montaigu College," in *Studies in Spanish Renaissance Thought* (The Hague, 1975), p. 14.

35. Cited by Elie, "Quelques maîtres," p. 210.

36. Noreña, *Studies in Spanish Renaissance Thought*, pp. 14-15.

37. Durkan, "John Major: After 400 Years," *The Innes Review* 1 (1950): 137-38.

38. Ibid., p. 134.

39. Ibid.

40. Major, *In Mattheum ad literam expositio* (Paris, 1518).

41. Carl Prantl, *Geschichte der Logik im Abendlande*, 4 vols. in 2 (Leipzig, 1927), III, pp. 204-9.

42. To Grey, *EE* I, p. 190, ll. 8-10; trans. *CWE* I, p. 135.

43. Durkan, "John Major," p. 131.

44. E.g., Petrarch, *Invective contra medicum* 2. 439-40, ed. Pier Giorgio Ricci (Rome, 1950), p. 52.

45. Cited by J. H. Burns, "New Light on John Major," *The Innes Review* 5 (1954):87.

46. Major, *Octo libri physicorum* (1526), v ii r⁰ A, v v r⁰ A, cited by ibid., pp. 86-87.

47. See my "Folly Plus: Moria and More," in press.

48. Cited by Durkan, "John Major," p. 132.

49. *Moria, ASD* IV-3, p. 74, ll. 57-60.

50. Cicero, *Partitiones oratoriae* 18. 61-62; see also 23. 62; trans. H. Rackham (Loeb ed.; London and Cambridge, Mass., 1942), p. 359.

51. Cicero, *Topica* 22. 83; trans. H. M. Hubbell (Loeb ed.; London and

Cambridge, Mass., 1949), p. 447. See also *Rhetorica ad C. Herennium* 4. 50. 63.

52. *De copia verborum ac rerum, libri duo* (1512), *LB* I, 77E–F, and to 82D; trans. Betty I. Knott, *CWE* XXIV, p. 577.

53. Anselm, *Proslogion* 1–3; trans. M. J. Charlesworth, *St. Anselm's Proslogion* (Oxford, 1965), pp. 117, 119.

54. André Hayen, "The Role of the Fool in St. Anselm and the Necessarily Apostolic Character of True Christian Reflection," in *The Many-Faced Argument: Recent Studies on the Ontological Argument for the Existence of God,* ed. John Hick and Arthur C. McGill (New York, 1967), pp. 162–82; rpt. and trans. from "S. Anselme et S. Thomas: la vraie nature de la théologie et sa portée apostolique," *Spicilegium Beccense* (Paris, 1959), pp. 69–85.

55. G. R. Evans, *Anselm and a New Generation* (Oxford, 1980), pp. 34–68; idem, *Old Arts and New Theology: The Beginings of Theology as an Academic Discipline* (Oxford, 1980), pp. 137–66.

56. See Enid Welsford, *The Fool: His Social and Literary History* (London, 1935); Barbara Swain, *Fools and Folly during the Middle Ages and the Renaissance* (New York, 1932).

57. Hayen, "The Role of the Fool in St. Anselm."

58. Anselm, *De concordia,* in *Opera,* ed. F. S. Schmitt, 6 vols. (Edinburgh, 1938–61), II, p. 258, ll. 2–3.

59. Gaunilo, *Quid ad haec respondeat quidam pro insipiente,* in trans. Charlesworth.

60. Anselm, *Quid ad haec respondeat editor ipsius libelli,* praef.; trans Charlesworth, p. 169.

61. *Moria, ASD* IV–3, p. 158, l. 524–p. 168, l. 674.

62. Evans, "The 'Secure Technician': Varieties of Paradox in the Writings of St. Anselm," *Vivarium* 13 (1975):1–21; and for the historical context, idem, *Anselm and a New Generation,* pp. 111–22.

63. *Pace* Evans, whose understanding of "rhetorical paradoxes" depends on Colie's analysis, which I criticize below. But for a more agreeable discussion of Anselm's rhetorical skill, see Evans, "St. Anselm's Analogies," *Vivarium* 14 (1976):81–93.

64. Evans, *Anselm and Talking about God* (Oxford, 1978), pp. 36, 93–94.

65. Desmond P. Henry, *The Logic of St. Anselm* (Oxford, 1967), pp. 12, 18, 107; "Saint Anselm's Nonsense," *Mind* 72 (1963):57, although the argument about paradox is mine.

66. Evans, *Anselm and a New Generation,* pp. 34–68.

67. William Willeford, *The Fool and His Sceptre: A Study in Clowns and Jesters and Their Audience* (n.p., 1969), p. 10.

68. Sebastian Brant, *Das Narrenschiff,* ed. Manfred Lemmer (Tübingen, 1962). The English translation (*The Shyp of Folys*) was published in the same year as the composition of the *Moria* (London, 1509; rpt. Amsterdam, 1970).

69. *Moria, ASD* IV–3, p. 106, ll. 625–53; trans. Radice, pp. 105–7. For the

identification of Stoic paradoxes in this passage, see Miller, ed., p. 107 nn. 642, 643.

70. Ibid., p. 88, l. 316-p. 90, l. 318. See my *Christening Pagan Mysteries: Erasmus in Pursuit of Wisdom* (Toronto, 1981), p. 50.

71. *Moria, ASD* IV-3, p. 180, l. 919-p. 188, l. 140.

72. For Moria as religiously "adorable," see my *Christening Pagan Mysteries*, pp. 29-61.

73. *Ratio*, in *Ausgewählte Werke*, ed. Hajo Holborn with Annemarie Holborn (Munich, 1964), p. 180, ll. 21-24; p. 193, ll. 18-22. See my *Erasmus on Language and Method in Theology* (Toronto, 1977) for his methodology, and for analysis of his rhetorical theology in its most historically important expression, see my *Rhetoric and Reform: Erasmus' Civil Dispute with Luther* (Cambridge, Mass., 1983).

74. For *memento mori*, see my *Christening Pagan Mysteries*, pp. 34-53.

75. *Moria, ASD* IV-3, p. 72, ll. 30-34; trans. Radice, p. 65.

76. Ibid., p. 74, ll. 55-56; trans. p. 66.

77. Cicero, *Orator* 13. 42. For the genre, see Theodore C. Burgess, *Epideictic Literature* (Chicago, 1902).

78. Rosalie L. Colie, *Paradoxia Epidemica: The Renaissance Tradition of Paradox* (Princeton, 1966), pp. 3-4; Burgess, *Epideictic Literature*, pp. 157-66.

79. Even Colie admits concerning the model paradox, The Liar, that "if someone else were to formulate the statement, the paradox would dissolve into a simple affirmation, the truth or falsity of which could be more or less accurately tested," *Paradoxia Epidemica*, pp. 6-7. Yet she states that "rhetorical paradoxes" are also logical ones, since they involve the self-contradiction of praising the unpraisable. My argument is precisely that the "rhetorical paradoxes" she cites are not *self*-contradictions, and therefore do not serve as counterparts to the logical model of self-contradiction, The Liar. Erasmus' *Moria*, therefore, is not a "rhetorical paradox," but rather a rhetorical treatment of a logical one. When Erasmus himself uses the term "paradox" he refers to its classical denotation, not its connotations in modern literary criticism. See my "Stoic Luther: Paradoxical Sin and Necessity," *Archiv für Reformationsgeschichte* 73 (1982):69-93. Colie imputes to Erasmus and to the classical authors she considers his model the meanings of "paradox" that developed only later—the OED gives no examples earlier than ca. 1570—when certain aspects of The Liar subsumed the much more sophisticated, and more varied, meanings of the term. There is, I suggest, in both literary criticism and theological analysis much glib writing about "paradoxes" in historical texts whose authors would never have recognized their figures of speech as anything more than oxymorons, antitheses, or types of ambiguity.

80. To Thomas More, *EE* II, p. 460, l. 25-p. 461, l. 38 (Ep. 222, 9 June 1511); trans. *CWE* II, 163. For these examples see Arthur S. Pease, "Things without Honour," *Classical Philology* 21 (1926):27-42; and

for some distinctions between them and the *Moria*, Sr. M. Geraldine Thompson, "Erasmus and the Tradition of Paradox," *Studies in Philology* 61 (1964):41–42. Erasmus also included in his list some jesting precedents not of the epideictic genre.

Two classical examples of self-praise have been identified as Poverty's paradoxical encomium in Aristophanes, *Plutus* 507–610, and Phalaris' in Lucian's *Phalarides*, as cited by Moria herself, *ASD* IV–3, p. 74, l. 48. Miller, ed., p. 20.

81. See Alexander Rüstow, *Der Lügner: Theorie/Geschichte und Auflösung* (Leipzig, 1910), pp. 19–98; Benson Mates, *Stoic Logic* (Berkeley and Los Angeles, 1971), p. 84.

82. Galileo, *Dialogo sopra i due massimi sistemi del mondo tolemaico e copernico* (1632), trans. Stillman Drake, *Dialogue Concerning the Two Chief World Systems* (Berkeley, 1953), p. 42; cited by Colie, *Paradoxia Epidemica*, pp. 509–10.

83. Paul V. Spade, "The Origins of the Mediaeval *Insolubilia* Literature," *Franciscan Studies* 33 (1973):292–309.

84. For a list of texts from the beginning of the thirteenth to the end of the first quarter of the fifteenth centuries, see idem, *The Mediaeval Liar: A Catalogue of the Insolubilia Literature* (Toronto, 1975); for a history, Francesco Bottin, *Le antinomie semantiche nella logica medievale* (Padua, 1976); and further bibliography on particular authors, Ashworth, *The Tradition of Mediaeval Logic and Speculative Grammar from Anselm to the End of the Seventeenth Century: A Bibliography from 1836 Onwards* (Toronto, 1978). See also Alan R. Perreiah, "*Insolubilia* in Paul of Venice's *Logica Parva*," *Medioevo, Rivista di Storia della Filosofia Medievale* 4 (1978):145–71.

85. William Kneale and Martha Kneale, *The Development of Logic* (Oxford, 1962), pp. 227–29.

86. Ashworth, "The Treatment of Semantic Paradoxes from 1400 to 1700," *Notre Dame Journal of Formal Logic* 13 (1972):34–37.

87. Ibid., 37–45; idem, *Language and Logic in the Post-Medieval Period*, pp. 101–17; idem, "Thomas Bricot (d. 1516) and the Liar Paradox," *Journal of the History of Philosophy* 15 (1977):267–80.

88. *Moria, ASD* IV–3, p. 71, l. 4; trans. Radice, p. 63.

89. See my *Erasmus on Language and Method in Theology*.

90. *Moria, ASD* IV–3, p. 72, ll. 23–28; trans. Radice, p. 64.

91. Ibid., p. 74, ll. 62–64; trans. p. 69.

92. Ibid., p. 92, ll. 383–85; trans. pp. 90–91, which incorrectly conflates "soritis, ceratinis" as "the Horned Sorites." The Latin terms refer rather to two distinct paradoxes: "the heap" or "the bald man," also known as the sorites, and "the horned." For the revival of "the crocodile" see Ashworth, "The Treatment of Semantic Paradoxes from 1400 to 1700," pp. 39–40.

93. *Moria, ASD* IV–3, p. 113, l. 794–p. 114, l. 795; trans. Radice, p. 116.

94. Ibid., p. 116, ll. 868–70; trans. p. 120.

95. See my "Folly Plus: Moria and More."

96. *Moria, ASD* IV-3, p. 140, ll. 302-3; trans. Radice, p. 147.

97. See the bibliography in *The Paradox of the Liar,* ed. Robert L. Martin (New Haven and London, 1970), pp. 135-49.

98. Marvin Minsky, an expert in artificial intelligence and Donner Professor of Science at the Massachusetts Institute of Technology, as interviewed by Jeremy Bernstein for "Profiles," *The New Yorker,* December 14, 1981, p. 125.

99. *Moria, ASD* IV-3, p. 106, l. 613; trans. Radice, p. 105.

100. Ibid., p. 110, l. 706-p. 112, l. 754; trans. pp. 111-12.

101. Ibid., p. 106, ll. 613-19; trans. p. 105.

102. Ibid., p. 130, ll. 96-102; trans. p. 135. For the Academic Skepticism of Erasmus, see my *Rhetoric and Reform.*

103. Ibid., p. 148, ll. 411-13; trans. p. 155.

104. To More, *EE* I, p. 461, ll. 50-53; trans. *CWE* II, p. 164.

Poetry and Politics in *Jorge Manrique's* Coplas por la muerte de su padre

DAVID H. DARST

Jorge Manrique's moving elegy to his father has been a perennial favorite with the masses as well as the critics since its diffusion shortly after the soldier poet's own death in 1479.[1] Since the appearance of Pedro Salinas's fundamental study of the poem in 1947,[2] this monument of fifteenth-century Spanish poetry has received an especially large number of valuable studies.[3] The political background has been exhaustively detailed by Antonio Serrano de Haro;[4] and the basic three-part structure, consisting of exposition (strophes I–XIII), evocation of don Rodrigo Manrique's generation (strophes XIV–XXIV), and laudatory dirge (strophes XXV–XL), has been analyzed repeatedly, most recently by Charles V. Aubrun and Gustavo Correa.[5] Few scholars, however, have bothered to examine the interrelationship between the content of each section and the way Jorge Manrique chose to express it. The only significant advance in that direction has been by Leo Spitzer, who tentatively approached Manrique's manipulation of language and syntax in a 1950 essay, noting a number of peculiarities. One of the most striking, according to Spitzer, was "la manera 'temática,' como de predicador en el púlpito, de adelantar lo que se piensa será su sujeto, reforzándolo con un demonstrativo, sin preocuparse de la alteración sintática en que la oración acabará por resolverse: '*Esos* reyes poderosos / . . . fueron *sus* buenas venturas / trastorna-das' (XIV), 'Pues *aquel* grand Condestabe / . . . non cumple que *dél* se hable' (XXI), 'tantos duques excelentes, / . . . di, Muerte, dó *los* escondes' (XXIII)."[6]

It is not by pure chance that Spitzer's examples are all from the second section of the *Coplas* (strophes XIV–XXIV), which describes "lo d'ayer" (XV) in Castile and Aragon. The demonstrative adjective *aquel*, for example, appears only once in the first part (strophes I–XIII): "Aun *aquel* fijo de Dios" (VI). The pronoun also occurs in a single stanza: "*aquél* sólo m'en-comiendo, / *aquél* sólo invoco yo" (IV).[7] It is significant that these uses are metonymical references to Jesus Christ, and the only other appearance of *aquél* outside the central stanzas is as a metonymical pronoun in strophe XXV: "*Aquel* de buenos abrigo," which refers to the poet's father. In contrast

197

Medievalia et Humanistica, New Series, Number 13 (Paul Maurice Clogan, ed.). Rowman & Allanheld, Totowa, NJ. 1985.

to this sparse use in the first and last sections, strophes XIV–XXIV contain abundant instances: "*Esos* reyes pederosos" (XIV), "lo d'*aquel* siglo passado" (XV), "¿Qué se hizo *aquel* trovar / . . . / ¿Qué se hizo *aquel* dançar, / *aquellas* ropas chapadas" (XVII), "Pues *aquel* grand Condestable" (XXI), and "*aquella* prosperidad" (XXII).

Spitzer's last example concerned the adjective *tanto*. It is interesting that this word does not even appear in the first thirteen stanzas, and the adverb *tan* has only two uses: "*tan* callando" (I) and "*tan* crescida" (X). In the second part, however, one finds "¿Qué fue de *tanto* galán, / ¿qué de *tanta* inuinción" (XVI), "las vaxillas tan fabridas / . . . / tan sobrados" (XIX), "iqué corte *tan* excellente" (XX), "*tan* privado" (XXI), "maestres *tan* prosperados / . . . / truxieron *tan* sojuzgados / . . . / qu'en *tan* alto fue subida" (XXII), "*Tantos* duques excelentes, / *tantos* marqueses e condes / e varones / como vimos *tan* potentes" (XXIII). In the description of don Rodrigo that forms the third section of the poem (strophes XXV–XL), one could deduce that there would be a dearth of phrases with *tan* and *tanto*, yet those stanzas in fact possess eight items: "el maestre don Rodrigo / Manrique, *tanto* famoso e *tan* valiente" (XXV), "fizo tratos *tan* honrosos" (XXX), "*tantas* vezes por su ley / al tablero; / después de *tan* bien servida / . . . / después de *tanta* hazaña" (XXXIII), "fezistes *tan* poca cuenta" (XXXIV), and "Non se vos haga *tan* amarga" (XXXV).

The question that arises from this selective usage of the demonstrative *aquel* and *tan* and *tanto* is why Jorge Manrique would write his verses in such a way. Depending on the section of the *Coplas*, the poet evidently has either stated things that do not require these forms, or he has omitted or inserted them to enhance the sense of the phrases in which they appear. The latter is more plausible, for the many uses of *aquel* and *tanto* in strophes XIV–XXIV add nothing to the content or the meaning of the poem. Their function is therefore principally formal and—*mutato nomine*—poetic.

What is it about the second, "lo d'ayer" section that is so different from section one? Principally, as Pedro Salinas reiterated throughout his study of the *Coplas*, stanzas I–XIII present ideas in general formulations, while the later sections offer progressively more particular examples of the general rules.[8] The first six stanzas thus elaborate various metaphors on the *Peregrinatio Vitae* (I–VI), and the next seven declare the transitoriness of "las cosas" (VIII), "la hermosura" (IX), "la sangre de los godos" (X), "los estados e riqueza" (XI), and "los plazeres e dulçores" (XIII). The next eleven stanzas particularize these five generalized ephemeralities.

Clearly, neither Manrique nor any other moralist of his age considered goods, beauty, noble blood, riches, and pleasure to be ends in themselves or laudable aspects of a proper spiritual life; and the poet stresses that point in strophe VII with his juxtaposition of "corporal" and "angelical." As in the other *De Contemptu Mundi* poems of the time, such as Ferrán Sanchez Calavera's famous *Decir*, material goods are no more than "las vanidades del mundo". and should be eschewed. Likewise, it is not without significance that six of the seven personages cited in the second section of the poem were known by all to be bitter enemies of Jorge's father.[9] Juan II, the Infantes de Aragón (don Enrique in particular), and Enrique IV are treated as one group (XVI-XIX); don Alonso "el inocente," whom Rodrigo Manrique tried to make king in 1465, is given a laudatory strophe to him alone (XX),[10] and the three *maestres* Alvaro de Luna, Juan Pacheco, and Pedro Girón are treated as another group (XXI-XXII).[11] There is thus a cleverly contrived progression from the first section to the second that moves from general things one should abhor to particular things one should abhor. The poet has arranged the syllogistic argument of his elegy in such a way that even if the readers were predisposed toward the people he mentions, the cumulative advance of the poem would induce them to consider those persons unfavorably.

Manrique reinforces his subtle predisposition of the readers to hold common general and specific particular examples in contempt by accentuating the things he will want the readers to despise with those very terms lacking in the first section. All the adjectives, nouns, pronouns, and infinitives that follow *aquel* and *tanto* are held in disrespect by the poet, including the gilded clothes, dancing, and singing of the ladies and gentlemen at court. Manrique utilizes his linguistic articulations most especially for the abuses of Enrique IV, Alvaro de Luna, and the other two *maestres*, where every *tan* is followed by a denunciatory term: "fabridas," "sobrados," "privado," "prosperados / como reyes," "sojuzgados / a sus leyes," "alto . . . subida," etc. The *aquello* functions to set the same contemptuous tone. "Aquel siglo passado," "aquel grand Condestable," and "aquella prosperidad" all breathe an overbearing air of denunciation of the referent.

Added to these linguistic manipulations, already noted by Spitzer, are others that also serve to turn the reader's allegiance from the people and things mentioned in the center part of the poem. The very nature of the rhetorical questions "¿Qué se hizo . . . ?" requires the answer to be negative, which in turn nullifies any regard for the deeds of the subject.[12] For this reason, the phrase "¿Qué se hizo . . . ?" is not used at all to describe the faithful don Alonso "el inocente," who receives an affirmative *¡Qué!* and a *¡Cuánto!* instead (strophe XX). This technique in turn reflects by contrast the derogatory use of the same exclamations in strophe XVIII, where *¡Cuánd!* in reference to Alonso's impotent brother was followed by the insulting terms "blando," "halaguero," "enemigo," "contrario," "cruel," etc.

To summarize, the poetic and linguistic techniques used in stanzas XIV-XXIV are there to predispose and sway the reader to view the people and things mentioned in an unfavorable way. The obvious reason Manrique would want to do this is because the personages to whom he refers were all enemies of his father. Now, however, Manrique has the creative problem of relating his father's deeds, which he obviously desires to extol and hold up for the reader's esteem, within a denunciatory context, since the *laudatio* follows twenty-four stanzas intended to force the reader to hold anything mentioned in contempt, especially particular political figures personifying authority, nobility, and the life at court.[13] How can he sway the reader to glorify these very characteristics in don Rodrigo while still retaining instilled disdain for the other people in the poem?[14]

The poet initiates the endeavor by opening the third and final section of his elegy with the phrase "aquel de buenos abrigo," whose only antecedent outside the middle portion was in reference to Christ. This does not mean that Manrique wishes the reader to see his father as a Christomimetes, but it is patent that the son has created at least some resemblance between don Rodrigo and Christ wherein his father would function analogically on a secular level the way Christ does on a religious one. The "oración" at the end (strophe XXXIX) is clearly an epitomized credo and a summary, *mutatis mutandis*, of travails in Rodrigo Manrique's life. The parallelism also appears in the last stanza, where Manrique writes "*Dio* el alma a quien gela *dio*."

It is also in stanza XXV that Jorge Manrique returns to the fundamental idea of remembrance and oblivion that has reverberated throughout the poem by stating that he will not praise his father (which is precisely what he will do) because everyone is cognizant of the Maestre's deeds:

> sus hechos grandes e claros
> non cumple que los alabe,
> pues los vieron;
> ni los quiero hazer caros,
> pues que el mundo todo sabe
> cuáles fueron.

These words belie everything the poet has said in the earlier fifteen strophes, where all was described repeatedly as "olvidado." The contrast later becomes the keystone of the poem's structure because Manrique will end what began with the exordium *Recuerde* by noting that the greatest consolation for his father's death was "que aunque la vida perdió, / dexónos harto consuelo / su *memoria*" (XL).

The poet also establishes a number of brilliant contrastive relationships between his father and the personages in the middle section of the *Coplas*. First, he uses the adverb *tan* in reference to his father for opposite values: "famoso," "valiente," "honrosos," "bien servida," "poca cuenta / por la fama," etc. The contrast created to the earlier stanzas is startlingly polar, especially in regard to the three *maestres*, who were so different from the final *maestre*, "el maestre don Rodrigo." Second, Manrique lauds his father with the same technique of the exclamatory *¡Qué!* that he used for don Alonso, which countermines radically the interrogative and negative *¿Qué?* employed to describe "lo d'ayer." In effect, the entire final section contains no interrogatives at all, whereas every stanza dedicated to the six personages in section two contained them. By the same token, and as would be expected, the first thirteen stanzas lack interrogatives also, creating thereby a pattern of affirmation-negation-affirmation for the three parts. Third, Manrique places a number of names—fifteen Roman ones, to be exact—in this last section (strophes XXVII–XXVIII) to contravene the personages cited in the middle portion of the elegy. It is significant that all the classical allusions appear as predicate nominatives of his father: Rodrigo Manrique was "en ventura, Octaviano," etc. Since the poet has repeatedly told the reader that all past heroes have been forgotten, the roster of these fifteen arrests the mind and leads to the observation that the Romans he mentions are remembered solely by reference to don Rodrigo, who, by reincarnating their attributes, gives cause for their rescue from oblivion. Fourth, Manrique makes direct comparisons between don Rodrigo's actions and those of his contemporaries by repeating words and phrases, but with opposite connotations. Enrique IV had "los *edificios reales* / llenos d'oro" (XIX), while don Rodrigo ended his life "en la su *villa* d'Ocaña" (XXXIII). Enrique lunched on "las *vaxillas* tan fabridas" and possessed "los enriques y reales / del *tesoro*" (XIX), while Manrique's father "Non dexó grandes *tesoros*, / ni alcançó muchas riguezas / ni *vaxillas*" (XXIX). In the same vein, don Alvaro de Luna was known for "sus infinitos *tesoros*, / sus *villas* y sus lugares" (XXI), and don Rodrigo found "sus *villas* e sus tierras, / ocupadas de tiranos" (XXXII).

These are only a few of the many syntactical and verbal similarities among the poem's parts. More exist, ranging from direct juxtaposition of words, where Enrique IV is "cuánd enemigo" (XVIII) and don Rodrigo "enemigo de enemigos" (XXVI), to subtle comparisons of meaning, as noting that the *maestres* had everyone "tan sojuzgados / a sus leyes" (XXII) while don Rodrigo was "¡Qué benino a los sujetos!" (XXVI), or that Pedro Girón and Juan Pacheco were "tan prosperados / como reyes" (XXII) while Manrique's father died "después de tan bien servida / la corona de su rey verdadero" (XXXIII).[15]

Finally, Manrique manipulates his subject matter in such a way as to guarantee eternal salvation for his father and, by default, eternal damnation for the enemies discussed in section two. After the extensive description of don Rodrigo's career (XXVI–XXXIII), Death arrives to tell the warrior—and the readers—that eternal life, the third and final one attainable,[16]

> non se gana con estados
> mundanales,
> ni con vida delectable
> donde moran los pecados
> infernales;

> mas los buenos religiosos
> gánanlo con oraciones
> e con lloros;
> los caballeros famosos,
> con trabajos e aflicciones
> contra moros.

The A–B / B′–A′ parallelism of the verses brilliantly summarizes the dirge's progress. "Estados / mundanales" is a clear reference to the second portion of "duques," "marqueses," "condes," and "varones" (strophe XXIII); and "vida delectable" epitomizes the "cosas," "hermosura," "sangre," "riqueza," and "placeres" of the first section (especially strophes VIII–XIII). As opposed to the latter, Manrique offers "los buenos religiosos," who deny the delightful life with prayers and tears. As opposed to the worldly estates, the poet puts forward "los caballeros famosos" who won their fortresses and villages with travails and afflictions. Since no religious personages are even mentioned in the poem, the only ones who could go to the heaven mentioned by Death are therefore the warriors. Did the Infantes de Aragón or the courtiers around the throne of Enrique IV or any of those other people from "lo d'ayer" fight against the Moors? On the contrary, they participated solely in fake battles— "las justas e los torneos" (XVI)—or in civil wars among themselves (strophe XXIV). Don Rodrigo, by contrast, "fizo guerra a los moros, / ganando sus fortalezas / e sus villas" (XXIX). Therefore he alone, as Death makes clear in strophe XXXVII, will gain fame as well as eternal life:

> E pues vos, claro varón,
> tanta sangre derramastes
> de paganos,
> esperad el galardón
> que en este mundo ganastes
> por las manos;
> e con esta confiança
> e con la fe tan entera
> que tenéis,
> partid con buena esperança,
> qu'estotra vida tercera
> ganaréis.

Manrique thus achieves for his father in one stroke of the pen what he has earlier denied to the family's enemies. All of those who populated the immediate past are forgotten: "Vengamos a lo d'ayer, / que también es olvidado / como aquello" (XV). In fact, they and "lo d'aquel siglo passado" are the *only* ones for whom the term "olvidado" is applied, since in the first thirteen stanzas Manrique never described how people and things have been forgotten, but merely how all inevitably passes away. For don Rodrigo, however, solely "esta vida mesquina" (XXXVIII) is lost by death; "la fama glorïosa" (XXXV) remains, and eternal life is gained. No one else in the poem is granted either the one (based on memory) or the other (based on wars against the Moors).

In closing, while it is certainly true that *Coplas por la muerte de su padre* is "el gran poema consolatorio de la lírica española, . . . la gran elegía del hombre en la tierra,"[17] it is equally correct to view the epicedium as a direct and often sarcastic political statement about the times immediately preceding the successful overthrow of the Trastámaras and their Portuguese allies by Fernando de Aragón and Isabel de Castilla.

NOTES

1. Edition consulted: Jorge Manrique, *Poesía*, ed. Jesús-Manuel Alda Tesán (Madrid, 1976), pp. 144–63.
2. Pedro Salinas, *Jorge Manrique o tradición y originalidad* (Buenos Aires, 1947).
3. See Matjastic M. Appolonia, *The History of Criticism of "Las coplas" of Jorge Manrique* (Madrid, 1979).
4. Antonio Serrano de Haro, *Personalidad y destino de Jorge Manrique* (Madrid, 1966).
5. Aubrun: "La mort du père (*Coplas* de Jorge Manrique): Structure et signification," *Mélanges de langue et de littérature médiévales offerts à Pierre le Gentil* (Paris, 1973), pp. 75–84. Aubrun separates the poem into the following parts: Introspection (I–III), Invocation (IV–V), Distanciation (VI–IX), Oraison (X–XIII), Evocation du passé (XIV–XXIV), Dithyrambe (XXV–XXXIII), Débat tragico-lyrique (XXXIV–XXXVIII), Prière et finale (XXXIX–XL). Correa: "Lenguaje y ritmo en las coplas de Jorge Manrique a la muerte de su padre," *Hispania* 63 (1980):184–94: "1) unidad tématica inicial (5 estrofas, I–V); 2) tema ético de la desvaloración de las cosas mundanas en oposición a la valoración de las eternas (9 estrofas, VI–XIV); 3) tema de la evanescencia de las cosas humanas, a través de casos recientes a la vida del poeta o contemporáneos con ella (10 estrofas, XV–XXIV); 4) elogio del muerto don Rodrigo (9 estrofas, XXV–XXXIII); 5) muerte de don Rodrigo y su oración final (6 estrofas, XXXIV–XXXIX); 6) pervivencia del desaparecido en el recuerdo del poeta (1 estrofa, XL)," pp. 189–90.
6. Leo Spitzer, "Dos observaciones sintáctico-estilísticas a las *Coplas* de Manrique," *Nueva Revista de Filología Hispánica* 4 (1950):9.
7. The "aquél" in the fifth line of strophe VI is discounted because it is juxtaposed to "Este mundo" in the first line.
8. Salinas, *Jorge Manrique*, pp. 156, 160, et passim.
9. For a historical survey of the epoch and the role the Manrique family play in it, consult Serrano de Haro (note 4) and Gualtiero Cangiotti, *Le "Coplas" di Manrique tra Medioevo e Umanesimo* (Bologna, 1964).

10. Don Alonso also occupies the central strophe (XX) of the poem. For a lucid discussion of the Infante's role in the elegy, see Peter Dunn, "Themes and Images in the *Coplas* of Jorge Manrique," *Medium Aevum* 33 (1964):169–83.

11. As Salinas astutely noted, the order of personages is not chronological, but hierarchical: "Primero los reyes, don Juan y don Enrique, en seguida el príncipe don Alfonso, después el gran Condestable don Alvaro y los dos maestres" (p. 177). Alda Tesán adds: "Puede notarse también cómo esa ordenación está relacionada con la estrofa VIII, en la que habla de las cosas desaparecidas por la edad, o términos naturales, por *casos desastrados*, o desastres súbitos, y por caídas de la privanza" (p. 58).

12. In effect, Manrique never answers his own rhetorical questions, since he avoids citing any "hechos" for his father's contemporaries. As explained by Enrique Moreno Castillo: "Cuando se pasa revista a los altos personajes ya desaparecidos se habla de lo que poseyeron, de lo que disfrutaron; nunca de lo que hicieron. . . . En el caso de don Rodrigo, por el contrario, lo que resalta es su actuar: *hizo* guerras, *ganó* fortalezas, *venció* lides, *ganó* rentas y vasallos, *hizo* tratos honrosos, *alcanzó* dignidades, *cobró* sus villas y sus tierras y, finalmente *consintió* en su morir. La diferencia es perceptible incluso a nivel gramatical: los personajes de la segunda parte no suelen ser sujetos de verbos de acción" ("Vida y muerte en las *Coplas* de Jorge Manrique," *Papeles de San Armadans* 82 [1976] :151).

13. It goes without saying that Francisco Caravaca's thesis postulated in "Foulché-Delbosc y su edición 'crítica' de las *Coplas* de Jorge Manrique," *Boletín de la Biblioteca de Menéndez Pelayo* 49 (1973):229–79, claiming anteriority for strophes I–XXIV, is patently false. The linguistic and argumental cohesiveness of all forty stanzas is undeniable.

14. One thing Manrique does *not* do is to relate the bare facts about his father. María Rosa Lida de Malkiel noted some time ago "la intencionada vaguedad de las *Coplas*" when compared to the true history of Rodrigo Manrique: "Reticencia inicial (25g y sigs.), gracias y virtudes agrandadas por ponderaciones admirativas (26) o por referencias a los arquetipos antiguos (27 y 28), hechos de armas patéticamente encuadrados por sus abnegadas hazañas de Reconquista (29 y 33), confirmadas en las últimas palabras de la Muerte (37). La acomodación de la turbulenta biografía a la vida ejemplar de 'caballero famoso' equiparable a Fernán González o al Cid queda cumplida con sutil perfección" (*La idea de la fama en la edad media castellana* [Mexico, 1952], p. 292 n. 122).

15. The adjective *verdadero*, preceded by a reference in strophe XXXII to "nuestro rey natural," was a blatant sarcastic remark directed at the pretentions of the unnatural, false monarch Juana la Beltraneja, whose claim to the throne was advanced by those two brothers Juan Pacheco and Pedro Girón.

16. Cangiotti astutely observes that "il *llamar a su puerta* (vv. 395–96) della morte si carica di un suo significato molto preciso, ancora una volta in contrasto con versi 286–88 ['cuando tú vienes airada,/ todo lo passas de claro / con tu flecha'] " (p. 100). The significance of the

three lives is discussed admirably by Stephan Gilman, "Tres retratos de la muerte en las *Coplas* de Jorge Manrique," *Nueva Revista de Filología Hispánica* 13 (1959):305–24.

17. Salinas, *Jorge Manrique*, pp. 230–31.

Chivalry and Its Historians

MICHAEL ALTSCHUL

Joachim Bumke, *The Concept of Knighthood in the Middle Ages*. New York: AMS Press, 1982. Pp. viii, 268. $29.50.

J. J. N. Palmer, ed., *Froissart: Historian*. Totowa, New Jersey: Rowman & Littlefield, 1981. Pp. xii, 203; 4 maps, 2 tables. $47.50.

Malcolm Vale, *War and Chivalry: Warfare and Aristocratic Culture in England, France, and Burgundy at the End of the Middle Ages*. Athens, Georgia: University of Georgia Press, 1981. Pp. x, 206; 1 map, 29 plates. $25.00.

Perhaps no subject more central to our perception of medieval secular society has been as widely recognized, yet so little understood, as chivalry. Patterns of aristocracy and aristocratic values, the ethos of knighthood, and the theory and practice of warfare are, of course, subjects that have had their commentators almost as long as they have had their lineages. Only in recent years, however, has a new generation of social, cultural, and literary historians penetrated beyond the standard generalizations of older scholars, in particular the classic formulation of Johan Huizinga, to breath new life, both in method and in interpretation, into the subject. The books under consideration here form, along with the studies of scholars such as Maurice Keen, P. S. Lewis, J. R. Hale, and Philippe Contamine, a representative sampling of this important new work.[1]

Late medieval chivalry had a long innings, and has had an even longer bad press. It has been dismissed as heartless, deceptive (because masking, or indeed romanticizing, brutality and brute force), superficial, and impossibly phantasmic. At the same time it has been contrasted with a supposed earlier, pristine, and wholesome set of relations and ideals, generally located in, or at least flowering in, the twelfth century. The pejorative interpretation of later chivalry owes much to a negative attitude toward Froissart that dismisses his work as inaccurate escapism, and his age, by extension, as decadence. It owes still more to the brilliant imaginative powers of Huizinga, conjuring a portrait of an increasingly anachronistic, self-deluding, and self-devouring elite. Huizinga's work is not entirely without validity and merit; Margaret Aston's sensitive appreciation shows us the ways in which his arguments, and the tone or mood he conveys, may still be fruitfully applied, for example, to late medieval England.[2] Yet the seminal article by Maurice Keen points scholars at last on the paths toward a wider and truer understanding, by

Medievalia et Humanistica, New Series, Number 13 (Paul Maurice Clogan, ed.). Rowman & Allanheld, Totowa, NJ. 1985.

demonstrating the essential continuities among early medieval, later medieval, and Renaissance chivalry, and by demonstrating further that the concept of "decline" is equally valid, or more precisely equally invalid, for all these periods.[3]

The books under discussion here triumphantly vindicate Keen's outlook and arguments. Professor Bumke's work, originally published under the title *Studien zum Ritterbegriff im 12. und 13. Jahrhundert*, and now superbly translated by W. H. T. Jackson and Erika Jackson, is already justly celebrated and will now command the even wider audience it deserves. Besides treating a chronologically earlier period than the other works, it deals exhaustively with German literature and its vocabulary as sources for social-institutional history, a most welcome addition to the traditional Francophone (and Francophile!) approach. Its findings are fundamental, albeit negative. The term *Ritter* could be applied to anyone who fought on horseback, whether noble or ignoble, indeed whether free or non-free; the essential characteristics of the knight prior to the thirteenth century were service to and dependence upon another, both military and non-military. The "aristocratization" of *Ritter*, and indeed the conceptualization of knighthood (*Rittertum*) itself, were essentially thirteenth century and later phenomena, influenced heavily by French courtly conventions and the clerical ideal of the knight as *miles Christi*. Even then, what exists is not so much a rising knightly class, as "the elevation of the word 'knight'" in literature (p. 143, and cf. p. 153). Thus stripped of its sentimentality and its contrived juridical-sociological classification, German knighthood, and the chivalric ideals to which it is only fitfully and partially assimilated, provide instructive contrast—and, it may be hoped, a spur to future comparative investigation in social and literary texts—with what such scholars as Duby and Genicot have taught us about France.[4]

To mention the word "chivalry" is almost automatically to evoke the name of Froissart. Dr. Palmer and his collaborators have undertaken a much-needed task, to rehabilitate Froissart and to define the proper criteria for that rehabilitation. The controlling theme throughout is Froissart as artist and as historian, or better, as artistic historian of the Hundred Years' War as chivalric epic. Yet the very design of the book to some extent rehearses the episodic patterns of the original. The majority of the chapters treat Froissart's historicity, with contributions on individual reigns (Henneman on Charles V, Sherborne on Charles VI and Richard II), regions and localities in chronological sequence (Jones on Brittany, Russell on Spain, Van Herwaarden on the Low Countries, and Tucoo-Chala on the Midi), with a singular "topical" chapter, on the art of warfare (Contamine). Richard Barber, in his chapter on Froissart's portrait of the Black Prince, comes closest to combining the artistic and the historical dimensions (cf. p. 54), which are at the forefront of the most wide-ranging chapters that open and close the book: by Palmer himself on Froissart's Book I, showing the various texts to have been not so much sequential revisions, as simultaneous and alternative versions; and by George Diller, analyzing the influence of patrons and patronage on Froissart's art. The basic message is, in a sense, not surprising. Froissart wrote largely in the 1390s, during what proved to be a lull in the War, to revive stories of great men and great deeds for the enjoyment and (moral) edification of his audiences. To preserve examples of honor, of bravery, and of martial valor, and thereby to stimulate their emulation—such is Froissart's own stated purpose in his very first sentence, a design faithfully pursued throughout the enormous bulk of his work. But preservation involves also transformation, artistic selection, and an imagination at times more deliberately poetic than prosaic. Thus using literary techniques, along with direct "journalistic" experience and prior sources, Froissart endows the age with a kind of unity and cultural integrity by treating war and chivalry as its constant *motifs*, subordinating (or at times sacrificing) factual accuracy to this higher literary objective. If Froissart is impressionistic, therein precisely lies his purpose and his enduring value. As literary historian he has neither the tragic sense, nor tragic scope, of the great writers of antiquity or—to anticipate—of the Renaissance or Enlightenment; he is light and discursive, and his "lessons" are both surface and easy, perhaps too easy, particularly for a modern sensibility. Yet he succeeds, imperishably, in conveying a mood, a texture, a chivalric tableau that both outlasts, and indeed supersedes, more mundane considerations of his factual accuracy. Might not Huizinga usefully come to mind here? It is not too fanciful—nor disrespectful to either—to suggest that Froissart and Huizinga might have more in common, for all their obvious differences of time, professional procedures, and audience, than either, perhaps, might have cared to admit.

If Froissart is long, and discursive, and an "entertainment," then Dr. Vale's book is brief, concise, and serious. It demands and will repay the most careful study, being, in my judgment, the most plausible and successful effort to rehabilitate the centrality and earnestness of the chivalric ethos to have appeared in the sixty-five years since the first (Dutch) edition of Huizinga's *Waning*. Vale marshals a host of literary references to show chivalric notions of honor as an essentially aristocratic variant on the wider and more ancient theme of public service, and he demonstrates that educational ideals (themselves flowing into, and then diffused by Castiglione's *Cortigiano*) were significant steps in revitalizing chivalric prestige in the face of competition from new, non-martial elites. In subsequent chapters Vale proves that the aristocracy made willing and intelligent adjustments to new military technology, and argues (not always, but almost always convincingly) that the tournament, ritual behavior and display, and the proliferation of new chivalric orders served serious rather than escapist purposes, and were progressive rather than retrogressive or decadent in spirit. If serious relations between ideals and behavior, and if warfare as a way of life and justification for continued aristocratic privilege and prestige, were either lacking or were rapidly disappearing, then historians have a number of embarrassing facts to explain away: the intense cultural and public interest in all things aristocratic, indeed the entire aristocratic *ancien régime*, that long outlasted the late Middle Ages. It is the great merit of Vale's book to have shown how the aristocracy, purposefully and imaginatively, reformed or transformed its place in social structures and social values, to give itself a new and by no means useless lease on life for centuries to come. In a very real sense, Vale's book is an elaboration on, and an elaborate confirmation of, Keen's signal article published in this journal a half-dozen years ago. Far from confirming a decline from an earlier (and largely imaginary) pristine chivalry, therefore, historians are now enriched as never before by a sense of the fifteenth-century "modernization," as it were, of the chivalric tradition, and its connections, both backwards and forwards in time, with literary *topoi*, with social realities, and above all, with the European code, or set of codes, of masculine honor.

Finally, taken as a whole, the three books demonstrate afresh the significance and the enduring fascination of chivalry and its associated themes in the study of medieval society and culture. In terms of historians of chivalry, Froissart may rightfully be taken to be the first; but Bumke and Vale are only among the most recent, assuredly not the last. If chivalry itself has long since ceased to flourish, the books discussed here suggest, happily, the opposite experience for its historians. "It is impossible to be chivalrous without a horse," to quote Denholm-Young's vivid aphorism;[5] it is now also impossible to study chivalry without reading Bumke, Palmer, and Vale.

NOTES

1. Johan Huizinga, *Herfsttij der Middeleeuwen* (Haarlem, 1919) (English translation entitled *The Waning of the Middle Ages*, London, 1924). Of the later scholars mentioned in the text, the following may be taken as their basic or most illustrative contribution to the subject: M. H. Keen, *The Laws of War in the Late Middle Ages* (London, 1965); P. S. Lewis, "Decayed and Non-feudalism in Later Medieval France," *Bulletin of the Institute of Historical Research* 37 (1964):157–84, and, more generally, *Later Medieval France: The Polity* (London, 1968); J. R. Hale, "War and Public Opinion in Renaissance Italy," *Italian Renaissance Studies*, ed. E. F. Jacob (London, 1960), pp. 94–122, and "Fifteenth and Sixteenth-Century Public Opinion and War," *Past & Present* 22 (July 1962):18–33; Philippe Contamine, *Guerre, état et société à la fin du moyen âge* (Paris, 1972).

2. Margaret Aston, "Huizinga's Harvest: England and *The Waning of the Middle Ages*," *Medievalia et Humanistica*, n.s. 9 (1979), pp. 1–24. See also, for more general considerations and reflections, R. L. Colie, "Johan Huizinga and the Task of Cultural History," *American Historical Review* 69 (April 1964):607–30.

3. Maurice Keen, "Huizinga, Kilgour and the Decline of Chivalry," *Medievalia et Humanistica*, n.s. 8 (1978), pp. 1–20.

4. Georges Duby's numerous article studies have been conveniently collected in *Hommes et structures du moyen âge. Recueil d'articles* (Paris, 1973) and (in translation by Cynthia Postan) *The Chivalrous Society* (London, 1977). For Genicot, see, *inter alia*, Léopold Genicot, "La noblesse au moyen âge dans l'ancienne 'Francie'," *Annales. Economies, sociétés, civilisations* 17 (Jan.–Feb. 1962):1–22. Among German-language scholars, the most important are Arno Borst, Karl Bosl, Walter Kienast, Gerd Tellenbach, and Walter Schlesinger. Relevant studies are conveniently listed in Bumke's exhaustive bibliography (pp. 162–81), an outstanding feature of his book; but special mention should be made of Bosl's own article collection; Karl Bosl, *Frühformen der Gesellschaft im mittelalterlichen Europa* (Munich, 1964).

5. Noël Denholm-Young, "The Tournament in the Thirteenth Century," *Studies in Medieval History Presented to Frederick Maurice Powicke*, ed. R. W. Hunt, W. A. Pantin, and R. W. Southern (Oxford, 1948), pp. 240–68, at p. 240.

Books Received

Adams, J. N. *The Latin Sexual Vocabulary*. Baltimore: The Johns Hopkins Univ. Press, 1982. Pp. 272. $27.50.

Alexander, David. *Eerdmans' Handbook to the Bible*. Grand Rapids: William B. Eerdmans Publishing Co., 1983. Pp. 680. $24.95.

Alighieri, Dante. *The Divine Comedy: Paradiso, Text and Commentary*. Trans. Charles Singleton. Princeton: Princeton Univ. Press, 1982 (second printing). Pp. 610. $16.50.

Anderson, David. *Pound's Cavalcanti*. Princeton: Princeton Univ. Press, 1983. Pp. 297. $25.00.

Anderson, J. J., ed. *Newcastle upon Tyne*. Toronto: Univ. of Toronto Press, 1982. Pp. 217. $45.00.

Armour, Peter. *The Door of Purgatory: A Study of Multiple Symbolism in Dante's Purgatorio*. Oxford: Clarendon Press, 1983. Pp. 217. $29.95.

Ashtor, Eliyahu. *Levant Trade in the Later Middle Ages*. Princeton: Princeton Univ. Press, 1984. Pp. 599. $60.00.

Axton, Marie, ed. *Three Tudor Classical Interludes*. Totowa, NJ: Rowman and Littlefield, 1982. Pp. 237. $47.50.

Baker, Donald C., ed. *A Variorum Edition of the Works of Geoffrey Chaucer, Vol. II, Part 10: The Manciple's Tale*. Norman: Univ. of Oklahoma Press, 1984. Pp. 146. $28.50.

Barber, Richard, ed. *Arthurian Literature III*. Totowa, NJ: Barnes & Noble Books, 1984. Pp. 136. $37.50.

Barkan, Leonard, ed. *Renaissance Drama*: New Series 13, *Drama and Society*. Evanston: Northwestern Univ. Press, 1982. Pp. 212. $24.95.

——. *Renaissance Drama*. New Series 14. Evanston: Northwestern Univ. Press, 1983. Pp. 195. $24.95.

Barlow, Frank. *William Rufus*. English Monarch Series. Berkeley: Univ. of California Press, 1984. Pp. 490. $24.95.

Barricelli, Jean-Pierre, and Joseph Gibaldi, eds. *Interrelations of Literature*. New York: Modern Language Association of America, 1982. Pp. 329. $9.50.

Bazire, Joyce, and James E. Cross, eds. *Eleven Old English Rogationtide Homilies*. Toronto: Univ. of Toronto Press, 1982. Pp. 142. $32.50.

Beadle, R., ed. *The New York Plays*. Bedford Square: Edward Arnold Ltd., 1982. Pp. 537. $98.50.

Benton, John F., ed. *Self and Society in Medieval France: The Memoirs of Abbot Guilbert of Nogent*. 1970. Toronto: Univ. of Toronto Press, 1984. Pp. 260. $8.95.

Benzie, William. *Dr. F. J. Furnivall: Victorian Scholar Adventurer.* Norman, OK: Pilgrim Books, 1983. Pp. 302.

Berman, Harold J. *Law and Revolution: The Formation of the Western Legal Tradition.* Cambridge: Harvard Univ. Press, 1983. Pp. 657. $32.50.

Birch, David. *Early Reformation English Polemics.* Elizabethan and Renaissance Studies 92:7. Salzburg: Universität Salzburg, 1984. Pp. 131. $25.00.

Birnbaum, Henrik, and Michael S. Flier, eds. *Medieval Russian Culture.* California Slavic Studies 12. Berkeley: Univ. of California Press, 1984. Pp. 396. $35.00.

Bloch, R. Howard. *Etymologies and Genealogies: A Literary Anthropology of the French Middle Ages.* Chicago: Univ. of Chicago Press, 1983. Pp. 282. $29.00.

Boccaccio, Giovanni. *Decameron.* The John Payne Translation Revised and Annotated by Charles S. Singleton. 3 vols. Berkeley: Univ. of California Press, 1984. $145.00.

Bogdanos, Theodore. *Pearl: Image of the Ineffable.* University Park: Penn State Press, 1983. Pp. 165. $17.95.

Boitani, Piero, ed. *Chaucer and the Italian Trecento.* New York: Cambridge Univ. Press, 1983. Pp. 313. $49.50.

Bony, Jean. *French Gothic Architecture of the 12th & 13th Centuries.* Berkeley: Univ. of California Press, 1983. Pp. 626. $95.00.

Booth, Wayne C. *The Rhetoric of Fiction.* 1961. Chicago: Univ. of Chicago Press, 1983. Pp. 552. $9.95, paper.

Bornstein, Diane. *The Lady in the Tower: Medieval Courtesy Literature for Women.* Hamden, CT.: The Shoe String Press, 1983. Pp. 152. $15.00.

Braswell, Mary F. *The Medieval Sinner.* East Brunswick, NJ: Fairleigh Dickinson Univ. Press, 1983. Pp. 160. $22.50.

Bray, Alan. *Homosexuality in Renaissance England.* London: Gay Men's Press, 1982. Pp. 149. $5.95.

Bregman, Jay. *Synesius of Cyrene: Philosopher-Bishop.* Berkeley: Univ. of California Press, 1982. Pp. 206. $25.00.

Breisach, Ernst. *Historiography: Ancient, Medieval, and Modern.* Chicago: Univ. of Chicago Press, 1983. Pp. 487. $13.50.

Brewer, Derek. *Tradition and Innovation in Chaucer.* Atlantic Highlands, NJ: Humanities Press, 1982. Pp. 181. $42.00.

Brown, R. Allen, ed. *Proceedings of the Battle Conference on Anglo-Norman Studies IV 1981.* Totowa, NJ: Boydell & Brewer Ltd., 1982. Pp. 237. $49.50.

Brown, R. Allen, ed. *Proceedings of the Battle Conference on Anglo-Norman Studies V 1982.* Totowa, NJ: Boydell & Brewer Ltd., 1983. Pp. 233. $49.50.

Brucker, Gene A. *Renaissance Florence.* Berkeley: Univ. of California Press, 1983. Pp. 320. $7.95, paper.

Bumke, Joachim. *The Concept of Knighthood in the Middle Ages.* Trans. W. T. H. and Erika Jackson. New York: AMS Press, 1982. Pp. 268. $29.50.

Burnley, David. *A Guide to Chaucer's Language.* Norman: Univ. of Oklahoma Press, 1984. Pp. 264. $22.50.

Burrow, J. A. *Essays on Medieval Literature*. Oxford: Clarendon Press, 1984. Pp. 218. $29.95.

——, ed. *Sir Gawain and the Green Knight*. New Haven: Yale Univ. Press, 1982. Pp. 176. $4.95, paper.

Burton, Rosemary. *Classical Poets in the Florilegium Gallicum*. Frankfurt: Verlag Peter Lang, 1983. Pp. 405. SFR 84,000.

Bynum, Caroline Walker. *Jesus as Mother: Studies in the Spirituality of the High Middle Ages*. 1982. Berkeley: Univ. of California Press, 1984. Pp. 279. $7.95, paper.

Byrne, Muriel St. Clare, ed. *Lisle Letters*. Chicago: Univ. of Chicago Press, 1983. Pp. 436.

Byzantine and Western History and Literature from the Late Classical to the Early Modern Period. Catalog 27. San Francisco: Bernard M. Rosenthal, 1981. Pp. 58.

Calin, William. *A Muse for Heroes: Nine Centuries of the Epic in France*. Toronto: Univ. of Toronto Press, 1983. Pp. 513. $47.50.

Cameron, Angus, Allison Kingsmill, and Ashley Crandell Amos. *Old English Word Studies: A Preliminary Author and Word Index*. Toronto: Univ. of Toronto Press, 1983. Pp. 190. $60.00.

Campbell, A. *Old English Grammar*. Oxford: Oxford Univ. Press, 1983. Pp. 423. $19.95.

Carruthers, Mary J., and Elizabeth D. Kirk. *Acts of Interpretation*. Norman, OK: Pilgrim Books, 1982. Pp. 385.

Castor, Grahame, and Terence Cave, eds. *Neo-Latin and the Vernacular in Renaissance France*. Oxford: Clarendon Press, 1984. Pp. 279. $45.00.

Chaucer, Geoffrey. *The Canterbury Tales*. Ed. N. F. Blake. London: Edward Arnold Ltd., 1980. Pp. 707.

Chrisman, Miriam Usher. *Lay Culture, Learned Culture: Books and Social Change in Strasbourg, 1480–1599*. New Haven: Yale Univ. Press, 1982. Pp. 401. $35.00.

Cipolla, Carlo M. *The Monetary Policy of Fourteenth-Century Florence*. Berkeley: Univ. of California Press, 1983. Pp. 114. $14.95.

Clanchy, M. T. *England and Its Rulers: 1066–1272*. Totowa, NJ: Barnes & Noble Books, 1984. Pp. 317. $27.50.

Colish, Marcia L. *The Mirror of Language: A Study in the Medieval Theory of Knowledge*. 1968. Lincoln: Univ. of Nebraska Press, 1983. Pp. 339. $25.00.

Collins, Louise. *Memoirs of a Medieval Woman: The Life and Times of Margery Kempe*. New York: Harper & Row, 1983. Pp. 269. $6.95, paper.

Contamine, Philippe. *War in the Middle Ages*. Trans. Michael Jones. New York: Basil Blackwell, 1984. Pp. 387. $24.95.

Coogan, Robert. *Babylon on the Rhone: A Translation of Letters by Dante, Petrarch, and Catherine of Siena on the Avignon Papacy*. Potomac: Studia Humanitatis, 1983. Pp. 134. $19.50.

Cooke, Thomas D., ed. *The Present State of Scholarship in Fourteenth-Century Literature*. Vol. 13. Columbia: Univ. of Missouri Press, 1982. Pp. 323. $23.80.

Damıco, Helen. *Beowulf's Wealtheow and the Valkyrie Tradition.* Madison: Univ. of Wisconsin Press, 1984. Pp. 270. $35.00.

Defaux, Gerard, ed. *Montaigne: Essays in Reading.* New Haven: Yale Univ. Press, 1983. Pp. 308. $10.95.

Devereux, E. J. *Renaissance English Translations of Erasmus: A Bibliography to 1700.* Toronto: Univ. of Toronto Press, 1983. Pp. 212. $35.00.

Dubois, Page. *History, Rhetorical Description and the Epic.* Totowa, NJ: Boydell & Brewer Ltd., 1982. Pp. 131. $35.00.

Dyer, James. *The Penguin Guide to Prehistoric England and Wales.* New York: Penguin Books, 1981. Pp. 384. $7.95.

Edwards, Mark U., Jr. *Luther's Last Battles: Politics and Polemics, 1531–46.* Ithaca and London: Cornell Univ. Press, 1983. Pp. 254. $19.95.

Farmakides, Anne. *Advanced Modern Greek.* New Haven: Yale Univ. Press, 1983. Pp. 469.

Ferguson, Margaret W. *Trials of Desire: Renaissance Defenses of Poetry.* New Haven: Yale Univ. Press, 1983. Pp. 257. $22.50.

Ferry, Anne. *The "Inward" Language: Sonnets of Wyatt, Sidney, Shakespeare, Donne.* Chicago: Univ. of Chicago Press, 1983. Pp. 285. $25.00.

Flannery, Austin, ed. *Vatican Council II: The Conciliar and Post Conciliar Documents.* Northport, CT.: Costello Publishing Co., 1980. Pp. 1062.

——. *Vatican Council II: More Postconciliar Documents.* Grand Rapids: Wm. B. Eerdmans Publishing Co., 1982. Pp. 920.

Fleming, John V. *From Bonaventure to Bellini: An Essay in Franciscan Exegesis.* Princeton: Princeton Univ. Press, 1983. Pp. 171. $25.00.

——. *Reason and the Lover.* Princeton: Princeton Univ. Press, 1984. Pp. 196. $20.00.

Forcione, Alban K. *Cervantes and the Humanist Vision: A Study of Four Exemplary Novels.* Princeton: Princeton Univ. Press, 1982. Pp. 411. $37.50.

——. *Cervantes and the Mystery of Lawlessness: A Study of El casamiento enganoso y El coloquio de los perros.* Princeton: Princeton Univ. Press, 1984. Pp. 243. $35.00.

Ford, Boris, ed. *Medieval Literature: Chaucer and the Alliterative Tradition.* Pt. 1, the New Pelican Guide to English Lit. New York: Penguin Books, 1982. Pp. 647. $5.95.

Ford, Patrick K., ed. *Celtic Folklore and Christianity: Studies in Memory of William W. Heist.* Los Angeles: Univ. of California, 1983. Pp. 225. $18.00.

Fossier, François. *Etude des Manuscrits Latins et en Langue Vernaculaire.* La Bibliothèque Farnese, III, 2. Palais Farnese: Ecole Française de Rome, 1982. Pp. 508.

Frantzen, Allen J. *The Literature of Penance in Anglo-Saxon England.* New Brunswick, NJ: Rutgers Univ. Press, 1983. Pp. 238. $27.50.

Freedman, Paul H. *The Diocese of Vic: Tradition and Regeneration in Medieval Catalonia.* New Brunswick, NJ: Rutgers Univ. Press, 1983. Pp. 230.

Ganim, John M. *Style and Consciousness in Middle English Narrative.* Princeton: Princeton Univ. Press, 1983. Pp. 177. $23.00.

Garbáty, Thomas J., ed. *Medieval English Literature*. Lexington, MA: D. C. Heath & Co., 1984. Pp. 974.

Geanakoplos, Deno John. *Byzantium: Church, Society, and Civilization Seen Through Contemporary Eyes*. Chicago: Univ. of Chicago Press, 1984. Pp. 485. $27.50.

Geiringer, Karl. *Haydn: A Creative Life in Music*. Berkeley: Univ. of California Press, 1983. Pp. 404. $8.95.

Georgianna, Linda. *The Solitary Self*. Cambridge: Harvard Univ. Press, 1981. Pp. 169. $5.95.

Gerald of Wales. *The History and Topography of Ireland*. Trans. J. J. O'Meara. New York: Penguin Books, 1982. Pp. 136. $5.95.

Gibson, Margaret. *Boethius*. Oxford: Basil Blackwell, 1983. Pp. 451. $48.00.

Ginsberg, Warren. *The Cast of Character: The Representative of Personality in Ancient and Medieval Literature*. Toronto: Univ. of Toronto Press, 1983. Pp. 202. $27.50.

Glare, P. G. W., ed. *Oxford Latin Dictionary*. Oxford: Clarendon Press, 1982. Pp. 2126. $145.00.

Goitein, S. D. *A Mediterranean Society: The Jewish Communities of the Arab World as Portrayed in the Documents of the Cario Geniza. Vol. IV: Daily Life*. Berkeley: Univ. of California Press, 1984. Pp. 492. $38.50.

Grassi, C., M. Ciatti, and A. Petri, eds. and trans. *Regia Carmina*. 2 vols. Prato: Gruppo Bibliofili Pratese, 1982. Pp. 144 & 64. Peso Kg. 2.500.

Gray, Douglas, and E. G. Stanley, eds. *Middle English Studies Presented to Norman Davis*. Oxford: Clarendon Press, 1983. Pp. 288. $67.00.

Greene, Thomas M. *The Light in Troy: Imitation and Discovery in Renaissance Poetry*. New Haven: Yale Univ. Press, 1982. Pp. 354. $27.50.

Hall, J. R. Clark. *A Concise Anglo-Saxon Dictionary*. 4th ed. 1960. Toronto: Univ. of Toronto Press, 1984. Pp. 432. $15.00.

Hanna, Ralph III, ed. *The Index of Middle English Prose, Handlist I: A Handlist of Manuscripts Containing Middle English Prose in the Henry E. Huntington Library*. Totowa, NJ: Boydell & Brewer Ltd., 1984. Pp. 81. $39.50.

Hanning, Robert W., and David Rosand, eds. *Castiglione: The Ideal and the Real in Renaissance Culture*. New Haven: Yale Univ. Press, 1983. Pp. 215. $22.50.

Hansen, William F. *Saxo Grammaticus and the Life of Hamlet: A Translation, History and Commentary*. Lincoln: Univ. of Nebraska Press, 1983. Pp. 202. $17.95.

Harvey, E. Ruth, ed. *The Court of Sapience*. Toronto: Univ. of Toronto Press, 1984. Pp. 217. $35.00.

Hollander, John. *Rhyme's Reason: A Guide to English Verse*. New Haven: Yale Univ. Press, 1981. Pp. 54. $3.95, paper.

Huetér, John E. *Now Judas and His Redemption*. Boston: Branden Press, 1983. Pp. 199.

Hulliung, Mark. *Citizen Machiavelli*. Princeton: Princeton Univ. Press, 1983. Pp. 299. $22.50.

Ihle, Sandra Ness. *Malory's Grail Quest: Invention and Adaptation in Medieval*

Prose Romance. Madison: Univ. of Wisconsin Press, 1983. Pp. 199. $22.50.

Jackson, W. T. H. *The Hero and the King: An Epic Theme.* New York: Columbia Univ. Press, 1982. Pp. 141. $20.00.

Jantzen, Hans. *High Gothic: The Classic Cathedrals of Chartres, Reims, Amiens.* Trans. James Palmes. 1962. Princeton: Princeton Univ. Press, 1984. Pp. 181. $7.95, paper.

Joannides, Paul. *The Drawings of Raphael with a Complete Catalogue.* Berkeley: Univ. of California Press, 1983. Pp. 272. $110.00.

Johnson, Lynn Staley. *The Voice of the Gawain-Poet.* Madison: Univ. of Wisconsin Press, 1984. Pp. 276. $32.50.

Jones, Hugh Lloyd. *The History of Classical Scholarship.* Baltimore: The Johns Hopkins Univ. Press, 1982. Pp. 189. $20.00.

Keefe, Thomas K. *Feudal Assessment and the Political Community under Henry II and His Sons.* Berkeley: Univ. of California Press, 1984. Pp. 294. $29.50.

Keen, Maurice. *Chivalry.* New Haven: Yale Univ. Press, 1984. Pp. 303. $25.00.

Kent, D. V., and F. W. Kent. *Neighbours and Neighbourhood in Renaissance Florence: The District of the Red Lion in the Fifteenth Century.* New York: J. J. Augustin, 1982. Pp. 192. $22.00.

King, Edward B., and Jacqueline T. Schaefer, eds. *Sewanee Medieval Colloquium Occasional Papers,* Vol. I, No. 1. Sewanee; Univ. Press, 1982. Pp. 59.

Kittelson, James M., and Pamela J. Transue, eds. *Rebirth, Reform and Resilience: Universities in Transition 1300–1700.* Columbus: Ohio State Univ. Press, 1984. Pp. 367. $25.00.

Kitzinger, Ernst. *Early Medieval Art.* Rev. Ed. Bloomington: Indiana Univ. Press, 1983. Pp. 127. $10.95.

Kolve, V. A. *Chaucer and the Imagery of Narrative: The First Five Canterbury Tales.* Stanford: Stanford Univ. Press, 1984. Pp. 551. $39.50.

Kouwenhoven, Jan Karel. *Apparent Narrative as Thematic Metaphor: The Organization of the Faerie Queene.* Oxford: Clarendon Press, 1983. Pp. 232. $37.50.

Krautheimer, Richard. *Lorenzo Ghiberti.* Princeton: Princeton Univ. Press, 1982. Pp. 461. $19.50.

——. *Three Christian Capitals: Topography & Politics.* Berkeley: Univ. of California Press, 1983. Pp. 168. $27.50.

Kristeller, Paul Oskar, and Hans Maier. *Thomas Morus als Humanist: Zwei Essays.* Germany: Bamberg, 1982. Pp. 61.

Kuhn, Sherman M. *Studies in the Language and Poetics of Anglo-Saxon England.* Ann Arbor: Karoma Publishers, 1984. Pp. 232.

Lainez, Manuel Mujica. *The Wandering Unicorn.* New York: Taplinger Publishing Co., 1983. Pp. 325. $16.95.

Landes, David S. *Revolution in Time: Clocks and the Making of the Modern World.* Cambridge: Harvard Univ. Press, 1983. Pp. 428. $20.00.

Lanham, Richard A. *The Motives of Eloquence*. 1976. New Haven: Yale Univ. Press, 1983. Pp. 234. $7.95, paper.

Latham, Robert, ed. *The Illustrated Pepys: Extracts from the Diary*. Berkeley: Univ. of California Press, 1983. Pp. 240. $15.95.

Lathan, Robert, and William Matthews, eds. *The Diary of Samuel Pepys Vol. X: Companion*. Berkeley: Univ. of California Press, 1983. Pp. 656. $35.00.

——. *The Diary of Samuel Pepys Vol. XI: Index*. Berkeley: Univ. of California Press, 1983. Pp. 368. $35.00.

Law, Vivien. *The Insular Latin Grammarians*. Woodbridge, NJ: Boydell & Brewer Press, 1983. Pp. 131. $49.50.

Leitch, Vincent B. *Deconstruction Criticism: An Advanced Introduction*. New York: Columbia Univ. Press, 1982. Pp. 290. $8.95 (paper).

Lerner, Robert E. *The Powers of Prophecy: The Cedar of Lebanon Vision from the Mongol Onslaught to the Dawn of the Enlightenment*. Berkeley: Univ. of California Press, 1983. Pp. 250. $32.50.

Lester, G. A. *Sir John Paston's 'Grete Boke': A Descriptive Catalogue with an Introduction of British Library MS Lansdowne 285*. Totowa, NJ: Boydell & Brewer Ltd., 1984. Pp. 197. $35.00.

Logan, George M. *The Meaning of More's "Utopia."* Princeton: Princeton Univ. Press, 1983. Pp. 296. $27.50.

Lucas, Peter J., ed. *John Capgrave's Abbreuiacion of Cronicles*. Oxford: Oxford Univ. Press, 1983. Pp. 410. $84.00.

Lumiansky, R. M., and David Mills, eds. *The Chester Mystery Cycle: Essays and Documents*. Chapel Hill: The Univ. of North Carolina Press, 1983. Pp. 339. $40.00.

McEvoy, James. *The Philosophy of Robert Grosseteste*. Oxford: Clarendon Press, 1982. Pp. 560. $74.00.

Mack, Maynard, and George deForest Lord, eds. *Poetic Traditions of the English Renaissance*. New Haven: Yale Univ. Press, 1982. Pp. 319. $22.50.

Mâle, Emile. *Religious Art: From the Twelfth to the Eighteenth Century*. 1949. Princeton: Princeton Univ. Press, 1982. Pp. 208. $8.95.

Maltby, William S. *Alba: A Biography of Fernando Alvarez de Toledo, Third Duke of Alba 1507–1582*. Los Angeles: Univ. of California Press, 1983. Pp. 377. $29.50.

Mancing, Howard. *The Chivalric World of Don Quixote: Style, Structure, and Narrative Technique*. Columbia: Univ. of Missouri Press, 1982. Pp. 240.

Mandelbaum, Allen, trans. *The Aeneid of Virgil*. Berkeley: Univ. of California Press, 1982. Pp. 413. $10.95.

Manning, Alan. *The Argentaye Trace: Edited from Paris, BN, fonds français 11,464*. Toronto: Univ. of Toronto Press, 1983. Pp. 145. $35.00.

Marrone, Steven P. *William of Auvergne and Robert Grosseteste*. Princeton: Princeton Univ. Press, 1983. Pp. 319. $32.50.

Masi, Michael. *Boethian Number Theory*. Amsterdam: Editions Rodopi, 1983. Pp. 197. $27.75.

Miller, Clarence H., Leicester Bradner, Charles A. Lynch, and Revilo P. Oliver, eds. *The Complete Works of St. Thomas More*, Vol. 3, Part 2. New Haven: Yale Univ. Press, 1984. Pp. 787. $60.00.

Millett, Bella, ed. *Hali Meidhad*. London: Oxford Univ. Press, 1982. Pp. 84. $13.95.

Minnis, A. J., ed. *Gower's Confessio Amantis: Responses and Reassessments*. Totowa, NJ: Boydell & Brewer Ltd., 1983. Pp. 202. $49.50.

Mitchell, Bruce, and Fred C. Robinson. *A Guide to Old English*. Rev. Ed. Toronto: Univ. of Toronto Press, 1982. Pp. 271. $15.00.

Montgomery, Robert L. *Giacopo Mazzoni on the Defense of the Comedy of Dante: Introduction and Summary*. Gainesville: Univ. Press of Florida, 1983. Pp. 149. $15.00.

Morris, Rosemary. *Character of King Arthur in Medieval Literature*. Totowa, NJ: Rowman and Littlefield, 1982. Pp. 175. $47.50.

Mueller, Janel M. *The Native Tongue and the Word: Developments in English Prose Style 1380–1580*. Chicago: Univ. of Chicago Press, 1984. Pp. 429. $27.50.

Murphy, James J., ed. *Renaissance Eloquence: Studies in the Theory and Practice of Renaissance Rhetoric*. Berkeley: Univ. of California Press, 1984. Pp. 474. $27.50.

Nichols, Stephen G., Jr. *Romanesque Signs: Early Medieval Narrative and Iconography*. New Haven: Yale Univ. Press, 1983. Pp. 248. $23.50.

Nigg, Joe. *The Book of Gryphons*. Cambridge: Apple-wood Books, 1983. Pp. 111. $19.95.

Noble, Peter S. *Love and Marriage in Chrétien de Troyes*. Cardiff: Univ. of Wales Press, 1982. Pp. 108. $15.00.

Ogilvy, J. D. A., and Donald C. Baker. *Reading Beowulf*. Norman: Univ. of Oklahoma Press, 1983. Pp. 221. $17.95.

Olson, Glending. *Literature as Recreation in the Later Middle Ages*. Ithaca: Cornell Univ. Press, 1982. Pp. 245.

Pace, George B., and Alfred David, eds. *The Minor Poems: Part One. A Variorum Edition of the Works of Geoffrey Chaucer*, Vol. 5. Norman: Univ. of Oklahoma Press, 1982. Pp. 223. $38.50.

Palmer, Robert C. *The Whilton Dispute, 1264–1380: A Social-Legal Study of Dispute Settlement in Medieval England*. Princeton: Princeton Univ. Press, 1984. Pp. 295. $28.50.

Papuli, G., ed. *Bollettino Di Storia Della Filosofia Dell'Universita Degli Studi Di Lecce*, Vol. 7. Lecce: Edizioni Milella, 1979. Pp. 410.

Patrides, C. A. *Premises and Motifs in Renaissance Thought and Literature*. Princeton: Princeton Univ. Press, 1982. Pp. 236. $20.00.

Pearsall, Derek, ed. *A Variorum Edition of the Works of Geoffrey Chaucer. Vol. II: The Canterbury Tales, Part 9: The Nun's Priest's Tale*. Norman: Univ. of Oklahoma Press, 1984. Pp. 284. $42.50.

Peck, Russell A. *Chaucer's Lyrics and Anelida and Arcite: An Annotated Bibliography 1900 to 1980*. Toronto: Univ. of Toronto Press, 1983. Pp. 226. $36.00.

Pelikan, Jaroslav. *The Christian Tradition: A History of the Development of*

Books Received 221

Doctrine. Vol. 4: Reformation of Church and Dogma (1300–1700). Chicago: Univ. of Chicago Press, 1984. Pp. 424. $27.50.

Pellegrin, Elizabeth, Jeannie Fohlen, Collette Jeudy, and Yves-Francois Riou. *Les Manuscrits Classiques Latin de La Bibliothèque Vaticane.* Paris: Editions du Centre National de La Recherche Scientifique, 1982. Pp. 685. 570 French francs.

Pickford, C. E., R. W. Last, and C. R. Barker, eds. *The Arthurian Bibliography II Subject Index.* Totowa, NJ: Boydell & Brewer Ltd., 1984. Pp. 117. $49.50.

Price, Lorna. *The Plan of St. Gall: In Brief.* Berkeley: Univ. of California Press, 1982. Pp. 100. $55.00.

Ramsey, Lee C. *Chivalric Romances: Popular Literature in Medieval England.* Bloomington: Indiana Univ. Press, 1983. Pp. 245. $17.50.

Renard the Fox. Trans. Patricia Terry. Boston: Northeastern Univ. Press, 1984. Pp. 178. $11.95.

Rollason, D. W. *The Mildrith Legend.* Atlantic Highlands, NJ: Humanities Press, 1982. Pp. 171. $42.00.

Roskell, J. S. *The Impeachment of Michael de la Pole, Earl of Suffolk in 1386, in the Context of the Reign of Richard II.* Manchester: Manchester Univ. Press, 1984. Pp. 216. $27.50.

Ross, Thomas W., ed. *A Variorum Edition of the Works of Geoffrey Chaucer, Vol. II: The Canterbury Tales, Part Three, The Miller's Tale.* Norman: Univ. of Oklahoma Press, 1983. Pp. 274. $38.50.

Rowse, A. L. *Eminent Elizabethans.* Athens: Univ. of Georgia Press, 1983. Pp. 199. $19.00.

Ruggiers, Paul G., ed. *Editing Chaucer: The Great Tradition.* Norman, OK: Pilgrim Books, 1984. Pp. 301. $34.95.

Russell, Rinaldina. *Generi Poetici Medioevali.* Corso Umberto: Sen, 1982. Pp. 209. $10.00.

Salter, Elizabeth. *Fourteenth-Century English Poetry: Contexts and Readings.* Oxford: Oxford Univ. Press, 1983. Pp. 224. $37.50.

Saul, Nigel. *Batsford Companion to Medieval England.* Totowa, NJ: Barnes & Noble Books, 1983. Pp. 283. $27.50.

Scattergood, John, ed. *John Skelton: The Complete English Poems.* London: Yale Univ. Press, 1983. Pp. 573. $9.95.

Schell, Edgar. *Strangers and Pilgrims: From the Castle of Perseverance to King Lear.* Chicago: Univ. of Chicago Press, 1983. Pp. 214. $22.50.

Schnerbe-Lievre, Marion, ed. *Le Songe du Vergier,* 2 vols. Paris: Editions du Centre National de la Recherche Scientifique, 1982. Vol. 1: pp. 501; Vol. 2: pp. 496.

Schultz, James A. *The Shape of the Round Table: Structures of Middle High German Arthurian Romance.* Toronto: Univ. of Toronto Press, 1983. Pp. 249. $25.00.

Shakespeare, William. *Henry V.* Ed. Gary Taylor. Oxford: Clarendon Press, 1982. Pp. 350. $19.95.

——. *The Taming of the Shrew.* Ed. H. J. Oliver, Oxford: Clarendon Press, 1982. Pp. 248. $19.95.

Shakespeare, William. *Troilus and Cressida.* Ed. Kenneth Muir. Oxford: Clarendon Press, 1982. Pp. 205. $19.95.

Shell, Marc. *Money, Language, and Thought: Literary and Philosophic Economies from the Medieval to the Modern Era.* Berkeley: Univ. of California Press, 1982. Pp. 240. $22.50.

Shereshevsky, Esra. *Rashi: The Man and His World.* New York: Sepher-Hermon Press, 1982. Pp. 265. $17.50.

Shideler, John. *A Medieval Catalan Noble Family: The Montcadas 1000–1230.* Berkeley: Univ. of California Press, 1984. Pp. 254. $34.50.

Shoaf, R. A. *Dante, Chaucer, and the Currency of the Word: Money, Images, and Reference in Late Medieval Poetry.* Norman, OK: Pilgrim Books, 1983. Pp. 312.

Silverstein, Theodore, ed. *Sir Gawain and the Green Knight: A New Critical Edition.* Chicago: Univ. of Chicago Press, 1984. Pp. 268. $15.00.

Specht, Henrik. *Poetry and the Iconography of the Peasant: The Attitude to the Peasant in Late Medieval English Literature and in Contemporary Calendar Illustration.* Copenhagen: B. Stouggard Jensen, 1983. Pp. 103.

Spisak, James W., William Matthews, and Bert Dillon, eds. *Caxton's Malory: A New Edition of Sir Thomas Malory's Le Morte D'Arthur.* Berkeley: Univ. of California Press, 1984. Pp. 922. $85.00.

Stafford, Pauline. *Queens, Concubines and Dowagers: The King's Wife in the Early Middle Ages.* Athens: Univ. of Georgia Press, 1983. Pp. 248. $22.50.

Staines, David. *Tennyson's Camelot: The Idylls of the King and Its Medieval Sources.* Waterloo: Wilfrid Laurier Univ. Press, 1982. Pp. 218. $18.50.

Stanley, E. G., and Douglas Gray. *Five Hundred Years of Words and Sounds.* Totowa, NJ: Boydell & Brewer Ltd., 1984. Pp. 177. $49.50.

Starn, Randolph. *Contrary Commonwealth: The Theme of Exile in Medieval and Renaissance Italy.* Berkeley: Univ. of California Press, 1982. Pp. 207. $24.50.

Stock, Brian. *The Implications of Literacy.* Princeton: Princeton Univ. Press, 1983. Pp. 604. $45.00.

Summers, Joseph H. *George Herbert: His Religion and Art.* Binghamton, NY: Center for Medieval and Early Renaissance Studies, 1981. Pp. 147. $12.60.

Tasso, Torquato. *Tasso's Dialogues: A Selection with the Discourse on the Art of the Dialogue.* Trans. C. Lord and D. A. Trafton. Berkeley: Univ. of California Press, 1984. Pp. 268. $7.95.

Taylor, Beverly, and Elisabeth Brewer. *The Return of King Arthur.* Totowa, NJ: Barnes & Noble Books, 1983. Pp. 382. $35.00.

Taylor, Gary, and Michael Warren, eds. *The Division of the Kingdom: Shakespeare's Two Versions of King Lear.* Oxford: Clarendon Press, 1983. Pp. 489. $67.00.

Taylor, Simon, ed. *Anglo-Saxon Chronicle: A Collaborative Edition*, Vol. 4. Totowa, NJ: Boydell & Brewer Ltd., 1984. Pp. 75. $30.00

Thomson, Rodney M. *Manuscripts from St. Albans Abbey 1066–1235.*

Part I: Text. Part II: Plates. Woodbridge, NJ: Boydell & Brewer Ltd., 1982. Pp. 152. $120 set.

Trimpi, Wesley. *Muses of One Mind: The Literary Analysis of Experience and Its Continuity*. Princeton: Princeton Univ. Press, 1983. Pp. 413. $40.00.

Trinkaus, Charles. *The Scope of Renaissance Humanism*. Ann Arbor: Univ. of Michigan Press, 1983. Pp. 479. $28.50.

Tripp, Raymond P., Jr. *More about the Fight with the Dragon: Beowulf 2208b–3182, Commentary, Edition, and Translation*. New York: Univ. Press of America, 1983. Pp. 480.

Troyes, Chrétien de. *Perceval, or the Story of the Grail*. Trans. Ruth Harwood Cline. Elmsford, NY: Pergamon Press, 1983. Pp. 247. $30.00.

Vale, Juliet. *Edward III and Chivalry*. Totowa, NJ: Boydell & Brewer Ltd., 1983. Pp. 207. $49.50.

Van Engen, John H. *Rupert of Deutz*. Berkeley: Univ. of California Press, 1983. Pp. 395. $35.00.

Váňa, Zdeněk. *The World of the Ancient Slavs*. Detroit: Wayne State Univ. Press, 1984. Pp. 240. $35.00.

Verdon, Timothy, ed. *Monasticism and the Arts*. Syracuse: Syracuse Univ. Press, 1984. Pp. 354. $16.95.

Vergara, Lisa. *Rubens and the Poetics of Landscape*. New Haven: Yale Univ. Press, 1982. Pp. 207. $35.00.

Vos, Catherine F. *The Child's Story Bible*. Grand Rapids: Wm. B. Eerdmans Publishing Co., 1977. Pp. 382.

Walsh, P. G. *Andreas Capellanus on Love*. London: Duckworth, 1983. Pp. 329. $14.95.

West, Delno C., and Sandra Zimdars-Swartz. *Joachim of Fiore: A Study in Spiritual Perception and History*. Bloomington: Indiana Univ. Press, 1983. Pp. 136. $20.00.

Wilson, Katharina M., ed. *Medieval Women Writers*. Athens: Univ. of Georgia Press, 1984. Pp. 363. $12.50.

Wood, Charles T. *The Quest for Eternity: Manners and Morals in the Age of Chivalry*. Hanover: Univ. Press of New England, 1983. Pp. 172. $7.95.

Wood, Chauncey. *The Elements of Chaucer's Troilus*. Durham: Duke Univ. Press, 1984. Pp. 204. $35.00.

Yerkes, David, ed. *The Old English Life of Machutus*. Toronto: Univ. of Toronto Press, 1984. Pp. 185. $45.00.